THE GREAT
AUSTRALIAN
BEER GUIDE

For Tara, to whom I should listen more.
And Matilda and William, whom I couldn't love more.

THE GREAT
AUSTRALIAN
BEER GUIDE

hardie grant books

INTRODUCTION
PAGE **10**

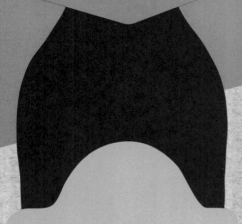

LAGERS
PAGE **28**

SESSION BEERS
PAGE **48**

PALE
ALES

PAGE **66**

IPAS

PAGE **86**

BRITISH & IRISH ALES

PAGE **114**

REDS & AMBER ALES

PAGE **132**

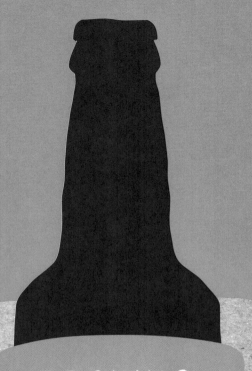

BROWNS, DARKS & PORTERS

PAGE **152**

STOUTS & IMPERIAL STOUTS

PAGE **170**

FRENCH &
BELGIAN ALES

PAGE **188**

WHEAT
BEERS

PAGE **206**

HOW THE BEERS WERE CHOSEN
PAGE **238**

INDEX
PAGE **240**

SPECIALTY BEERS

PAGE **214**

HOW TO USE THIS BOOK

BEER STYLE

ALCOHOL BY VOLUME – STRENGTH

BREWER'S SUGGESTED SERVING TEMPERATURE

BREWER'S SUGGESTED SERVING VESSEL

Beer in Australia:
An Introduction

It's remarkable how much can change in two years. At the time of writing the introduction to this book's predecessor, *150 Great Australian Beers – Your guide to craft beer and beyond,* it felt like the Australian craft beer industry was reaching critical mass.

Thirty years on from the first glass of Anchor Special Bitter being poured at the Sail & Anchor in Fremantle, and with the second wave of small, independent breweries gaining momentum and numbers for more than a decade, any fears that this second wave would go the same way as the first had been dispelled. It was too big – even at just a fraction of the total beer industry, too legion, too noisy and had too many passionate disciples for it to fail. Naysayers, whether in hope or mere observation, could no longer dismiss it as a fad.

And so it has proved. Craft beer has become an intrinsic part of the contemporary Australian food and drink scene to the extent that terminology from its world has been co-opted by marketers in other fields. Bundaberg's flavoured ginger beers are 'craft brewed' according to TV ads. Bertocchi hams are 'hand crafted'. Craft beer is no longer a dirty word but used instead by many businesses who would once have disparaged it and its drinkers as a lure

with which to draw in customers. As a result, while today you'll find even more of the impassioned people we described in the intro to *150 Great Australian Beers* – those with a collection of T-shirts 'adorned with cartoon hop flowers and the names of breweries from all over the world' – there is, to an extent, a more relaxed feel around the craftier realms of the Australian beer world, or at least an acceptance that certain battles require less expending of energy that is now better employed elsewhere.

There's less need for those fighting the cause of small, independent breweries to wave their pitchforks so vehemently in the direction of the major breweries because the battle first fought and lost in the 1980s and 1990s, when the first wave of small breweries rose then crashed, has been won. The country is, inexorably, well on the way to becoming one that boasts a spectacular diversity of breweries from coast to coast, breweries that serve up plenty for those seeking something other than the

simple lagers on offer from the likes of Lion and CUB.

There's no hyperbole in the use of the phrase 'spectacular diversity' either. With well in excess of 300 brewing companies operating at the time of writing, from tiny, shed-based 'nano' operations through brewpubs of all shapes and sizes to larger production breweries as well as 'gypsy' or contract brewers who don't own their own kit, it's the most kaleidoscopic of mosaics.

And even more than the nature of the breweries or the characters behind them, the diversity of beers on offer now is little short of incredible. The vast majority of beer consumed remains common or 'garden lager', while even in the craft beer sector pale and golden ales of a similar strength to those lagers are dominant. Yet the past two years have seen levels of innovation and experimentation rise rapidly from what was already an impressive base in 2014.

Not everyone has the skills to carry off some of the wilder ventures, but there are brewers here who are creating wonderful things with barrels and bacteria, who are mastering the art of creating extremely high or low ABV beers, who are creating hybrid styles with aplomb or who are finding ways of making the native flavours of Australia – even their very own pieces of the country – part of their beers.

That said, there's little point pretending that with the smaller, independent brewers having taken an unshakeable foothold in the market, at least when grouped as a whole, we've entered some utopian paradise where all is wonderful, everyone sings from the same hymn sheet and all that matters is quality, innovation and bringing joy to the world. Challenges remain for brewers in all parts of the industry, challenges that are considered later in this chapter.

Yet, if it was easy to declare the local beer culture in rude health two years ago, it's ruder still today. The monoculture that dominated much of the 20th century continues to be eroded away; the exact nature that its replacement takes on in the coming years remains to be seen but it will be one in which concerns such as flavour, aroma and provenance play a far greater role than they did for a long, long time. And anyone with a passing interest in the content of their glass will surely want to drink to that.

The original 'craft' beers

Back in the early days of the colonies, breweries were local and brewed a range of beers, such as English-inspired ales, porters and stouts. The stories of the country's first two acknowledged brewers, James Squire and, to a lesser extent, John Boston, have been retold in picture book fashion via contemporary brands that bear their names but, as settlers spread across Australia, breweries sprung up with them. The standard of their output may have been variable – brewers may have particularly struggled in the heat of summer due to a lack of refrigeration – but these small breweries, without distribution networks, would serve a handful of local outlets and offer a variety of beers.

With these local beers available alongside ales imported from England, Australian drinkers through much of the 19th century had a reasonable choice of tipples. Towards the end of that century there were around 300 breweries in Australia – at a time when the population was still fewer than four million.

Change was coming, however, with its genesis towards the end of the 19th century. Some of the larger, city-based breweries had begun establishing 'tied' houses: pubs that they owned and that would only serve their beer, a tactic that gave them an advantage over many smaller, suburban and regional breweries. These challenges were exacerbated by the economic depression of the 1890s, during which many breweries closed.

It wasn't purely economics that threatened the existence of many smaller breweries, either. Drinking habits were to change, too. Gambrinus, a brewer from Germany, set up shop in Melbourne in 1885 and started brewing the country's first lager, bringing with them the means of refrigeration that allowed them to serve their beers chilled. Two years later, the American Foster brothers followed suit, with Castlemaine opening in Brisbane before the decade was out. As these breweries grew, the popularity of ice-cold, pale lagers – ideally suited to the hot Australian climate – took off.

The passing of the Commonwealth Beer Excise Act in 1901, which imposed heavy penalties on brewers who failed to meet its regulations, posed another threat to smaller breweries and led to further closures. While they shut their doors, the larger breweries with better technology, distribution networks and, ultimately, greater economies of scale, expanded rapidly. The shrinking of the industry was dramatic. According to *The Breweries of Australia*, by 1910 there were only 157 breweries left operating in Australia; a decade later that number had dwindled to just 77.

Beer's peak and nadir

Fast forward to the 1970s and rationalisation had reached its peak – or nadir, depending on which side of the fence you sit. Beer consumption was at its highest level in Australian history and beer had the greatest share of the total alcohol market in the country. But punters were drinking pretty much the same beer – pale lager measuring something in the region of 5 per cent ABV – and they were drinking it in pubs that were generally rough, poorly maintained and predominantly the preserve of men. (Sure, there would be a room somewhere for the ladies to knit and sip Stone's Ginger Wine, but the front bar was for blokes. Should a woman venture in and assert her right to remain, in some places there was a risk she might face arrest.)

The industry was dominated by a handful of large breweries that serviced their home states, the likes of Castlemaine Perkins, CUB, Tooheys, Swan and the South Australian Brewing Company, each of whom focused predominantly on brewing one style of beer consistently and efficiently.

Imported beer was practically non-existent, certainly outside a handful of traditional Irish pubs and the Lowenbrau Keller in The Rocks. Towards the end of the 1960s, even the previously ale-only Coopers Brewery in South Australia had released its first lager in more than a century of unbroken brewing.

It was a period in which, according to Phil Sexton, one of the pioneers of Australia's craft beer renaissance: "Beer was nothing more than a fast-moving consumer good, and any discussion about quality or flavour was secondary."

Australia was not alone in experiencing this change. Globally, large, efficient brewers of pilsner-style beers dominated. And if anyone had wanted to set up a smaller brewery they would have struggled. In Australia, when the major breweries upgraded their equipment, the redundant gear was destroyed to ensure there was no secondary market. And no manufacturer of brewing equipment anywhere in the world built anything suitable for a microbrewery setup.

However, the first stirrings of a beer renaissance had begun elsewhere. In the UK, the Campaign for Real Ale (CAMRA) was on the rise, trying to save and then re-popularise Britain's real ale tradition. And, in the US, Fritz Maytag had taken over Anchor Steam Brewery, which had started brewing beers such as the hoppy Liberty Ale; famous names such as Sierra Nevada, which was founded in 1980 and now has a sizeable presence in Australia after finally relenting to years of persistent requests from local importers, were soon to follow.

A new beginning

Inspired by time spent in the UK and Europe, and visits to some of the fledgling craft breweries in the States, Sexton, along with hang-gliding mates from university, Garry Gosatti and John Tollis, felt compelled to rejuvenate Australia's bleak beer landscape. In 1984, they first turned Fremantle's dilapidated Freemasons Hotel into the Sail & Anchor, complete with its own microbrewery, then built the original Matilda Bay Brewery, backed by colourful entrepreneur Peter Briggs, before establishing venues across Australia and challenging many accepted norms in the industry.

They were soon joined by other pioneers. In 1986, Blair Hayden returned from the UK and started pouring English-inspired ales at the Lord Nelson in The Rocks, thus kick-starting three decades and counting of brewing at one of the finest pubs in Australia. Geoff Scharer, who died in 2012, began brewing Scharer's Lager at Scharer's Little Brewery at the George IV Inn in Picton, New South Wales. And, in 1988, American brewmaster Chuck Hahn opened Hahn Brewery in the Sydney suburb of Camperdown and began brewing an authentic pilsner called Hahn Premium (a beer he tried to return to its early glories in recent years and which appeared in *150 Great Australian Beers*, but which has since been deleted by Lion).

Other small enterprises sprung up elsewhere but, of those to commence brewing in the 1980s, only those mentioned above and Grand Ridge in Victoria, which started brewing in 1989, are brands that continue to this day, with Matilda Bay left by its owners to become a pale shadow of what it once was and could potentially have been.

Problems such as under-capitalisation and poor or inconsistent product meant that many ventures in this first wave of Australian craft breweries were short-lived. Matilda Bay was bought by Foster's at the start of the 1990s, and Hahn was snapped up by Lion Nathan (now Lion) in 1993, with the Camperdown site renamed the Malt Shovel Brewery and becoming the home for the James Squire range of beers under Chuck Hahn's guidance. While CAMRA enjoyed success in the UK and the American craft beer revolution took hold, Australia appeared to have suffered a false start.

That said, Coopers was on the rise. The brewery began producing draught beer for the first time in the 1980s, a decade that also saw the company take ownership of several hotels through which it was able to sell its beers, a move that mirrored the approach the first iteration of Matilda Bay had so successfully taken to retail. A handful of imports from Europe and North America were becoming available to those who wanted to hunt them down and, with Matilda Bay and James Squire offering alternatives (albeit alternatives that were still owned by major breweries), there was a semblance of choice.

A tiny number of breweries that still operate to this day did open in the 1990s: Last Drop in the Perth Hills and Bootleg Brewery in Margaret River, for example. But it was not until the end of that decade that microbrewing in Australia began to grow in earnest. In the last years before the millennium, some of the most respected names in Australian craft beer today released their first beer: Mountain Goat in Melbourne, Nail Brewing in Perth, and Holgate Brewhouse in Woodend, Victoria.

Perhaps the biggest single moment that kick-started the second wave of craft brewing in Australia, however, was an echo of the very first. Sexton, who had returned to his first love, wine, and spent time in the US working with friends at BridgePort Brewing Company where he's credited with designing the first American IPA, was enticed back to Australia by former colleagues from Matilda Bay. Nic Tromboli and Howard Cearn saw an opportunity to start another brewery in WA, driven in part by displeasure with the direction in which Foster's had taken their earlier creation.

They opened Little Creatures on the Fremantle waterfront, a spectacular venture in a building that formerly housed a crocodile farm. It took the brewpub concept to another level in Australia and also brought with it a beer that was to revolutionise the country's drinking habits. Originally called Little Creatures Live, then renamed Little Creatures Pale Ale, this US-inspired ale featured the wonderfully aromatic, citrusy hops of the Pacific Northwest and was based on the hoppy pale ales and IPAs that were leading the charge for American craft brewers, tweaked by Sexton and fellow winemaker Janice McDonald for the Australian palate.

While growth of craft beer remained steady rather than spectacular and its market share was negligible, the early years of the new millennium saw a steady growth in the number of breweries, many opening up in popular wine and tourism regions – some among them now recognised as the best in the country, including Feral Brewing in Swan Valley and Bridge Road Brewers in Beechworth.

Often they were opened by people who had experienced beer epiphanies while travelling through the States, the UK or Europe, and decided to change careers. But there were also those who were starting to view small-scale brewing as a viable career option. The number and diversity of quality imports available in Australia continued to rise too, opening palates and minds to the possibilities inherent in beer.

Despite this, there were plenty who doubted beer could follow the same trajectory enjoyed by Australian wine from the 1980s onwards. Commonly tagged 'boutique beer' (a term that could not be less appropriate for describing the ethos or, indeed, the personalities, of many involved in the Australian microbrewery scene and one which has now, thankfully, almost disappeared), it was frequently written off as a fad that would die a similar death to the first wave.

The doubters had plenty of ammunition. It was a challenge for these breweries to find venues that would stock their beer, while a lack of brewing knowledge and ordinary equipment contributed to beer of a quality that was variable at best for many of the start-up breweries. Even a few years ago, you could find breweries that were seemingly founded on a belief that their point of difference and location in a popular tourism region would be reason enough for people to visit and drink their beers – quality be damned. Indeed, one suspects some owners figured (with good reason) that Australian beer drinkers wouldn't

know what many of the styles of beers they were claiming to brew should taste like and thus wouldn't know whether they were good or bad. As long as it tasted 'different', it might be enough.

However, despite the naysayers, grow it did. What was increasingly being named 'craft beer' was taking off in many other countries. Information on techniques, new beer styles, new ingredients and more was being shared freely on the internet, giving brewers unprecedented access to a wealth of previously unavailable or hard-to-source information. In Australia, there was also a vibrant home-brewing culture developing. And a handful of visionary bar owners realised what was happening and resisted the temptation to take lucrative contracts or deals from the major breweries and instead operated as free houses, filling their taps with beers from these small local breweries. Suddenly, brewers had a means to get their beer to the public even if they didn't have a cellar door or brewery bar of their own.

Gaining traction

As the availability of craft beer grew, so did the breadth of styles available either by import or from local breweries. Standards improved and, as beer drinkers became more knowledgeable about what various beers should taste like and started expecting more, there was less room in the market for substandard beers from local breweries. A handful of breweries closed, but in most cases they just started making better beer or brought in new brewers who could. By 2010, an industry that had been growing steadily for a decade began expanding faster and faster. Since then, growth in every aspect has been little short of phenomenal. It is not uncommon to find breweries reporting 100 per cent year-on-year growth, even several years into their existence. At times, it feels like

there must be a small flotilla of ships making its way to Australia all year round, bringing nothing other than stainless steel fermenters and brewhouses from Europe, North America and China to satisfy Australians' voracious appetite for better beer.

Perhaps the best example of this phenomenal growth is Stone & Wood. The brewery was only opened in Byron Bay in 2008 by three mates who had previously worked in various roles at CUB, and latterly at Matilda Bay where head brewer Brad Rogers was responsible for creating a series of eye-catching beers. Today, it is the largest independent Australian brewery outside of the 150-plus-year-old Coopers and is busy diversifying the businesses within the Stone & Wood Group. Its story is told elsewhere in this book (page 65) and its rapid rise looks set to be followed by others that have opened in the past year or two, most notably Hawkers Beer and Pirate Life Brewing.

These two brewers launched their first beers within ten days of each other in early 2015 and both enjoyed a phenomenally successful opening 12 months in business. Each built a brewery as big or bigger than any other microbrewery in their respective home states (Hawkers in Victoria and Pirate Life in South Australia) yet soon had to expand significantly and rapidly and, at the time of writing, were hitting targets they'd set for their third, fourth or fifth years.

While there are stark differences in the way each has chosen to operate – in terms of beer styles, branding, and their targeting of various Australian markets, for example – there are similarities that underline why they have exploded onto the scene. Indeed, it is typically by addressing the major reasons why most businesses in the first wave failed.

They are well resourced, well run by teams that possess experience outside the Australian beer industry (Hawkers co-founder Mazen Hajjar founded the Middle East's first craft brewery, 961 Beer, for example), both brew great beer consistently, have identifiable brands and, in their different ways, are forceful, but not unpleasantly so, in getting their product and brands noticed and into people's hands. Of the newest arrivals on the local scene, they're the two who could set the template for many other brewery owners looking to make a noise on a national scale in a hurry.

Yet they are far from alone in working frantically to meet demand. As sales for many of Australia's biggest brands continue to falter and overall beer consumption steadily declines, the clamour for the best local beers is so high that many brewers struggle to meet their own state's demands, and have to bat away requests from eager bar owners and drinkers elsewhere. It is not uncommon to ask a brewer how things are going since their new, larger setup was installed and discover they are hitting capacity again and are bringing forward plans for the next stage of expansion. Some brewers have been forced to find alternative means of brewing their beer, outsourcing production of some of their main lines, at least in packaged form, to external operators that specialise in brewing for other businesses.

The third wave

When you consider that the brewers who kick-started the second wave referred to above are, for the most part, in rude health, either sitting comfortably on what they've built or, more often, continuing to build and innovate, it might seem odd to talk of a third wave. Yet there has been a notable change of direction – or at least the addition of some delightful tangents – within the Australian beer industry in the past five years.

The brewers I refer to are those who entered the industry with little regard for perceived norms, in their own way doing what Phil Sexton, Chuck Hahn, Geoff Scharer and their ilk did in the 1980s, but in a rather more twisted and experimental manner. Inspired by the 'no rules' ethos of many American brewers, they ignored, and continue to ignore, what was seen as the sensible approach – essentially, create a core range featuring something approachable like a golden ale and back it up with something fruity (a wheat beer), something a little hoppy (pale ale) and something darker (porter or stout) – and instead did it their own way.

Sure, by 2010 or 2011, there were already many breweries across Australia producing innovative and often unusual beers as limited releases, but no one for whom that was the very *raison d'être* driving their output from day one.

Kick-starting this third wave as much as anyone was Moon Dog. Based in a small industrial unit in Abbotsford, equidistant from CUB's headquarters and a brothel, their first official releases were a barrel-aged wild black ale featuring cherries called Perverse Sexual Amalgam and a cognac barrel–aged imperial IPA called Skunkworks. Today, the two brothers and their mate that started the brewery have deviated a little towards the norm. They opened 2016 by adding a pale ale and a hoppy dark ale to their core range. Old Mate and Mack Daddy joined the 5 per cent ABV hoppy lager Love Tap to give them a trio of still colourfully conceived and presented yet rather more 'normal' beers, but they continue to push the boundaries with most of their beers, their names and their labels.

In 2015 alone, with a former winner of the Champion Australian Brewery title added to the brewing team, they released a beer that pulled off a fine impression of champagne (Bad Boy Bubbly) without

using anything other than beer's four main ingredients, a pair of beers sold as a two-pack designed to be blended together to form their take on an Old Fashioned cocktail, and a delicious fruit stout that featured 5,800 Redskin lollies.

They're not alone. HopDog BeerWorks has been knocking out increasingly better beers that explore crazy hopping regimes, odd ingredients and infected barrels with equal relish, while their success has inspired others to leap straight into the deep end too, launching with beers that are close to their hearts rather than those they believe would have reasonable mass-market appeal. Among them are the likes of 7 cent, whose most eye-catching beers include a sour cherry porter that was 18 months in the making, and Kaiju! Beer with their fondness for throwing preposterous amounts of hops at beers.

Others combine the production of beers of broad appeal with those of a more idiosyncratic bent; none more so than Boatrocker Brewery. The Braeside-based company launched initially as a contract brewer, with beers such as the Alpha Queen pale ale and Hoppbier pilsner brewed under license. Since opening its own brewery, it has embarked on an ambitious barrel program: a two-pronged one that sees the brewers ageing big beers such as imperial stouts and barley wines in whisky and bourbon barrels while developing a large stock of various funky and sour beers inspired by Boatrocker founder Matt Houghton's beloved Belgium.

Not too far away in Melbourne, La Sirène has its own barrel and coolship program up and running and is, like Tasmania's unique Two Metre Tall, exploring spontaneous fermentation – where beer is fermented only by the wild yeasts present in the local atmosphere rather than any house or packet yeast. Even White Rabbit, the younger sibling to Lion-owned Little Creatures, opened its own barrel room in Geelong in 2015 and is producing some sour styles.

It is not just the beers available that are changing. As more young brewers look to turn their dreams into commercial reality, they are seeking ever more creative ways to break into the industry. There used to be pretty much three choices: find half a million dollars or more and build your own brewery; come up with a brand and pay someone else to brew for you; or cobble something together from repurposed milk and cosmetic vats or tanks intended for winemaking.

More recently, however, some have branded themselves as 'gypsy' or 'nomad' brewers – those without their own equipment who travel from brewery to brewery, creating their beers on other people's gear.

There are others exploring another avenue too. A small number of 'communal breweries' have opened. Some created by design, others more by accident, they are typically owned by one brewery that invites other brewing companies to buy their own fermenters to be installed alongside their host's. The brewing companies brew on the host brewery's equipment but have their own space in which to ferment and condition beer without tying up their host's capacity.

Young Henrys in Newtown once offered space to The Grifter Brewing Company, allowing three talented young brewers a foothold in the market they otherwise would not have been able to afford before they both outgrew each other and Grifter set out to build their own home in Sydney's inner west. Cavalier in Melbourne's west has welcomed a horde of brewers to its warehouse, with many of them since leaving to open their own brewery having established their brand. Indeed, in a couple of cases, brewers who were part of the crowd at Cavalier have since paired up, such as Exit Brewing,

whose founders now brew at Kaiju!. In Adelaide, Big Shed Brewing was set up with this approach in mind; the owners 'rent' their brewery and fermenters to other brewing companies, although, as with Young Henrys and Grifter, Big Shed and their main customer Mismatch's success means they're outgrowing each other.

Collaboration brews, which, two years ago, I tagged a 'notable trend', having risen in prominence rapidly since 2010, are now utterly commonplace. Brewers still collaborate with each other, often for special events, but also brew with bands, artists, farmers, writers, roasters, venues, beard gum makers – you name it, if someone's game and has an idea or an ingredient to offer then there will be a brewery happy to work with them.

In *150 Great Australian Beers*, I also wrote about the rise of the specialty beer bar. Such venues, at which the range and presentation of beer is the centre point of the experience, remain an intrinsic and increasingly commonplace part of the beer world, so much so they're almost past being worthy of comment. What is worthy of comment is where they can now be found, with excellent pubs and bars serving a multitude of fine beers found in country and coastal towns as well as the major centres. Many of the best cocktail bars now offer a fine line in quality beer, with Boilermakers – the pairing of beer and whisky that are served together – are also increasingly common.

Complementing that, it's becoming increasingly common for hotels and pubs you would never tag as 'specialist beer bars' to dabble in craftier waters. With Lion, in particular, having been smart in building a diverse portfolio this might be little more than beers from the likes of James Squire or Little Creatures, which are still a step or two away from XXXX Gold and Pure Blonde. But many are also being

won over by smaller, independent brewers too, with publicans dipping their toes in the water, discovering there are people looking for something different in all corners of the country and that they can make greater margins on craft beer too.

And it's here that smaller brewers would be wise to focus much of their attention in building their own – and their peers' – audience in the coming years. Dedicated beer venues will take their beers, but likely rotate them one or two kegs at a time and will be selecting from scores of local brewers plus a growing number of often excellent imports. With more venues moving away from the strict contracts signed with the country's major players and hotel owners increasingly aware that there's something else on offer and it's not going away, it should be imperative for small brewers to be hitting up and befriending every beer-selling outlet in their locality, no matter how unlikely it might seem for them to take a chance on their products. After all, if there are no rules when it comes to brewing, why should there be in terms of where they should be sold?

More than beer

It is not just Australian brewers making their mark either. Over the past decade, Hop Products Australia, the country's largest grower of commercial hops, has changed tack significantly to focus on creating a greater number of aroma and flavour hops. Some, particularly Galaxy and Ella, are in great demand the world over. Victorian grower Ellerslie Hop added its own new aroma hop, Melba, in 2015 and has a second, Astra, making its first appearances in commercial brews in 2016.

The beer festival has come into its own too, and not those of the large Oktoberfest bent either, which are typically driven by misogynistic advertising and the swilling of as much imported lager as possible. These are instead festivals of varying sizes and format that are linked by a desire to put small producers and their beers front and centre. Where once there was a small number of these one- or two-day beer festivals in the annual calendar, now – particularly in summer – they are found all over the country, the biggest of them attracting thousands of attendees.

The beer week also continues to come into its own. Just as WA was the first state to have craft beer, it was the first with a beer week, although the one operated by the state's brewing association has tended to be a small, niche affair compared to those that have come later, even if it is building year on year.

It was the arrival of Good Beer Week in Melbourne in 2011 that took things to another level. Run in conjunction with the long-running Australian International Beer Awards and now also incorporating the huge Great Australasian Beer SpecTAPular (GABS) within its nine days, it has become an event with global reach, regularly enticing brewers from all over the planet to Australia for an array of events – 270 of them in 2016 – celebrating beer and beer culture in every way imaginable. (Full disclosure: I am a co-founder and former festival director of Good Beer Week.) It has spawned city- and state-based beer weeks in Sydney, Brisbane, Canberra and Hobart, as well as the five-day Good Beer Wheaty in Adelaide, while GABS has become a touring affair, taking its converted shipping containers, from which pour 120 brand new beers each year on the road, initially from Melbourne to Sydney in 2015 and adding Auckland in 2016.

The combination of so much growth in so many areas, not to mention the businesses developing as a result of craft beer's rise – small maltings and hop farms, specialist tap handle and decal producers, for example – makes for a potent brew.

The landscape has never been as colourful or delicious, particularly as standards, for the most part, rise in tandem with sales.

The landscape also has a more even spread of breweries and beer venues now; in the past two years alone, things have changed markedly. Melbourne and Victoria long led the way, before the slumbering giant that was Sydney finally came alive, aided by a rising number of small breweries and a thriving small bar scene; indeed, Sydney's inner west is the most populous area in Australia for brewery venues.

As recently as 2012, there were those that questioned whether Brisbane would ever embrace craft beer but it now has its own independent, week-long beer festival, Brewsvegas, while the Gold Coast held its own beer week in 2015 and will have three significant breweries operating by the time you read this. The Tasmanian brewing industry comprised the same eight or nine names for years but now has twice that number, with Hobart in particular developing quite a buzzing little scene. South Australia has erupted too, with a big increase in breweries matched by venues supporting them since scores of new small bar licenses were granted.

Out west, the state in which the contemporary beer industry had its first stirrings has welcomed a few new players into what was already a populous brewing state and, finally, Perth has a handful of beer venues worthy of the name. The country's capital is increasingly well served too, with the legendary Wig & Pen safely ensconced in a new home, its trophy-winning former head brewer, Richard Watkins, now running the superb BentSpoke with his partner Tracy Margrain, and new brewing company Pact Beer joining Zierholz to make four. In the Northern Territory, One Mile Brewery is the lone microbrewery although Darwin does have a small number of venues offering a choice of beers now.

Yet, as mentioned above, challenges remain for those at all levels of the beer world.

The country's long dominant twosome, Lion (owned by Japan's Kirin) and CUB (owned by SABMiller and, maybe by the time of publication, part of the behemoth that is AB InBev), continue to see sales of their flagship brands struggle and face a future in which such beers will probably never again command the monopoly they enjoyed throughout much of the 20th century.

Other major players are looking to flex their muscles too. Asahi's purchase of Melbourne's Mountain Goat on the eve of the latter's 18th anniversary sent shockwaves through the industry. It should bring the Japanese giant more success than its prior purchase of Cricketers Arms, even if the initial period following the sale saw many of Goat's independent stockists take their business elsewhere. The Japanese brewer has approached other storied local names too, so don't be surprised if others follow Goat's lead.

Asahi's purchase of Goat and Lion's acquisition of Little World Beverages in 2012 (which owned Little Creatures and White Rabbit) were, at the time of writing, the only big brewery buyouts of any significance in Australia. Elsewhere, particularly in the States, they have been happening around once a month, with some phenomenal prices paid and some big names in the craft beer world, including those who played upon their outlaw status, succumbing to the lure of the big pay cheque. Without fail, their new owners claim to have nothing but love and respect for the businesses they've acquired and have the means to help them grow; how the stories will develop and the impact on those who either aren't offered a cheque or who choose to remain independent is one of the more fascinating aspects of the near future for anyone with an interest in beer and business.

WHAT IS CRAFT BEER?

In some ways, this has been the craft beer world's million-dollar question: just how do we define what we are and what we aren't? Associations in different parts of the world have come up with definitions that lean on parameters such as ingredients, size or ownership. In Australia, the CBIA's definition favours the abstract – 'craft beer is born of a mindset, an idea between art and science executed by the dedicated skill of a brewer' – which leaves anyone wanting to understand who is on the bus and who isn't little the wiser.

In New Zealand, Epic Beer's Luke Nicholas has argued that it may be wiser to define 'industrial beer' – that produced by 'big mega breweries' whose 'near beer' wort streams he calls 'a disgrace to the history of all brewers'. Craft beer, maybe even beer itself, is what this is not, he suggests.

Take any of the parameters used by those seeking to define and it becomes possible to pick holes in them. If independence or ownership is important then did Mountain Goat's beers stop being craft beer once the business was sold lock, stock and Belgian quad-filled Lark Distillery whisky barrels to Asahi? If it comes down to ingredients and flavours, then what about the rare occasions a brand bought from a contract facility by one of the country's supermarket chains and given prominence – and a far cheaper price point than the beers it mimics – tastes good? If it comes down to size, you end up with a situation like that in the States where the Brewers Association has to keep raising its upper limit so it can keep the biggest breweries that meet all of its other criteria in the club.

In *150 Great Australian Beers* I favoured a line from beer writer -turned-Seven Sheds brewer Willie Simpson. In trying to capture what craft beer was, he quoted from *The Castle*: "It's the vibe."

Certainly, if you do care about beer on levels other than whether it's cold, wet and will make you feel warm and fuzzy, and have some knowledge of the beer world, then you'll know what he means. There is a vibe, albeit one that is defined differently from person to person, as each drinker will have their own parameters for what is acceptable to them. Like any purchase, some people will just want the cheapest or most readily available, while others will look for qualities such as locally made, organic, sustainable and so on.

Like many brewers who include 'love' as an ingredient on their labels, I believe that love plays an integral part in craft beer too: love for your business, your beer, the way it's presented, the wider industry as a whole. But, without wishing to get too cosmic, how can we ever really know someone's true intentions and whether a claim of 'love' is little more than a marketing ploy? What's more, there will be brewers out there who pour love into their business and beers but might also have a beer they knock out as cheaply as possible as a volume shifter to prop up the stuff they really love.

Right now, the term 'indie beer' is gaining credence, particularly on the back of the takeovers of leading craft brewers. To those who care about the provenance of their beers and where their money will end up, this declaration of independence is perhaps most useful of all.

I would suggest that the ultimate solution isn't to try to define at all but to leave the decision making in drinkers' hands. For this to happen, there would need to be absolute transparency and honesty applied to the labelling of beers. Brewers should list all ingredients, who owns the brand or business right up to the top of the chain (as Lion does with its sub-brands now), and where the beer is brewed, be that by the brewing company itself or under license for them by another.

This way, a discerning drinker has all the information they need to make a choice. Is it made with all natural ingredients? OK, that's acceptable to me. Is it owned by a small, independent, local company? OK, I like that too. And do they brew it themselves? Yes. Great, let's hope it tastes awesome.

Most drinkers don't and won't care, but for those that do take an interest in what they buy, this provides the information they need to make their decision. Then it's up to a brewer to ensure that the beer is good enough that they come back for more.

For now, however, while many scribes have taken delight in declaring the term 'craft beer' dead – and at some point in the future it probably all will become just beer – I believe it still has great relevance. We may not know or agree with exactly what it means, but we do know that it is something that barely existed 30 years ago, after the local beer industry was crushed of all diversity and colour, and which well and truly exists now, more diverse and colourful than ever.

As a result, today's beer world really is a place where four ingredients – water, malt, hops and yeast – combined with a brewer's ingenuity, can create endless possibilities. ●

Back in Australia, Lion and CUB have been joined by others with deep pockets and global reach. The joint venture between Yellow Tail wine manufacturer Casella and Coca-Cola Amatil (CCA), Australian Beer Co, continues to look for ways to break into the market in a big way. Neither the Arvo lagers or Alehouse beers cut through, but Yenda, the brand they present as a cutesy little rural operation, is more visible and the company started 2016 by launching a range of Yellow Tail beers.

Add in Adelaide's family brewery Coopers and the home brands from the country's dominant retailers (Steamrail, Lorry Boys and 3 Pub Circus from Coles; Sail & Anchor and John Boston from Woolworths, which also has a 25 per cent stake in Gage Roads) and you've got a fair number of players with significant resources and the ability to shape what the public sees on shelves.

And then you have the 300-odd smaller, independent players. They include a handful that are becoming truly national, such as Stone & Wood, 4 Pines and Feral, far more that operate on a regional level, plus all manner of brewpubs and locally focused businesses. For all to succeed, they need to keep chipping away at the market share of the big breweries and to tell and sell the story of why they should be supported – provenance, integrity, independence, flavour and so on – rather than engaging in internecine warfare, intentional or otherwise.

Their collective fight to see craft beer secure a solid foothold in Australia may be won, but other fights such as those concerning excise tax or the inflated cost of ingredients and supplies continue, while yet more take shape. Above all, they need to ensure that they are brewing to the best standard they can, then keep improving on that best standard because, while the audience is going to grow, it will have more choice and those who fail to deliver will be shunned, allowing natural selection to weed them out.

As for the size of that audience, it is without doubt bigger than the official figures released by survey companies claim. Their measures fail to take into account a huge chunk of sales, including those direct from breweries, and independent retailers such as specialist bottleshops and the hundreds of pubs and bars selling little other than beer from small producers. One industry stalwart who has been operating in the craft beer world since well before the term 'craft' was applied, told me he believes the true figure for craft beer as a percentage of the beer market in Australian to be closer to 10 per cent than the four often cited. That is, of course, if you include brands owned by the multinationals, such as Matilda Bay, Yak Ales, James Squire and Little Creatures.

Even without those he estimates the percentage share for which small, independent Australian brewers is responsible is far higher than official stats state, while growth among small, independents surely dwarfs the low double-digit figures often cited. However, with the main national body representing smaller brewing companies in Australia, the Craft Beer Industry Association (CBIA), as yet unable to persuade its members to share production figures, nailing an accurate figure would appear to be some way away.

What's certain, however, is that it is growing. And that, however you look at the beer industry in Australia today, is exciting – thrilling, even – with all the highs and lows that can accompany any exciting or thrilling moment.

Any questions over the size of the industry are now better focused on how much of the market the still-dominant major brands will lose and how big the loosely defined craft sector will grow; will it stop at 10 per cent, 20, 30? And who will own that 10, 20 or 30 per cent?

Will it be the major players wearing crafty clothes? Certainly, Lion above all others has been smart and, with James Squire, Kosciuszko, Little Creatures, White Rabbit and Knappstein, not to mention Emerson's in New Zealand, is well positioned to dominate.

How much room is there for bigger independents who want to play on a national scale? Will enough of the really small operators find their niche or be able to build up a strong and well resourced enough business to survive in more competitive waters? And will the term 'craft beer' even mean anything anymore? •

How Beer is Made

Stripped back to its very basics, beer is a remarkably simple thing. It is almost always made of just four ingredients: malt, water, hops and yeast. A wide variety of those four ingredients is available to brewers anywhere in the world, pretty much whenever they want them.

The process of combining those four ingredients to make beer is also, when stripped back to its very basics, remarkably simple. Malt is milled, then steeped in hot water to extract fermentable sugars. This sweet water is then boiled and hops are added before it is cooled and transferred to a fermenter where yeast is added. Over the course of a few days, it turns into what we know as beer.

The easiest way to think of it is like cooking: brewers follow a recipe and add the right ingredients at the right time to achieve the desired outcome. In fact, you can brew a beer on your stovetop at home using exactly the same ingredients as a commercial brewer.

Yet there is good beer and bad beer, so it can't be that easy, right? Furthermore, as you will discover while making your way through the beers in this book – which only represent a small percentage of the beers released in Australia in any one year – those four ingredients and that simple process can lead to vastly different outcomes.

There is a huge variety to choose from within each of beer's key ingredients, and they can be combined in any way a brewer sees fit. Even changing the make-up of the water can alter a beer. Likewise, any variation at any stage of the brewing process – be that the temperature of the water in which the malt is steeped in the mash tun; the length of time the sweet water (known as wort) is boiled in the kettle; how much, when and what type of hops are added; the temperature at which fermentation takes place; or even the vessel in which fermentation takes place – can change the character of the beer.

In reality, there are endless possibilities with these four ingredients, and this simple process, and the science, techniques and art of brewing, can become as complex as a student of beer wants it to be. But, for the purposes of this book, let's keep things as simple as possible.

First up, the basics of the brewing process...

The brewing process

Almost all beer begins with malted barley (see the ingredients section on the following page). A brewer will mill (essentially crush) their chosen blend of malts and add it to a mash tun where it will be mixed with hot water that is heated to a temperature dependent on what beer is being brewed. This process converts the starches in the malt into fermentable sugars that are dissolved into the water to form a sweet, sugary liquid known as wort. Usually, it takes about an hour to convert the starches into malt sugars.

At this point, the sweet wort is slowly separated from the grain in the mash tun, using the grain bed itself as a filter (in a process known as lautering). Water is gently sprayed over the grain, in a process known as sparging, to ensure that as much of the fermentable sugars have been extracted as possible. Once transferred to the brew kettle, the liquid is heated to boiling temperature.

It is here that hops are first added (except in very rare cases when brewers choose to add hops in the mash tun in a process known as mash hopping). Hops added early in the boil will give a beer bitterness, while those added towards the end of the boil, which typically lasts around 90 minutes, will lend beer flavours and aromas.

The boiling process can also aid clarity and the long-term stability of the finished beer by 'breaking' proteins that then drop out of suspension.

Once the boil is complete, the liquid is cooled rapidly, usually via a heat exchanger, and transferred to a fermentation vessel. It is at this point that the sugary, hoppy liquid will be transformed into beer. This happens when the final of the four key ingredients is added: yeast. These microscopic living organisms go to work, multiplying rapidly and devouring the fermentable sugars. As they do so, they create two useful byproducts: alcohol and carbon dioxide, as well as adding a range of flavours and aromas.

Several days later, the yeast's work is done and a brewer has beer. Some types of beer will be packaged at this point and sent straight into the market for consumption. Often, however, a brewer will allow a beer to condition longer in the tank, as this additional time allows yeast to settle out, leaving an end product with much greater clarity.

The vast majority of commercial beer is filtered, and in some cases pasteurised, before being force-carbonated with carbon dioxide and transferred into kegs or bottles. In some cases, particularly among craft brewers, beer undergoes a secondary fermentation in a bottle or keg, meaning live yeast remains in the beer so that it continues to develop and retains its spritzy carbonation.

The ingredients

MALT Along with malted barley, malt is beer's backbone – the source of the sugars that will be fermented into alcohol, and much of its flavour too. In today's rapidly evolving craft beer world, many drinkers are first lured in by hops, with their dramatic aromas like a moth to a light bulb. But while you can create beer without hops (in fact, beer existed for millennia before humans were even aware of hops), you cannot create beer without malt, water and yeast.

The vast majority of beers are brewed using varieties of malted barley. Once harvested, it goes through a process of steeping in water and then partial, controlled germination to encourage the production of enzymes and starches. After four or five days, and before the germinating grains begin to grow plants, they are kilned (or dried) to create malt. What type of malt is created depends on how long they are kilned for, at what temperature, and how much moisture is in the air (or indeed in the grains themselves) when they are kilned by the maltster.

The most commonly used base malts in beers are the palest; in other words those kilned for the least amount of time at the lowest temperatures. As malts become progressively darker, the flavours, aromas and colour they lend to a beer change accordingly. While the lightest of malts used alone will give a brewer pale-yellow or light-golden beers and lightly sweet, sometimes honey-like, flavours and aromas, as you move along the scale, malts will lend beers colours that range from copper, amber and red to various shades of brown and, ultimately, black. Flavours and aromas move from those akin to biscuit to caramel, nuts, chocolate and treacle to coffee and even fairly harsh, acrid roast bitterness, with many shades in between.

Malted barley may be the most common grain used in beer, but it is not the only one. Many beers also use a percentage of wheat, both malted and unmalted. It is found in high proportions in wheat beers (see the Wheat Beers chapter, page 206) and also in small amounts in other beers where it can help a brewer achieve a particular body, assist with head retention or add a dryness or tartness. Rye malt is becoming increasingly popular among craft brewers too. It can give beers a fuller, almost oily or slick, body, as well as adding a distinct and intense spicy flavour. Another ingredient often found in a grain bill is oats, particularly in stouts, where they help create a smooth, silky and creamy body. Brewers, particularly large commercial brewers, will also use rice and corn on occasion, often as adjuncts designed to affect the body of a beer as well as, to an extent, its flavour.

Then there are smoked malts. These fall into two main categories. There is the malted barley smoked over open wood fires, with beechwood the most popular fuel. They have been popularised by German brewers, with the best known of these being Schlenkerla. As well as lending a sweet smokiness to beers, the flavours and aromas are commonly described as meaty, in particular bacon-like.

Some brewers also use peated distilling malt on occasion. As the name suggests, this is a type of malted barley typically used by whisky distilleries. It is produced in peat-fueled kilns and comes in a range of intensities. Many brewers would run a mile rather than have such grains in their brewery due to their potency and persistence but, used in small amounts, they can add additional layers of character and complexity to a beer. In a couple of extreme cases, brewers have created beers using 100 per cent peated distilling malt, including Tasmania's Seven Sheds with its Smokin' Bagpipes, and Bacchus Brewing who created Islay, a high alcohol beer brewed with nothing but peated malt and then aged for months in former Islay whisky barrels.

In addition to these varieties, malt companies around the world are constantly developing new 'specialty malts'. Sometimes these are designed to give a particular colour to a beer without adding much in the way of flavour, including one known as Midnight Wheat that has become increasingly popular as a means of creating deeply dark beers without the associated roast or bitter flavours. There is also a small number of tiny 'craft' maltings starting up around Australia where the intention is to develop malts that will be of interest to craft brewers.

These days, it is worth adding that nothing is off-limits for brewers. Across the globe you will find limited-release beers using grains that are native to a particular area or ancient grains that may have been used to make beer hundreds or thousands of years ago. And then there are varieties such as sorghum and millet that are essential to the handful of brewers specialising in creating gluten-free beers for coeliacs. In 2013, Ballarat-based O'Brien won the first-ever gold medal awarded to a gluten-free beer in Australia.

HOPS These flowers are a relative newcomer to the world of beer. Historians and archaeologists have found evidence of brewing and beer consumption in the Middle East and former Mesopotamia stretching back several thousand years. Yet the earliest recorded use of hops in beer is 9th-century France. Prior to that, a wide variety of herbs and other less savoury ingredients – soot, anyone? – were used instead and their use in beer didn't become widespread for centuries after their first appearance.

The easiest way to understand what they contribute to beer is to return to the cooking analogy. Hops are like spices. They are added in the latter part of the brewing (or cooking) process and used predominantly to add three things to beer: bitterness, aroma and flavour. They have other useful properties, not least acting as a preservative, but it is those three areas in which they specialise.

The hop plant, *Humulus lupulus* (literally 'wolf in the woods'), is cultivated on hop farms. Hop bines grow up strings attached to trellises and can reach several metres in height. The parts that are of interest to brewers are the flowers of the female plants: bulbous, yellow-green cones that are harvested in early autumn. They grow between 35 and 55 degrees of latitude in both the northern and southern hemispheres, with the most famous hop-growing regions found across France, Germany and the Czech Republic, in Southern England, in America's Pacific Northwest, the north of New Zealand's South Island around Nelson, and in the Victorian High Country and Bushy Park in Tasmania.

At harvest time, they are dried within hours of being cut and are processed into one of a number of different formats. These include whole hop flowers, hop pellets, hop extract and hop oils.

As stated earlier, their primary use to a brewer is to deliver bitterness, flavour and aroma. The point at which hops are added in the brewing process dictates what characteristics a brewer will obtain. Adding them early in the boil, once the sweet wort has been transferred from the mash tun, delivers predominantly bitterness via a process called isomerisation, which occurs from boiling hops, typically for a period between one and two hours. Much of the flavour and aroma is lost to the atmosphere from hops added early in the boil. Those added later, either towards the end of the boil, after the boil or during or post fermentation, contribute little in the way of bitterness but instead deliver flavour and aroma from the essential oils particular to each variety. Part of the brewer's skill is to capture just the right amount and balance of these different characteristics from the hops.

Many contemporary craft brewers favour adding large amounts of hops late in the process, after the boil has been completed. This can be in a whirlpool or hop back (vessels through which the sweet, hoppy wort passes on its way to a fermenter), or in the fermenter itself in a process known as 'dry-hopping'.

The bitterness that hops lend to beers is measured on a scale called International Bitterness Units or IBUs. The human palate is said to be unable to detect an increase in bitterness beyond 100 to 120 IBUs, but this hasn't stopped some extreme brewers creating beers with theoretical bitterness levels in the hundreds, even one that claimed to have 1000 IBUs. Ultimately, however, any good beer will have a balanced bitterness wherein even if the number of IBUs is high, the perceived bitterness on the palate is balanced by malt sweetness. Think of it like adding chillies to a dish: get the amount right and you can add pleasant flavour and heat; go overboard and the heat will dominate all else.

For those of a technical bent, it's also worth pointing out that there are moves to give drinkers a more accurate idea of what the hops in their beer should be delivering as a simple measurement of IBUs is only helpful to a point. Former Moo Brew head brewer Owen Johnston, now working for Hop Products Australia, launched Hop Trial early in 2016 (too late to be considered for a full entry in this book). The brewing company will release nothing but single hop beers – beers brewed with just one hop variety – and the tap decals, which look like they're drawn from the periodic table, contain more information as to just how much of each of the hop's active ingredients has been used and at what point in the brewing process. This way those who are interested in learning more can gain a deeper understanding of exactly what to expect from each particular type.

As for the aromas and flavours a drinker can expect from hops, it depends on the variety. Certain common characteristics can be expected from hops native to certain regions of the world. The world's oldest and biggest hop-growing region, centred around southern Germany and surrounding countries, produces hops known for their subtlety and elegance, often possessing soft spice and lemon citrus aromas and flavours. Four varieties from the region are known as noble hops, originally developed in the wild, which are low in bitterness and high in aroma. They are Hallertau, Saaz, Tettnanger and Spalt, and many contemporary varieties have been developed from their parentage.

English hops are traditionally known for their floral and earthy nature and can give beers a gentle, broad and lingering bitterness. Those developed America's Pacific Northwest are typically much more powerful, known best for their pungent citrus, grapefruit and pine aromas and flavours, as well as an assertive bitterness.

A number of recently developed varieties of Kiwi hops are known for their tropical aromas, such as lychee and kiwifruit. One particularly distinctive variety is named Nelson Sauvin because of its similarity to sauvignon blanc grapes. Australian hop growers have been relative latecomers to the move towards aroma hops, but in recent years Hop Products Australia and Ellerslie Hop have developed a number of new breeds that are proving hugely popular throughout the beer world, with the passionfruit-like Galaxy leading the charge.

That said, new varieties are being developed every year by hop growers in order to satisfy the insatiable demand for new characteristics in beers. Many are also expanding their crops year on year in the hope of meeting demand, something that is becoming more challenging with each passing year. This is because

many contemporary brewers – and their audience – favour brewing aromatic hops and are thus chasing key varieties such as Galaxy, Nelson Sauvin, Mosaic, Citra and Amarillo. New, often small-scale, operations are being launched by farmers too, aware that this is an area of farming in which demand is only likely to increase.

To understand the different aromas and flavours particular hop varieties can lend to a beer, some brewers have created single-hop series, most notably Bridge Road Brewers in Australia. For these, they create a beer that is identical in every way – grain bill, alcohol content and yeast – but change the hops. For the most part, however, brewers will use a blend of different varieties at different stages in the brewing process to achieve balance and complexity of the flavours and aromas they desire. Doing so also gives them a better chance of coping with a shortage of a particular variety as they can adjust their blend accordingly and, with skill, still deliver the same end result in their beer.

YEAST Without yeast there would be no beer. Yet for most of beer's history, brewers of beer in its various historical forms had no idea that such a thing existed. They just knew that, given the right ingredients and certain conditions, the process that we now understand as yeast cells consuming fermentable sugars and creating alcohol and carbon dioxide would turn those ingredients into something that, when imbibed, would make them feel warm and fuzzy. Natural yeasts in the environment were doing the work for them.

Yeast is so central to beer, and indeed the creation of great, clean beer, that you will often hear brewers refer to themselves as 'yeast farmers'. By this, they are highlighting how their most important role, aside, perhaps, from recipe development, is creating the perfect conditions for their chosen yeast to go to work and

turn sugary, hoppy water into wonderful, aromatic, flavoursome and balanced beer. At one Belgian brewery I visited, Brasserie de la Senne, co-founder Yvan de Baets designed atypical wide and relatively flat fermenters in the knowledge they would treat his yeast kindly, yeast he refers to as 'she' and describes as "employee of the month every month – and I don't even have to pay her!"

To gain the best results, brewers need to use healthy yeast (yeasts can be pitched and re-pitched into beer, but they will mutate if used over long periods of time). And, in the vast majority of cases, it requires creating an environment free of potential contamination, and at an appropriate temperature where these unicellular organisms can multiply and feast.

As you will discover later in the book, different yeast strains will add a range of nuances to beer. Lager yeasts are typically described as 'clean' and, like many American ale yeasts, are 'neutral'; in other words they add little in the way of flavour or aroma to a beer. English ale yeasts are known for the fruity characteristics they can impart, while Belgian ale yeasts – those found in saisons, witbiers, dubbels, tripels and quadrupels, for example – as well as the yeast strains used in German wheat beers such as Hefeweizen, are responsible for some of the most dominant characteristics in those beers: typically of a fruity and spicy nature.

Different yeasts prefer different temperatures at which to operate, something that is touched upon in the introduction to the chapter on lagers (page 30). Typically, lager yeasts go to work between 6°C and 13°C, ale yeasts between 15°C and 24°C. But, while an individual yeast strain may have a preferred temperature range in which it would like to operate, brewers can play around with this to achieve different results in the end beer. In the hands of a skilled brewer, 'stressing' yeast by maintaining a temperature that is cooler or warmer than it would prefer can lead to some interesting and welcome flavours in a finished beer.

Not every brewer in Australia today is looking to operate a completely aseptic brewery all of the time, however. On the very fringes – the cutting edge, some might suggest – there are brewers playing with spontaneous fermentation. This sees them create their wort and then leave it open to the elements. It's a practice perfected by the lambic brewers of Belgium; visit Cantillon's working museum brewery in Brussels where you can walk through the brewery, even on brew days if you're there during the cooler months, to see perhaps the most famous example. And it's a practice that is gaining popularity in Australia.

Wild yeasts borne in the air around the brewery will ferment the beer, rather than any known yeast pitched into a sealed fermenter. The brewer will then wait and see what they – and any other bacteria or microflora in the atmosphere – will do to their wort and how the process will impact their beer. Often, such beers are then aged in barrels and, should the results be less than desirable, blended later or, in some cases, dumped. This might be a blend between multiple barrels or with another, frequently younger, beer to create the end product, in such cases creating what are referred to as mixed fermentation beers.

WATER While brewers do not have the vast array of options with water that they do with malt, hops or yeast, how they treat their water can affect the outcome of their finished beers. Different compositions of water in terms of its mineral content and acidity or alkalinity are best suited to different types of beers. This is best highlighted in a couple of classic beer styles.

The water in Pilsen, in the Czech Republic, is incredibly soft – not far from being as pure as filtered water. It is perfect for brewing pale beers, as during mashing brewers are able to reach the desired acidity for turning starches into fermentable sugars using just pale malts. The result is beers with soft malt flavours and aromas that allow the aromatics of noble hops, such as Saaz, to shine unhindered. The pilsner style born there has gone on to dominate the world of beer. In 2015, Seven Sheds in Tasmania brewed a pilsner using Cape Grim water, allegedly the purest on the planet, with the resultant beer one of the softest and creamiest I've encountered.

Conversely, the water in Burton-upon-Trent, in the heart of England, is hard. Its natural composition allowed the town's brewers to create paler, more assertively bitter ales than their peers in London in the 19th century, leading to a period of dominance for Burton's brewers. A chemist later discovered how to reproduce the water's mineral content, a process named Burtonisation, so that brewers anywhere could create such pale ales.

Today, with the importance of water's composition fully understood, brewers anywhere can use a range of key salts, such as calcium sulphate, calcium carbonate, sodium chloride and calcium chloride, to manipulate the water profile to suit the beer they intend to brew.

OTHER While this chapter opens by stating that brewers use four simple ingredients to make all beers, it's not strictly true. There are some classic styles that require the addition of other elements, such as coriander and Curaçao (and often other fruits and spices) in Belgian witbiers. Indeed, many beers from Belgium feature additions of candied sugar and/or spices.

In today's environment, brewers will look anywhere for new flavours, aromas or textures. Just as in pre-hop days when brewers would use all manner of additions to flavour or preserve their beer, now there is seemingly nothing that is off the table. While it risks the new wave of beer being dismissed as a novelty with 'weird ingredient' articles being something of a media staple, if brewers have the skills to use them to create great beers then there's no issue. In recent years, I have enjoyed excellent beers brewed with coffee, mussels and oysters, kids' lollies, wine wort, seawater, vanilla, native Australian plants, Weet-Bix, and all manner of fruit and more besides.

The use of barrels and, in rare cases in other countries, clay in which to ferment or age beer is also gaining in popularity. Many local breweries now have at least a handful of barrels to play with, some hundreds. The reasons for which they are used is touched upon in the introduction to the Specialty Beers chapter (page 214).

In many ways, this no-limits approach mirrors what is going on in some of the finest kitchens in the world, where award-winning chefs are seeking new ingredients and using innovative techniques to create wonderful new sensory experiences. Perhaps as the wider world awakes from the decades of brainwashing by dominant lager brewers, who have been hammering home the message that only their beer is real beer, the best of these experimental brewers will be viewed in the same light as the great chefs of the world. ●

Serving and Enjoying Beer

To get the best out of your beer, it should be served in optimum conditions. This can mean using an appropriate glass and drinking it at the right temperature. Better still, it should involve drinking it in the right setting and, ideally, with good company.

If this sounds a little over-the-top for beer, for which the choice of serving vessel has traditionally been stubby or can, pot, schooner or pint, then consider this: would you serve ice cream warm, on a plate, with a fork? Have you considered offering houseguests a pot of tea in which the teabags have been suspended in cold water straight from the tap? Would you serve shiraz cold in a tumbler?

The point is that beer, at least beer brewed to be savoured, deserves to be treated no differently than any other food or beverage. Steadily, Australians are waking up to that fact and are beginning to appreciate the diversity, versatility, quality and complexity inherent in good beer and according it similar respect to that granted to everything from wine to cheese to coffee. Once that is understood, it makes perfect sense to want to serve and enjoy every beer in the best way possible.

When you read through the list of beers in this book, you will see that the brewers of each beer have recommended the ideal temperature at which they should be enjoyed, as well as the most appropriate glassware. You'll find there will be common ground here for beers of the same or similar styles so, if you find yourself with a beer not listed in the book and are interested in trying to enjoy it at its best, then a safe guide is to find one of a similar style and go with that recommendation.

And, while I'm not suggesting you carry a thermometer and a padded rucksack containing a range of glassware with you at all times, where possible it is worth paying attention to brewers' suggestions as they will make a difference to the quality of your experience.

However, if you are drinking a beer you want to savour then the most important rule is this: use a glass.

I describe a number of different glass types below, but simply by using a glass rather than drinking straight from a bottle or can, you instantly enhance your appreciation. To fully enjoy a beer, we must engage our entire olfactory system, as what we actually taste via our taste buds – sweet, salt, bitter, sour and umami – is only a small percentage of the overall experience. Those tastes without the accompanying aromas tell only a tiny part of the story.

Think back to the last time you had a cold. Your nose was blocked and your head was stuffy: did food taste the same or did it appear bland? In effect, by drinking beer from a bottle or can you are creating for yourself that same handicap: locking in the aromas and only allowing yourself to experience a piece of what the brewer intended. Once the beer is poured into a glass, it opens up and releases those aromas in full: fruity, spicy, or earthy hops; sweet, nutty or roast malts; fruity, herbal, or peppery esters from the yeast. If a brewer is going to the trouble of creating a beer with aromas that could encompass orange blossom or coriander, pine cones or sherbet, lychees or leather, clotted-cream toffee or Vegemite, it's just rude to keep them under virtual lock and key.

The second most important rule when it comes to glassware is to ensure it is clean. This may sound like a case of stating the bleeding obvious, but with beer it is particularly important. Residue, even that left by washing-up liquid, can kill a beer's head, which isn't there just to look pretty but plays host to the aforementioned aromatics. A beer's head can also act as a form of 'liquid bottle-top', protecting the beer in your glass from the unwanted effects of oxygen, and can add a softer 'creamier' texture to the liquid as it is supped.

Beyond this, it depends how far you want to go. If you have room for just one beer glass in your cupboard, the best option is to go for some form of goblet with room in which to swirl the contents and release those all-important aromas. If you do wish to take things to another level, there are glasses designed for certain beer styles. Glassware manufacturers such as Spiegelau run eye-opening master classes that demonstrate the difference style-appropriate glassware can make to carbonation, aroma, mouthfeel and so on, while there are other manufacturers looking to push beer-specific glassware in Australia. If you want to go really fancy, check out CRAFTD. – a small Melbourne family business specialising in beautifully designed and branded beer glasses.

If you want to go further than the one-stop-shop of the goblet, there are specialist, beer-specific designs out there that allow you to serve every beer as the brewer intended. Some of the best-known and iconic style-specific glasses include those used for German weissbiers: they're tall, curvaceous, almost voluptuous, affairs designed to maintain the beer's thick, fluffy head. Pilsner glasses are traditionally tall and thin, highlighting the colour and clarity of their contents.

In Belgium, where beer is held in higher regard than any other country, you find some of the most beautiful glassware. Many brewers produce their own large, stemmed, tulip-shaped goblets designed to make the most of the beer's wonderful aromatics and retain its foamy head. Others, including the Trappist breweries, have their own particular design of glassware that is akin to a chalice. Some look almost too good to drink from, as if they should be perched on your mantelpiece; that is, of course, until

you sample the beer for which the glass is intended and realise, in many cases, that nothing could be too good for it.

In the past few years, Spiegelau released a number of unique glasses for particular beer styles, designed in conjunction with US breweries known for making great beers in those styles, including Dogfish Head, Rogue, Left Hand and Sierra Nevada. First was the IPA glass, which has a series of ripples or bumps in its lower half, which was followed by the development of specialist stout and wheat beer glasses.

Of course, while you may wish to dedicate an entire shelf to a range of glassware, any clean, stemmed wine glass will ensure your beer-drinking experience is far superior to merely knocking the cap off a bottle and glugging straight from the neck.

For the most part, when drinking in a pub you'll be handed a standard pot, schooner or pint glass. None are designed with any great focus on showcasing aromas and flavours at their best; the flip side is that, in most cases, if you're drinking at the pub the priority should be socialising rather than in-depth analysis of the contents of your glass. That said, many specialist beer bars have started using stemmed tulip glasses, while a handful even have some high-end glassware for use with their fanciest tipples.

As for temperature, it also plays a significant role in the enjoyment of beer. The colder a beer is, the less its aromas and flavours come into play. For pale lagers and pilsners, this is less of an issue as they are generally clean, dry beers – but serving many other styles too cold means locking away much that is good about them. Thus, particularly with richer, heavier, darker beers, it is best to remove them from the fridge and allow them to warm a while before consuming them.

Storing beer

With the vast majority of beer styles, the mantra 'fresh is best' is apt. More often than not, a beer will never taste better than the first day it is tapped, ideally at a bar at the brewery where it has been brewed. This is particularly true with lighter and hop-forward beers, with hop aromatics the first thing to fade in a beer in the months after it is released. Beer is also affected negatively by heat and light, so the best place to store most beers if you're not consuming straight away is in your fridge.

That said, there are certain beer styles that are suitable for ageing. These include strong Belgian ales, barley wines and imperial stouts and porters as well as many sour and farmhouse style beers, such as lambics, gueuzes and saisons. In the stronger beers, alcohol helps them stand up, while certain acids in the others are also a friend to people wanting to develop a cellar. Ideally, these beers should be kept in a cool cellar but, given most Australian homes don't come with cellars, the coolest, darkest spot you can find in your home (one that's not too moist or dry) may have to do. I know people who have invested in wine chillers they set at 10°C–12°C, and one with a tin-lined cupboard in his shed. Alternatively, an extra fridge set at a warmer (cellar-like) temperature than your main fridge could suffice, with the main goal being to ensure a steady temperature. I know my wife loves the fact I have two fridges at different temperatures for beer, yet still clog up the one supposedly for food...

Be prepared to play the lottery too. Even beers that should be perfect for ageing can deteriorate, so while a great barley wine might be wonderful three years on, it might also be good for nothing more than the sink. But if you're happy to win some and lose some, it's a fun and fascinating practice. ●

Beer and Food

Just as beer has come a long way from the days when choice meant 'Do you want one or not?', so has the concept of beer and food pairing moved on from pairing a snag in one hand with a tinny in the other.

Today you can invite someone to a beer dinner without expecting a response along the lines of, "Is that like a liquid lunch?" And, mercifully (if painfully slowly), it's getting rarer to flick past a 20-page wine list in an acclaimed restaurant only to alight upon a beer list comprising eight nigh-on-identical European-style lagers and a light beer – the equivalent of such a restaurant being proud to offer an exhaustive range of cask wines, although only, of course, white varieties.

Now that Australian drinkers are faced with a wonderfully diverse range of beers from which to choose, both brewed locally and imported from across the globe, they have an incredible range of flavours, textures and aromas to match with food. Where once there was a tiny number of advocates banging the drum for beer to be treated with similar respect to wine on the dining table, now it is not uncommon to find the occasional beer creeping onto leading restaurants' degustation menus, as at Noma's Sydney pop-up that opened with a barrel-aged beer–cider hybrid from Tasmania, or chefs

and brewers joining forces to combine each of their specialist subjects into a culinary feast.

Of course, just as craft beer is not something new, merely a renaissance of how things used to be (albeit with the condensed knowledge of thousands of years and with added bells and whistles), the pairing of beer and food is no modern invention. In fact, while brewers and advocates for better beer will use high-profile dinners as a means of showcasing beer to new and wider audiences, when you examine some of the classic pairings you'll find origins that stretch back long before Fritz Maytag bought Anchor Steam in California and kick-started the modern craft beer revolution.

Beer has been enjoyed with food for as long as it has existed. The difference now is the level to which beer and food pairing, and indeed cooking with beer, is sometimes taken. But, whether it is a drinker at home deciding which beer to pull from the fridge to have with dinner, or a brewer, sommelier and chef conferring in a Hatted restaurant ahead of a

degustation, the guiding principles remain the same. Ultimately, just as a brewer seeks to achieve balance in a beer, the aim when pairing beer and food should be to achieve balance, too.

Rather than attempt to explain how to do this with words and theory, this book offers 150 ways to understand how the two can work together in practice. As with serving temperature and glassware, the brewers of the beers featured here have suggested their favourite food match. By attempting these pairings yourself, your palate will tell you what works.

That said, armed with a few basic principles, you can begin to understand just why those pairings work and attempt to create your own.

One key consideration is assessing the weight or intensity of a particular beer or a dish that you intend to pair with beer. Beers that are lighter on the palate will pair better with lighter dishes, such as seafood with a Hefeweizen or witbier, while something heavier, such as a smoked brisket, sits perfectly with the rich, heavier malt flavours of a porter. Switch them around, and the porter would overwhelm a light seafood dish; the gentle sweetness and spiciness of either wheat beer would be no match for the meat.

When considering weight or intensity and beer, there are a number of aspects to consider, including bitterness, level of alcohol, richness, sweetness, carbonation and so on. Similarly, when assessing food, it is not just the core ingredient but also how it has been cooked or prepared, the heat or spices that have been added, and the texture, too.

You will often hear people talk about the 'three Cs' when discussing beer-and-food pairing: complement, contrast and cleanse. Keeping these in mind is another simple way to plan successful marriages.

Complement means to find common characteristics between what is on your plate and in your glass. This could be as obvious as the rich, dark malt flavours of an imperial stout with bitter chocolate or a fruity Belgian beer with a sweet, fruity dessert. Or it could be more subtle, perhaps a hint of orange zest within a sauce that reflects the citrus hop flavours of a particular beer.

Beer can also be used to contrast certain elements of a dish to create a balanced whole. Pairing a dry Irish stout with raw oysters is a classic for a reason. Pairing a sweeter, malty brown ale can take the edge off a hot chilli dish. That said, there are far more chefs and brewers I've come across who advocate combining hoppy ales or IPAs with hot, spicy dishes; such beers intensify the heat, particularly as alcohol content and bitterness rise, something that may not be to everybody's liking, but appeals to heat fiends.

When it comes to beer's cleansing properties, it can work in a number of ways. Highly carbonated beers can make heavier dishes seem lighter; similarly, well-hopped beers have the ability to cut through fatty, creamy or oily foods, refreshing the palate. Beers with high acidity are excellent for countering salty foods. Essentially, if you try to approach any pairing by considering beer as an additional ingredient of the dish as a whole you'll be on the right track.

Another phrase you may hear in relation to beer and food matching is 'What grows together, goes together.' When you think of such tried-and-tested traditional pairings as a German weissbier with weisswurst, commonly enjoyed with a pretzel as a late-morning snack throughout Bavaria, there is an appeal that is both evocative of a time and place and delicious on the palate.

With beer offering up such a vast and complex array of flavours, aromas and textures, there are endless possibilities when it comes to beer and food pairing. And, while there are classic matches and guiding principles, there is little that beats experimentation. Indeed, you can find that two beers of ostensibly the same character might work vastly differently with the same dish due to the difference in texture, alcohol or malt and hop choices.

As for the beer-versus-wine question that often raises its head: why not beer *and* wine? Within the broad spectrum of each, you can find characteristics that they share and others that are unique to one or the other. Certainly, the caramelised flavours that you can find in many beers is absent in wine and opens up many excellent pairings, while there are heavenly matches that wine can achieve with certain foods that beer cannot. In fact, once one heads down the path of seeking out perfect pairings to elevate both the beverage and cuisine to a higher plane, surely the only logical conclusion is to bring every single beverage into play. Not just beer, not just wine, and not just beer and wine.

There are many books dedicated to the art of beer and food pairing, most notably the classic *The Brewmaster's Table* by Garrett Oliver, for those wishing to take their understanding deeper. Another way to enhance your appreciation is to look out for the many beer dinners held regularly throughout Australia, particularly at the growing number of beer weeks taking place in most cities. Often the chef or host sommelier or brewer will be on hand to talk through their decision-making process and some see each course paired with a wine or cider too so you are able to understand the differences in how each pairing works.

Then there is self-exploration, and not just in the kitchen either. There is plenty to be said for picking up a selection of beers, some artisan cheeses and cured meats, and spending an evening seeing which work best together.

There is, of course, no need to devour books or work towards a PhD student's understanding of the science and theory behind why a saison works well with a particular washed-rind cheese. But, just as knowing a little bit about beer and its ingredients helps you enjoy beer a little more, so a little comprehension about how beer and food can work in harmony can enhance any meal.

If you do commit to exploring the world of beer and food, rest assured there will be revelations ahead. Perhaps it will be the first time you experience the right imperial stout with a chunk of creamy Stilton, or the moment a particular herb in a sauce sets off fireworks with the Belgian ale in your mouth. Whenever and whatever those matches and moments are, enjoy! ●

LAGERS

LAGERS

Lager occupies an interesting position in the Australian beer world right now. For years, it was the easy enemy for the vast majority of small brewers looking to change the country's beer culture from one of lager guzzlers to a more diverse and interesting community. They were the ones brewing characterful, bold ales while the 'fizzy yellow lagers' belonged to the big brewers who had crushed such diversity so successfully from the turn of the 20th century onwards.

Yet, now, as consumption of Australia's major beer brands falls dramatically, while still totally dwarfing that of anything else, many of those smaller brewers are looking to add lagers to their own rosters. And not just souped-up versions such as hoppy Indian pale lagers (IPL) or darker drops inspired by German dunkels either: straight down the line, Czech or German-inspired pilsners and helles lagers. Whether they all have the skills or tools to make them as cleanly as their bigger brethren is debatable, but it's an interesting turn of affairs; another sign, perhaps, that the small independents have 'made it', that craft beer is here to stay and there's other battles to be fought as well as that against the monolith of industrial lager and its promotional army.

That pale lagers came to achieve almost total dominance in Australia, and much of the rest of the world, is a legacy of the phenomenal growth in the 20th century of a handful of breweries and their success in capturing the Australian market. The local beer industry shrank from almost 300 breweries across Australia at the turn of the 20th century to a bare handful by the 1980s; the choice of beer in your local pub became similarly limited too: usually 'heavy' or 'light' from your state's main brewery.

This homogenisation of Australia's beer culture became possible for a number of reasons. Light lagers were well-suited to the country's hot climate, thus those who had the ability to make them – and make them well and consistently – were at an advantage. Too many breweries were making poor and inconsistent beer, allowing those with the best technology and skills to thrive. Innovations in refrigeration helped these pilsner-style beers thrive too, with pubs and hotels able to serve them ice cold.

The larger breweries also established their own extensive distribution networks and set up their own pub chains. These 'tied pubs' gave them the ability to lock their competitors out. And, as the rationalisation of Australian breweries reached its peak, each state's dominant brewer would focus on its own market, leaving its interstate peers alone to monopolise their local market in the knowledge they, in return, would do the same. Thus, when Phil Sexton secured Carlton Draught through a third party to pour at the Sail & Anchor in Fremantle in the mid-80s, it became the only place pouring the popular Victorian drop in WA and caused much consternation at Swan.

It was against such a backdrop that what has become known as the craft beer industry today began: as a rebellion against the commoditisation and mundanity of beer then and a desire to create something different, more interesting, with provenance and, usually, made with love.

Yet, three decades on from the opening of the Sail & Anchor and the work of the late Geoff Scharer, who brewed pioneering lagers in New South Wales at the same time, this alone does not explain the relative scarcity of 'craft' lagers and pilsners from Australia's 200-plus breweries and brewing companies, at least until the recent change of direction.

Brewing a lager properly takes time – the larger brewers might be able to use special techniques to turn around commercial lagers in as little as six days, but six weeks or more is regarded as an appropriate conditioning time for a pilsner-style beer. Indeed, the very term 'lager' comes from the German 'lagern', which means 'to store' and relates to the period of weeks or months these beers spend maturing at close to freezing point. For many smaller breweries already working at capacity, such time is a luxury they simply do not have; ales can progress from raw ingredients to packaged product in less than two weeks. Furthermore, creating a traditional German-style lager or pilsner – typically such clean, refined beers – leaves a brewer with nowhere to hide.

But what is lager, other than the beer poured from almost every tap at most pubs, hotels and sporting clubs in Australia? It is one half of the wider beer family, the other half being ale. And the one thing that distinguishes all lagers from all ales is its yeast.

Ale yeasts (*Saccharomyces cerevisiae*) generally ferment wort at relatively warm temperatures (15°C–24°C), while lager yeasts go to work at lower temperatures (6°C–13°C) and generally go about the business of turning wort into beer at a much slower rate. Lager yeasts also settle at the bottom of a beer, while ale yeasts are top-fermenting. For those of a historical bent, lager yeasts are known as both *Saccharomyces pastorianus*, named after Louis Pasteur, the chemist who discovered microbial fermentation (as well as vaccination and pasteurisation), and *Saccharomyces carlsbergensis*, in honour of Emil Christian Hansen, who first described the species when working for Danish brewery Carlsberg in the late 19th century.

So how does this help with your selection next time you're faced with a lineup of taps on a bar or several fridges full of bottles? The main difference when it comes to having a lager or an ale in your hand is that lager yeasts tend to deliver cleaner ferments. In other words, they give off less by-products that are noticeable in the finished beer. Whereas a brewer would expect to gain some fruity characteristics from an English ale yeast or spices from a Belgian witbier yeast, for example, lager yeasts are more neutral, allowing the characteristics of the malt, hops and, to a lesser extent, water to take centre stage. Hence talk of 'clean' or 'crisp' lagers.

This does not mean that all lagers, however, are pale, clean and/or crisp. The beers that have risen to dominance worldwide over the past century and a half, based upon the wonderful helles lagers from Bavaria and pilsners from the Czech Republic developed in the mid-19th century, may suit such descriptors. Yet lager yeast can be used with any combination of grain and hops, creating lagers that are dark, rich and heavy, too. Indeed, before the first pale lagers were created in Munich in the 19th century, lagers would, for the most part, have been dark.

Today, darker variants include copper-coloured Vienna lagers and Schwarzbiers (black beers), while Bocks (strong lagers) and their bigger variants Doppelbocks and Eisbocks are usually darker as well as boozier.

——— *A DOZEN MORE TO TRY* ———

HAWKERS BEER	**MOO BREW**
Pilsner	Pilsner
STONE & WOOD BREWING	**DAINTON FAMILY BREWERY**
Green Coast	Samurye Lager
AUSTRALIAN BREWERY	**MATILDA BAY BREWING**
The Pilsner	Dogbolter
LITTLE CREATURES	**COOPERS**
Original Pilsner	Premium Lager
BOATROCKER BREWERY	**BREWCULT**
Hoppbier	Beer Geek Quit Rage
HOLGATE BREWHOUSE	**RED HILL BREWERY**
Norton Lager	Crafty Pilsner

KUNG FOO RICE LAGER

2 BROTHERS BREWERY

 RICE LAGER 4.6% 2°C STRAIGHT-SIDED PINT GLASS

TASTING NOTES It seems a little odd to feature a lager from 2 Brothers, given the accolades they've attracted over the years for all manner of bigger, often malt-driven ales. Yet Kung Foo is a perennial favourite with tropical and citrus hops sitting on a soft malt (and rice) base, in a lager with character that's also a flexible friend at the dinner table.

THE STORY Brothers Andrew and David Ong fell in love with good beer while working in America – one as a bullet-dodging physio in the Bronx; the other as a number-crunching aeronautical engineer in Seattle – and bought their kit from a former brewpub in New York's Times Square, relocating it to an industrial unit in Moorabbin.

Without any attendant song and dance, they've carved a reputation as purveyors of consistently high quality beers in a broad range of styles, from lagers to Belgian ales to high ABV barley wines and much in between. They've proved a hit, particularly at their Beerhall in Moorabbin and across Melbourne's pubs, as well as with judges at the Australian International Beer Awards and voting punters at the annual Great Australasian Beer SpecTAPular.

Early in 2016, the brothers closed down their Beerhall and gave it a serious overhaul. By the time you read this, the new one will be open, featuring more taps, more beers, more space and a beer garden too.

ALSO TRY Voodoo Baltic Porter Grizz American Amber | BOOM! XPA Growler American Brown Ale James Brown Belgian Brown Ale

BREWER'S FOOD MATCH
A 30°C day ... or spicy Asian food

AVAILABILITY
Year-round

BREWERY & CELLAR DOOR LOCATION
4 Joyner Street, Moorabbin, VIC 3189

BREWERY WEBSITE
www.2brothers.com.au

ORIGINAL BOCK

BALMAIN

 BOCK   **5.5%**   **5°C**   **SOMETHING LARGE**

TASTING NOTES Given Balmain Brewing Company is a revival of a brewery of the same name, it was only right to bring back a beer inspired by the original brewery's most popular tipple. This isn't a replica of the Original Balmain Bock, but it is good. It pours a lovely, deep mahogany and emits big dark caramel, chocolate and cocoa aromas. Dark malts dominate the flavours too, with a touch of warming alcohol and soft roast to finish.

THE STORY The original Balmain brewery operated in the Sydney suburb in the 1980s before its owners received an offer for their land from developers and checked out. The brand sat idle until 2010 when it was re-registered and new owners set about relaunching Balmain with a pale ale brewed for them under license, then bringing in Glenn Cary, who had founded then sold the Byron Bay Brewery, as CEO.

They've since added a pilsner, summer ale and this Original Bock to the lineup and combined a prominent presence in several key Balmain pubs with growing distribution across Australia. This included them becoming the first local craft brewer to put cans into Aldi, while Balmain was launched in China at the start of 2016 too.

There are plans to make Balmain more than just a name borrowed from a brewery that once existed in the suburb. While efforts to find a location in Balmain itself have proved fruitless, there is hope that 2016 will see them open a venue somewhere within that area of Sydney. While most production would still be contracted, the talk is of having a small brewery onsite to act as a 'test pad' for future releases.

ALSO TRY Original Pale | Original Pilsner

BREWER'S FOOD MATCH
Game meats and casseroles

AVAILABILITY
Year-round

BREWERY LOCATION
Contract-brewed

BREWERY WEBSITE
www.balmainbrewing.com.au

STORMY LAGER

BARROW BOYS BREWING CO.

 DARK LAGER　 **4.7%**　 **6-8°C**　 **FLUTE**

TASTING NOTES There were few lagers available from Australian microbreweries when the team behind Barrow Boys was planning its launch; fewer still that were dark in colour and nature. They stepped into that void with a beer that's closest to a Marzen or Vienna Lager but darker in colour and richer in its biscuity, caramel flavours.

THE STORY Barrow Boys took an unusual decision when launching in 2014. While the vast majority of small brewing companies have launched with pale or golden ales, they opted for a lager – a dark one at that. They soon redressed the balance, following up with Pedlar's Pale, a second packaged beer that joined its bright orange sibling in garish lime-green livery. In addition to these core beers, former Little Creatures brewer Ash Hazell has brewed some fine draught-only beers at Temple Brewing, with the exquisite India Amber Ale one I'd love to see repeated.

At time of publication, Ash, backer Ross Sudano, marketing guy Justin Trail and 'spruiker' Dean Romeo, were still on the hunt for a place to build their own brewery, having originally hoped to open up in North Melbourne, whose old markets gave them the name 'Barrow Boys' in the first place. But the quality of their beers coming out of Hawkers Beer – and the other breweries where Ash creates their keg-only limited releases – will be easing the pain.

ALSO TRY Pedlar's Pale | India Amber Ale
Black Market Porter

☆

BREWER'S FOOD MATCH
Spicy pork sausages or pulled-pork dishes

AVAILABILITY
Year-round

BREWERY LOCATION
'Gypsy' brewed

BREWERY WEBSITE
www.barrowboysbrewing.com.au

UNFILTERED LAGER

BLACKMAN'S BREWERY

 LAGER   **4.6%**   **4–5°C**    **PILSNER OR PINT GLASS**

TASTING NOTES Initially trialled as an Oktoberfest special release, the first packaged beer from Blackman's is one of the best lagers you'll find in Australia. A finely judged take on the hard-to-master Munich-style Helles, it has a delicate honey malt, floral hops and soft bitterness balance to it, a sure sign that Renn Blackman is a young brewer to watch.

THE STORY After travelling Australia and the world learning the art of brewing, including stops at The Monk and Old Swan breweries in WA, Camden Town in London and former brewpub True South in Victoria, Renn Blackman returned close to home. In Torquay, he and girlfriend Jess Giudice, with family support, converted the popular Surfrider Café and Restaurant into Blackman's Brewery.

The beers and cider are named (mostly) after family members; more importantly, they're bloody good beers and have been collecting medals with impressive frequency to prove it. The venue does a fine line in beer food too, with the kitchen initially set up by Renn's old mate from The Monk and beer food guru Mitch of Beersine. He's not averse to the odd collaboration too, most notably with the owner of his alma mater, Camden

Town, brewers of a damn fine Helles themselves, good enough indeed for the Londoners to attract a multimillion dollar buyout from AB InBev.

Look out for Blackman's beers in tinny form too, after they installed their own canning line at the start of 2016.

ALSO TRY Ernie Golden Ale
Bob Witbier Reginald IPA
Arthur Smoked Porter

BREWER'S FOOD MATCH
Fish tacos, slaw, chipotle

AVAILABILITY
Year-round

BREWERY & CELLAR DOOR LOCATION
26 Bell Street, Torquay, VIC 3228

BREWERY WEBSITE
www.blackmansbrewery.com.au

COOL HOPS

EDGE BREWING PROJECT

 LAGER  4.6% 6°C **FOOTED PILSNER GLASS**

TASTING NOTES This New World lager has worked wonders for Edge, proving equally popular on beer geek rating sites and with beer judges here and overseas. Starting with a smooth and relatively full caramel and biscuit malt base, it layers on welcoming tropical and citrus hops to create a highly appealing lager.

THE STORY Originally a joint venture between Danish 'gypsy' brewer Christian Skovdal Andersen of Beer Here and the home-brewing importer, Adam Betts, who introduced his beers to the Australian market, Edge is now solely the latter's domain. And it's one upon which Adam is focusing ever greater attention – understandable given its successes in competitions here and abroad. He also runs the import/distribution business Northdown, Craft Beer Movement.

Brewing at various sites in Victoria, although usually at Hawkers Beer for his big batch beers and lagers, at smaller breweries for his for quirkier releases, Adam has proved himself adept at creating tight lagers while not being afraid to head to the other end of the scale and concoct big beers alongside those featuring unusual – often native to Australia – ingredients.

He's also been able to use his connections as an importer to line up collaborative brews too, with a Rye Pilsner created with New York-based Dane Evil Twin a real treat.

ALSO TRY Cereal Killer Red Lager SHIPA (Southern Hemisphere Imperial Pale Ale) | Rye Pilsner (collaboration with Evil Twin)

BREWER'S FOOD MATCH
Bourbon-marinated pork chops

AVAILABILITY
Year-round

BREWERY LOCATION
West Melbourne, VIC

BREWERY WEBSITE
www.edgebrewing.com.au

HUNTER BOCK

HUNTER BEER CO.

 BOCK   **6.0%**    **6°C**   **CHALICE OR STEIN GLASS**

TASTING NOTES Such is the diversity of beers brewed at Hunter Beer Co. that you could return every couple of months and find several taps pouring something different. One beer that sticks around is the Bock, a smooth, strong lager that collected Champion Dark Lager at the 2015 Craft Beer Awards. Pouring an impenetrable dark brown, aromas of cola and noble hops give way to dark cocoa, nuts, toffee and sarsaparilla.

THE STORY Hunter Beer Co. enters its teens in 2016 yet, while the Australian beer industry has grown phenomenally since original brewer Luke Scott created its first batch of Kolsch in 2003, it continues to occupy a rather unassuming position. Its focus is first and foremost on running a brewpub-style operation; sure, the wide range of beers brewed by head brewer Keith Grice and his team can be found in select venues (mostly in New South Wales) but the best way to experience them is to head to Potters Hotel in the Hunter Valley.

There, attached to the main building and sharing grounds with old brick kilns and accommodation, is the small brewery where beers such as the Bock and Kolsch are brewed. The brewpub approach means there's no need to meet supply chain demand for big-volume core beers, so variety – as well as taking guests on laid-back brewery tours – is the name of the game. On my first visit it was Oktoberfest and half a dozen of the venue's taps featured German-inspired beers, while smoked beers, oyster stouts, eisbocks, IPAs and sours crop up from time to time.

Barrel-aged beers, making use of oak from the surrounding wineries, are an increasing feature, while the trophy for this Bock at the Craft Beer Awards in 2015, suggests Hunter's old-timers have still got it, too.

ALSO TRY Kolsch | Pale Ale
Various one-offs and seasonals

BREWER'S FOOD MATCH
Chocolate or, for a surprising treat, chilli chicken mole

AVAILABILITY
Year-round

BREWERY & CELLAR DOOR LOCATION
Wine Country Drive, Nulkaba, NSW 2325

BREWERY WEBSITE
www.hunterbeerco.com

PREMIUM LAGER

JAMES BOAG'S

 LAGER 5.0% COLD!  CHALICE

TASTING NOTES The sole 'industrial' lager to make an appearance in this book is one that has the qualities of consistency and cleanliness shared by its many peers that aren't here; the crucial difference is that it has appealing characteristics too. There's a touch of fruity hops up front, a soft malty body and a pleasant, gentle bitterness. Must be the pure waters of Tasmania...

THE STORY With so much interesting, increasingly good (and occasionally not so good) beer coming out of the country's rapidly growing number of small breweries, there's less and less reason to sample the wares from the country's major breweries – not to mention less opportunity as more venues switch to craft beer. Sure, they make technically high quality beers, but do so within realms of the flavour and aroma spectrum that offer little beyond benefitting from being consumed ice cold.

On the rare occasions there's no other choice (other than something other than beer, of course) – sporting events, gigs, out bush, for example – a couple of mouthfuls is usually enough reminder that I choose craft beer for more reasons than simply supporting the little guy. Yet Boag's Premium is an exception.

A few years back, in the Match Day Bar after a game at the 'G, a brewer friend and I were faced with a choice of Boag's or Boag's. Boag's it was, and what a pleasant surprise it was too, with a light, lifted hop character kicking things off. More recently, in a blind tasting I hosted of lagers from breweries big and small, it came top. With Hahn Premium abandoned, it's the best of the big brand lagers.

ALSO TRY Wizard Smith's Ale

BREWER'S FOOD MATCH
Ideal accompaniment to seafood or lamb

AVAILABILITY
Year-round

BREWERY & CELLAR DOOR LOCATION
69 The Esplanade, Launceston, TAS 7250

BREWERY WEBSITE
www.jamesboag.com.au

RESERVE LAGER

KNAPPSTEIN

 LAGER   5.6%   4–5°C   PILSNER GLASS

TASTING NOTES Fresh and at its best, Knappstein Reserve Lager is an explosion of fruity New Zealand hops, with the use of the Nelson Sauvin variety creating grapefruit, gooseberry and lychee aromas and flavours. Its relatively high alcohol content gives a full, creamy body too.

THE STORY Knappstein, in the Clare Valley, is first and foremost a producer of wine. Part of the Lion empire, in 2006 it added a wood-clad microbrewery to the interior of its striking, redbrick home in the heart of Clare. The brewery has only ever produced one beer, this Reserve Lager based on the clean, crisp lagers of southern Germany.

Once a much-loved beer among the country's small but growing band of discerning beer cognoscenti, it has since got a little lost within the machinations of its sprawling parent company. Noises from industry legend Chuck Hahn suggest he intends to see that rectified with investment in the brewery itself and a fresh push into venues. Here's hoping he succeeds as it's a big-natured lager several leagues in character above those that pay Lion's bills.

ALSO TRY N/A

BREWER'S FOOD MATCH
Rich Asian dishes

AVAILABILITY
Year-round

BREWERY & CELLAR DOOR LOCATION
2 Pioneer Avenue, Clare, SA 5453

BREWERY WEBSITE
www.knappstein.com.au

PILSNER

LAST DROP BREWERY

 PILSNER   4.8%  2–4°C   **STEIN OR PILSNER GLASS**

TASTING NOTES It had been a while since I'd last tried a beer from Last Drop but, wanting to include this slice of WA brewing heritage in the book, I sought the views of a few knowledgeable locals. "By far the best craft pilsner on the market," said one, so here it is: a Czech-style pilsner brewed by a Czech brewer with Czech hops adding subtle grassy, lemon and spicy characters to its soft, sweet malts.

THE STORY There are plenty of Australian micros with a lot of mileage on the clock these days, breweries that have celebrated a decade or more in the business. Not many have made it into a third decade yet, but that's the case for Last Drop, which served its first beers way back in 1992.

Yet, outside of WA, there will no doubt be plenty asking: "Last who?" Because, despite being well into a third decade of brewing, the beers are found only within the various Last Drop venues in WA, occasionally on taps at other beer venues in the state and very rarely at the country's bigger beer festivals.

When you do find them, they're predominantly of a European bent: lagers, wheat beers, farmhouse-style ales.

They're brewed on a setup salvaged from a brewery in Bavaria by Jan Bruckner, the Czech head brewer who's been at the helm for most of its 20-plus years, favouring traditional techniques: open fermenters, horizontal lagering tanks and, perhaps most crucially of all, maturation periods far in excess of those allowed at most modern breweries.

ALSO TRY Hefeweizen | Bock | Oktoberfest

BREWER'S FOOD MATCH
Pork ribs or sauerkraut-based dishes

AVAILABILITY
Year-round in Western Australia

BREWERY LOCATION
Bedfordale, WA

CELLAR DOOR
507 Nicholson Road, Canning Vale, WA 6155

BREWERY WEBSITE
www.lastdropbeer.com.au

STEFANO'S PILSNER

MILDURA BREWERY

 PILSNER 4.7% 4°C LONG PILSNER GLASS

TASTING NOTES The beer that takes its name from the chef, Stefano di Pieri, who, along with wife Donata Carrazza, owns and runs Mildura Brewery alongside his restaurant. It's a beer designed with the dinner table in mind: a soft, subtle, spicy and gently bitter pilsner that's also a tribute to the beers Stefano's forebears would have enjoyed in Italy.

THE STORY Brewery homes in Australia don't come much grander than that of Mildura Brewery. It's found within the city's former Astor Theatre, a stunning Art Deco building that operated as a theatre from the 1920s to the 1960s. Today, it houses the brewery, pub and dining room, after being bought by Don Carrazza in 1989 and impressively brought back to life with beer and food providing the entertainment.

The brewery itself is one of the bigger setups in the local microbrewing landscape and, as such, brews beer for a number of other brewing companies under license. Its own offerings are based around a core range that covers styles from pilsner to strong ale, tending towards the safer end of each style.

That core range is embellished by occasional seasonal and short run releases, of which the highlight is Choc Hops, a chocolate and vanilla dessert-in-a-glass affair that was inspired by the iconic Youngs Double Chocolate Stout from the UK.

ALSO TRY Choc Hops | Astor Ale Mallee Bull

BREWER'S FOOD MATCH
Prawn linguine

AVAILABILITY
Year-round

BREWERY & CELLAR DOOR LOCATION
20 Langtree Avenue, Mildura, VIC 3500

BREWERY WEBSITE
www.mildurabrewery.com.au

LOVEDALE LAGER

SYDNEY BREWERY

 LAGER   **4.7%**   **COLD!**   **500 ML STEIN GLASS**
(OR 1 LITRE IF YOU'RE THIRSTY!)

TASTING NOTES The Sydney Brewery's brewery is no longer based in Sydney, but rather in Lovedale in the Hunter Valley. This lager takes its name from the new home and also takes home pretty much every trophy awarded for lager. An elegant, well-balanced take on Munich lagers, it has light lemon, citrus aromas, a soft texture, light biscuit malts and the gentlest of bitter finishes.

THE STORY The original Sydney Brewery was located in the basement of the Macquarie Hotel near Hyde Park; the sort of 'we'll fit it all in somehow' arrangement that you'll also find at the Lord Nelson in The Rocks. Originally called Schwartz Brewery, it mainly focused on the approachable end of the craft beer spectrum with the majority of beer sold through the owner's chain of hotels and bars.

A rebrand and move to one of those hotels in the Hunter took place in March 2014, where the Lovedale Brewery was opened. Head brewer Michael Capaldo transferred his skills there, taking his talent for making impeccably clean and tight beers to the new site. Those skills are best demonstrated in this multiple trophy-winning lager but can also be found in a wide range of ales and even ciders.

ALSO TRY Darlo Dark | Pyrmont Rye IPA
Surry Hills Pils

BREWER'S FOOD MATCH
Margherita pizza

AVAILABILITY
Year-round

BREWERY & CELLAR DOOR LOCATION
420 Wine Country Drive, Lovedale, NSW 2325

BREWERY WEBSITE
www.sydneybrewery.com

POWERSTANCE PILSNER

TEMPLE BREWING COMPANY

 PILSNER 5.1% 4–5°C PILSNER GLASS

TASTING NOTES Their Anytime IPA is a major trophy winner but whenever I call into Temple it's always the Powerstance (named after brewer Glenn Harrison's way of standing) that's first in my glass. Initially brewed with pilsner meister Frank Piefer, the former head brewer of Weihenstephan, at the other end of the phone, it's an outstanding recreation of a classic pilsner, capturing both the distinct pilsner malt character and the herbal, spicy nature of noble European hops.

THE STORY Temple Mk II rose from the remnants of the original brewing company that had made its name as a 'gypsy' brewery before opening the current brewery and venue just off Brunswick East's popular Lygon Street. Many, me included, wondered whether a new Temple could succeed, but have been swiftly put in our place as the reworked venue, including a beer garden always planned by the original owners, has become steadily busier (not least because the food is great) and the beers have lived up to the standards the old Temple set for themselves.

Former Hargreaves Hill brewer Glenn has embraced his first head-brewer role, reworking the Anytime IPA into an AIBA trophy winner and adding his own quality

creations. With bold plans for the future and financial backers who should make them possible, expect to see Temple grow in size in the coming years.

ALSO TRY Anytime IPA | Bicycle Beer New World Order American Stout Rye Hard IPA

BREWER'S FOOD MATCH
Scallops, fresh oysters, baked fish

AVAILABILITY
Year-round

BREWERY & CELLAR DOOR LOCATION
122 Weston Street, Brunswick East, VIC 3056

BREWERY WEBSITE
www.templebrewing.com.au

AMERICAN AMBER LAGER

VALE BREWING

 DARK LAGER 4.5% 3°C TULIP GLASS

TASTING NOTES The lager formerly known as DRK underwent a rebrand in 2015, as had the brewery behind it earlier in the year. Now tagged an 'American amber lager', the liquid itself hasn't changed and remains my pick of Vale's beers, a surprisingly luscious blend of caramel, mocha and milk chocolate, with a touch of fruity hops and a mild bitter finish.

THE STORY The brewery formerly known as McLaren Vale underwent a tweak in ownership and rebrand in 2015, becoming Vale Brewing. It had started out as a single beer, Vale Ale, venture that was as much marketing driven as anything else – beer brewed interstate while playing upon the McLaren Vale name – but for the past few years has brewed all of its keg beers at its home in Willunga.

The move 'home' allowed head brewer Jeff Wright to improve the quality and consistency of the draught product and also start releasing some pretty out-there one-off releases under the EXP banner. In 2015, they also launched a spin-off second brand, Fox Hat (see page 178), taking them ever further from their single beer origins and into the world of beer nerd credibility.

ALSO TRY IPA | Ale | EXP range

☆

BREWER'S FOOD MATCH
Pulled pork slider, Red Leicester cheese

AVAILABILITY
Year-round

BREWERY LOCATION
Willunga, SA

CELLAR DOOR LOCATION
187 McMurtrie Road, McLaren Vale, SA 5171

BREWERY WEBSITE
www.valebrewing.com.au

PIRATE LIFE BREWING

The beer scene in South Australia has been awakening for a couple of years. Initially, a number of breweries and contract or 'gypsy' brands had thrown their hat into the ring, joining the handful of existing microbreweries and, of course, Coopers. At the same time, a change was starting to spread through Adelaide's venues as more embraced a wider variety of beer on and behind their bars.

Yet, without wishing to downplay the role played in the ongoing transformation by a host of brewers – old and new, Adelaide-based and regional – no one has caused quite the commotion upon opening as did Pirate Life Brewing in early 2015. Not only did they shake up Adelaide, they caught the attention of beer lovers across the country, making 2015 more or less the year of the pirate.

The story of the threesome at the centre of the business starts in Aberdeen. There, two young brewers who both hailed from Western Australia met while working at BrewDog. Red Proudfoot and Jack Cameron ended up living, working, studying and drinking together before returning to their home state and continuing their brewing education, the former at Margaret River start-up Cheeky Monkey, the latter at Little Creatures.

The third soon-to-be Pirate was Jack's dad, Michael. He had his own links with BrewDog, having built their first bar, and also brought with him experience in various roles within the craft beer industry in Australia and the States.

A good couple of years before they launched, Red told me of a potential venture of his own. South Australia always looked to be the likely home for such a venture, with talk initially of setting up in one of the wine regions. Part of the thinking was that the state was, at that point, lagging behind much of the rest of Australia when it came to craft beer, while it also offered a central location for distribution to both coasts.

Yet, by the time the brewery started taking shape in Adelaide's Hindmarsh suburb, the SA scene was much livelier than it had been. Several breweries and brewing companies had opened within a couple of years of each other: the likes of Big Shed Brewing Concern, Mismatch, Prancing Pony and Clare Valley among others.

So, as Pirate Life set off on their journey from WA – literally as well as figuratively: they drove across the Nullarbor to their new home, documenting the trip as they went – I wondered whether their choice of destination would work. Was there less space for a new brewery, especially one set up by 'outsiders'? Or would there be a bigger and more engaged audience ready for something new?

I needn't have worried. The trio were thinking big. Indeed, along with Hawkers Beer, which launched in Melbourne the week before Pirate Life, they were thinking bigger from the off than any new brewing company in Australia in years – at least since Byron Bay's Stone & Wood. Like Hawkers, they brought experience from overseas: from working in more developed craft beer markets and both for and with large and mature microbreweries. And, like Hawkers, it was a case of hitting the ground sprinting.

Within months of launching their first three beers – a triptych of hoppy ales – they'd completed tours of parts of the east and west coasts, hitting up several venues a day and indicating that their staying power was as impressive as their brewing. And wherever they called in, they left a mark.

The main reason they did so – as it always has to be if a brand is going to thrive rather than be a flash in the pan – was the quality of the beers. Their Throwback IPA was a hopped-up mid-strength take on the loosely defined 'session IPA' category. Their West Coast USA-inspired Pale Ale was a true masterpiece that wove subtle complex layers of hops and malts upon one another, all with impeccable balance. And, as I've said elsewhere in this book (see page 105), their IIPA (imperial India pale ale) was the ultimate '#$%^ you!' statement of intent.

The last of these wasn't just a fine beer – it really was and has improved over time too – but it tipped the scales close to 9 per cent ABV and managed to squeeze in a mountain of hops without leaving a punishing or unpleasant bitterness. Most striking of all, where its siblings came in standard-size cans, this came in 500 ml tallboys. And in black.

The Pirate Life cocktail – great brewers fond of a good time, excellent beers that tap into Australia's fetish for American-style hoppy beers, intense determination and great branding (they've won trophies for their packaging as well as their beers) – has proven intoxicating to all who have consumed their beers. Within a year of opening, they had already significantly expanded capacity, collected a swag of gold medals and trophies and nailed three of the top 11 spots in the annual nationwide GABS Hottest 100 Aussie Craft Beers poll, a public vote for the top beers of the year.

Their arrival has put something of a cherry on the cake of Adelaide's beer renaissance. What's more, as with the aforementioned Hawkers, they are forcing a lot of local brewers to think bigger, to think better and to think differently. And, ultimately, that may prove to be their legacy as much as the beers they brew.

SESSION
BEERS

SESSION BEERS

Beer is a wonderfully subjective thing. Put a group of experienced brewers together at a table and ask them to judge a series of beers against strict style guidelines and you would expect them to come up with similar results. Give the same group of brewers the same series of beers and ask them which ones they like the best and, chances are, you would get very different results.

People's tastes differ. There will be those for whom a balanced IPA will be their choice when sitting down for the proverbial 'session'. So, as with *150 Great Australian Beers*, for the purposes of this collection of 'session ales', the peccadilloes of the more extreme or adventurous drinkers are ignored in favour of beers that the vast majority would consider sessionable.

This includes light beers, mid-strengths and approachable, light-coloured ales that might be tagged 'golden ales' or 'summer ales' or referred to as 'gateway' beers. In other words, those that offer newcomers to the world of craft beer a gentle introduction as they move away from generic lagers, as well as those packing enough flavour to keep confirmed craft beer drinkers happy while packing little in the way of booze so that they can enjoy a session without becoming inebriated.

Mid-strength as a category is self-explanatory: typically beers around 3.5 per cent ABV. It is one that is becoming more diverse and heavily populated in Australia. For years, drinkers looking for a fuller-flavoured mid-strength had little other than Rogers' from Little Creatures on offer. Today, while that beer remains a classic of its kind, it has been joined by a growing number from brewers looking to achieve the dual aims of lower alcohol content and higher flavour.

Two years ago, I wrote in this section about the appearance of 'tiny IPAs' and, while there are still new beers being released with such a title, the rise of the term 'session IPA' has, for the most part, superseded it. Taking a lead from what has been one of the fastest growing sectors in the States, it's a pretty fluid category of beers, with some more accurately tagged as hoppier (some would say, unbalanced) pale ales and thus appear in that section of the book. But there are some, like those tiny IPAs, that duck under the 4 per cent ABV mark.

As well as such beers in which brewers look to combine imposing hop aromatics and high bitterness at low alcohol levels, you can find beers inspired by English milds that are typically malt driven on many breweries' lineups, as well as reduced-alcohol German-style lagers.

Also at the lower end of the alcohol spectrum, although perhaps destined for the Specialty section of this book once there are enough of them brewed to a high standard consistently, are certain sour styles, such as the once almost forgotten German Berliner Weisse. A deliberately soured (by various methods) wheat ale, it is growing in popularity in Australia and typically these beers tip the scales around the 3–3.5 per cent ABV mark. The best, such as Feral's Watermelon Warhead, Mash Brewing's wax-sealed, comically grotesquely packaged series, plus a number from Boatrocker offer a refreshing, complex and satisfying option for anyone looking for something interesting in their glass but who need to remain clear headed.

However, while such beers exist very much in the fringes, it is a different story entirely when it comes to golden ales. The biggest growth within the craft sector in recent years has been pale and golden ales around the 4.5 per cent ABV mark. Huge numbers of breweries now have a golden or summer ale as part of their offering now; some even feel the need to brew golden, summer and pale ales that all occupy the same space on the spectrum of beer flavours and aromas. Whether it's down to the phenomenal success of Stone & Wood's Pacific Ale and James Squire's One Fifty

Lashes or the desire to try and capture the growing number of people taking their first steps outside the mainstream, 'golden' or 'summer' ales are nigh-on ubiquitous.

So what should drinkers expect from such beers? Aside from being golden in colour (or often in the case of summer ales, a lighter shade of yellow), they are beers in which malt character is restrained to the extent that the brewer's choice of hops can take centre stage, although with the focus on capturing hop aroma without significant bitterness. That said, there are golden ales out there in which hop character is also restrained, although none that make this book; surely a beer should have some character... Golden ales should finish dry too, something that is often achieved through the use of wheat malt, with this dryness lending them much of their refreshing character.

Golden ales of a British bent will tend to have a more floral hop aroma, but the vast majority of those brewed locally favour New World hop varieties, so, for the most part, expect more citrus or tropical characteristics.

A DOZEN MORE TO TRY

LITTLE CREATURES Rogers'	**MOUNTAIN GOAT** Summer Ale	**BOATROCKER BREWERY** Big Love Suburban Pale
NEWSTEAD BREWING 3 Quarter Time Session Ale	**TWO BIRDS BREWING** Golden Ale	**COLONIAL BREWING** Small Ale
PIRATE LIFE BREWING Throwback IPA	**MASH BREWING** Grasscutter	**NEW ENGLAND BREWING** Golden Ale
NAIL BREWING Golden Nail	**TEMPLE BREWING** Bicycle Beer	**YOUNG HENRYS** Newtowner

RESET ROBOT

BREWCULT

 SESSION ALE　　 3.5%　　 3–5°C　　 PINT GLASS

TASTING NOTES BrewCult founder Steve 'Hendo' Henderson is a fan of cramming as much hop character into his beers as possible, whatever their size. Reset Robot is perhaps the best example, a mere 3.5 per cent ABV bursting with lime and lychee, not to mention a bitterness that punches above its weight.

THE STORY One of the beer world's liveliest characters, 'Hendo' cut his teeth working for a number of breweries around Australia before setting up alone as BrewCult. While he's established himself as an advocate for hops – in particular the need for hoppy beers to be looked after and consumed fresh – he's often captured people's attention when stepping outside the world of hop-forward beers.

An early eye-catcher was Acid Freaks, a dark beer featuring barrel-aged balsamic vinegar made by his brother, and in 2015 he took out the People's Choice title at the Great Australasian Beer SpecTAPular (which attracted 22,000 attendees over its two sites) for Milk & Two Sugars, a milk stout that required Melbourne's Axil Coffee to produce 3,000 espresso shots and 120 litres of cold-drip coffee per batch.

ALSO TRY Hop Zone Session IPA
Beer Geek Rage Quit IPL
Thanks Captain Obvious IPA | Acid Freaks
The 'Psychedelic Series'

☆

BREWER'S FOOD MATCH
Barbecue, salad, the outdoors (now a food)

AVAILABILITY
Year-round

BREWERY LOCATION
Dandenong South, VIC

BREWERY WEBSITE
www.brewcult.com

DRAUGHT (FORMERLY KÖLSCH)

COLONIAL BREWING

 KOLSCH **4.8%** **COLD**  **STANGE GLASS**

TASTING NOTES Their hoppy, flip-top canned Small Ale could easily take this spot but their longstanding favourite Kölsch, now renamed Draught and available in cans too, still gets the nod. It's nothing flash, just an impeccably made drinking beer in which none of the constituent parts drown out the others, but instead sit together in lightly fruity, softly malty, gently bitter perfect balance.

THE STORY Exciting times for Colonial Brewing. The Margaret River brewery has long had one of the finest and most expansive cellar doors of any brewery in Australia as well as a number of popular venues within its Colonial Leisure Group arm pouring its beers in WA and Victoria. But it now has an eastern outpost too.

For years, there was talk of building a brewery at Cape Schanck but, with that proving problematic, they instead took over the former Matilda Bay brewery in Port Melbourne, installed a canning line to complement the one already in place at their original home and sent award-winning brewer Justin Fox over to run the joint. Given the brewers he left behind in WA have won plenty of awards themselves, it should just mean more well conceived and constructed beers – not to mention one-off releases called Gary – for anyone who wants them.

They have installed a second canning line in Melbourne, so look out for a lot more colonial brewing in a lot more places.

ALSO TRY Small Ale | Porter | Pale Ale The 'Project Beers'

BREWER'S FOOD MATCH
Oysters

AVAILABILITY
Year-round

BREWERY & CELLAR DOOR LOCATION
Osmington Road, Margaret River, WA 6285

BREWERY WEBSITE
www.colonialbrewingco.com.au

GOLDEN ALE

FORTITUDE BREWING COMPANY

 SESSION **4.5%**  **4-6°C** **TUMBLER**

TASTING NOTES Golden Ale by name but closer to contemporary pale ale by nature – which is no bad thing considering the insipid nature of much of what passes for a golden ale in Australia these days. Stone fruit, pine and citrus hops combine with light caramel malts in the brewery's fine flagship beer.

THE STORY Fortitude Brewing Company and sister label Noisy Minor (see page 148) started out on the tiny former Eagle Heights brewery in South East Queensland before taking over the much larger nearby Mt Tamborine brewery site, which they share, rather handily, with a cheesemaker. They still operate both, upon which they've developed one (or should that be two) of the most consistent ranges anywhere in Australia.

Head brewer Ian Watson is a well travelled brewer, whose prior post was at Murray's in NSW, and also someone steeped in beer's history and traditions. He's poured that knowledge and passion into a diverse collection of beers, although Fortitude remains the home for the more traditional releases, with the Golden accompanied in the realm of 'session ales' by the low ABV Pacer 2.8.

ALSO TRY Standard Lager | Stout Pacer 2.8

BREWER'S FOOD MATCH
Red Leicester cheese

AVAILABILITY
Year-round

BREWERY & CELLAR DOOR LOCATION
165 Long Road, North Tamborine, QLD 4271

BREWERY WEBSITE
fortitudebrewing.com.au

IPSWICH CHALLENGER

FOUR HEARTS BREWING

 LIGHT BEER   **2.9%**   **4-7°C**   **SCHOONER GLASS**

TASTING NOTES Spend time in Queensland when it's warm and humid and, while you might not like it, you'll better understand why a mid-strength, XXXX Gold, is the biggest selling beer there. Knowing his audience, Four Hearts founder Wade Curtis was quick to introduce the Ipswich Challenger: an English-inspired, malt led, gently floral 2.9 per-center. In summer, it's joined by a second light beer, the tropically Aussie-hopped Longshot.

THE STORY Wade Curtis made full use of his background in marketing when launching Four Hearts Brewing in Ipswich. Within months of brewing his first commercial beer, a pale ale, he'd garnered significant media attention for his mission to bring something a little different to the bars and hotels of his hometown – quite the task given how resilient the city was proving to the lure of craft beer, despite the revolution that was steadily gathering pace in nearby Brisbane.

While such beers' inroads into the broader Ipswich community remain hit and miss, for Wade it's a case of mission accomplished after he opened his own brewery and venue. He made a home for Four Hearts inside a former college dating from the 19th century on the site of a natural spring that originally supplied Ipswich's water. Today, Pumpyard Bar & Brewery supplies locals instead with 20 taps of beer – a mix of his and guests' – quality beer food and occasional special events.

His flair for catching the media's eye continues. He partnered with a local farmer to create a carrot beer, the Wabbit Saison, for the 2015 GABS festival, an idea that gained such traction for its quirkiness it was picked up by mainstream news outlets the world over.

ALSO TRY Pale Ale | Coal Miners Stout Longshot Session Ale | IPA

☆

BREWER'S FOOD MATCH
Good Queensland seafood, served fresh with lime (the food, not the beer!)

AVAILABILITY
Year-round

BREWERY LOCATION
88 Limestone Street, Ipswich, QLD 4305

BREWERY WEBSITE
www.4heartsbrewing.com

SINGLE FIN

GAGE ROADS

 SUMMER ALE   4.5%   4-6°C   PINT GLASS

TASTING NOTES The most recent addition to Gage Roads' revamped range is possibly its finest and an encapsulation of what the Woolies-backed WA brewery is about: approachable beers you can return to again and again. A cracking example of the modern Aussie summer ale, this pale golden beer uses local hops Enigma and Galaxy to create stone fruit and lime curd aromas.

THE STORY At a time when the issue of ownership in the Australian beer world is discussed perhaps more than ever before, Gage Roads occupies a unique position: a once small microbrewery in which Woolworths took a share that allowed for major expansion. It makes many of Woolies' other 'home-brand' beers, such as Sail & Anchor, plus beers for other brewing companies under license, but it has also revamped and shone a new focus on its own Gage Roads beers.

The results led to a shortlisting for Champion Large Australian Brewery at the 2015 Australian International Beer Awards and an improved and broadened core range. Despite their size, an annual Backyard to Bottleshop competition keeps them connected to local home brewers by offering customers the chance to have their beer brewed commercially and released nationwide.

ALSO TRY Narrow Neck Session Ale Sleeping Giant IPA | Premium Mid Pils Atomic Pale Ale

BREWER'S FOOD MATCH
Pairs well with seafood and outdoor dining, whether it's fish and chips at the beach or barbecue prawns alfresco

AVAILABILITY
Year-round

BREWERY & CELLAR DOOR LOCATION
14 Absolon Street, Palmyra, WA 6157

BREWERY WEBSITE
www.gageroads.com.au

SPOTTED ALE

PRICKLY MOSES

 SESSION ALE   4.5%   2–4°C   PILSNER OR IPA GLASS

TASTING NOTES As a beer, Prickly Moses Spotted Ale is one of the better takes on the tropically fruity golden/summer ales popularised by Stone & Wood's Pacific Ale. It's also one you can quaff with a healthy conscience as the brewery donates 100 per cent of profits towards the protection of the tiger quolls inhabiting their Otway Ranges home.

THE STORY Prickly Moses is one of Victoria's longest established microbreweries, producing a broad and ever-evolving range of beers in the Otway Ranges. For a long time, they were pretty much the only non mainstream beer found along the Great Ocean Road and are now found widely across the country.

You can pretty much split Luke Scott's beers into two categories: the playing-it-safe core range and bigger, more experimental limited and seasonal releases. In the latter there have been multiple beers playing with different fruits, one making use of wild hops found in a field near the brewery, a trio of French/Belgian-inspired ales and many barrel-aged experiments too.

Since 2015, the brewery has also operated the Great Ocean Road Brewhouse in the historic former Ballarat Hotel in Apollo Bay. You'll find their full range plus other guest brewers' beers pouring across more than two dozen taps.

ALSO TRY ChainSAW Chardonnay IPA Reserve de Otway | Tailpipe Brown Ale Otway Stout | Blueberry Hefeweizen

BREWER'S FOOD MATCH
Chicken green curry with another Spotted Ale to follow

AVAILABILITY
Year-round

BREWERY & CELLAR DOOR LOCATION
10–30 Hoveys Road, Barongarook, VIC 3249

BREWERY WEBSITE
www.pricklymoses.com.au

FEATHERWEIGHT ALE

PUBLIC BREWERY

 **LIGHT BEER** **2.9%** **6-8°C** **TULIP GLASS**

TASTING NOTES Conceived by the brewery's owner as part of a mission to show younger drinkers it's OK to have a drink without getting wrecked, brewer Brendan Guild has worked to retain as much body and citrus/stone fruit hop character – not to mention a pleasant, resinous bitterness – while staying under 3 per cent ABV.

THE STORY A quite remarkable tale here, in which Croydon's original café owner, the dreadlocked, skateboarding Dale Pope, decided to turn an old warehouse/auction room in the craft-beer-free suburb into a 'Brew Your Own' venue in which he'd like to hang out. Along with his business partners, he decided to install a small brewery alongside the mini-brewhouses as well as a bottleshop and bar serving only independent Victorian craft beer and Yarra Valley wine and cider, with a restaurant completing the picture.

They drew big crowds from day one, were later invited to be part of the huge redevelopment of Eastland shopping centre in Ringwood and did so with gusto, creating the mighty impressive three-storey Cellar Door, and have added a production facility in Warrandyte too. All while retaining their focus on independent, local and quality. Inspirational.

ALSO TRY Their Australian Pale Ale was still evolving at the time of writing, but the Funky Town Brown is a fine take on the hoppy American brown ale style.

BREWER'S FOOD MATCH
Chilli chicken wings

AVAILABILITY
Year-round

BREWERY LOCATION
Croydon, VIC

CELLAR DOOR LOCATION
The Cellar Door by The Public Brewery,
Townsquare, Eastland, Ringwood, VIC 3134

BREWERY WEBSITE
www.thepublicbrewery.com.au

GREENHILLS

SHARK ISLAND

 SUMMER ALE   **4.8%**   **4°C**   **PILSNER GLASS**

TASTING NOTES So far, Shark Island's brews have tended towards the broader appeal end of the craft beer spectrum, with Greenhills my favourite. Taking its name from a beach close to their Kirrawee brewery, it's a summer ale with distinctive and lively lime aromas and flavours. There's a relatively biting, resinous finish too, derived, like the lime, from the use of newly released Aussie hop variety Melba.

THE STORY Shark Island Brewing first came to my attention in less than ideal circumstances; indeed, they were circumstances that suggested the dream that mates Dion 'Driza' Dickinson and James Peebles had of opening their own brewery was to be nothing more than a nightmare.

They were one of many small businesses who lost tens of thousands of dollars in deposits, rent and earnings after an equipment supplier left them high and dry. Thankfully, while they never recouped their money or obtained promised equipment, friends and the beer industry rallied around and helped get their first beers to market while they looked at other options.

In the second half of 2015, they moved into the small offsite brewery set up by Blackhorse Brewhouse and have since made the Kirrawee site their own, adding a cellar door that's pulling bigger crowds each time it opens. The plan is to have a bigger – albeit still small – site by the end of 2016 as they work towards the ultimate goal of a larger packaging brewery. Having overcome the roughest of starts, you wouldn't bet against them getting there.

ALSO TRY El Mono Bolas | Pale Ale

BREWER'S FOOD MATCH
Balmain bugs with garlic and chargrilled lime

AVAILABILITY
Year-round

BREWERY & CELLAR DOOR LOCATION
Unit 8, 29–33 Waratah Street
Kirrawee, NSW 2232

BREWERY WEBSITE
www.sharkislandbrewing.com.au

THE SESH

STOCKADE BREW CO

 **SESSION ALE**   **4.1%**   **5-8°C**   **TULIP GLASS**

TASTING NOTES Of the three Stockade beers available for tasting at the time of writing, golden session ale 'The Sesh' was the pick, packing plenty of character for a beer measuring just 4.1 per cent ABV. Within its slightly hazy, relatively full golden body you find tropical and grapefruit hops and biscuity, caramel malts. Choosing the bitey Aussie hop Vic Secret ensures a resinous bitterness, too.

THE STORY The BrewPack brewery in Smeaton Grange, in Sydney's southwest, is one of the country's most popular contract brewing facilities, particularly among smaller Australian operations, brewing dozens of beers for other brands. Stockade is effectively BrewPack's in-house label, overseen by the family that owns the facility. It's something of a creative outlet for the team of brewers who otherwise spend their days making other peoples' beer.

They first used the name Stockade for a lager, pale and IPA brewed under their Macarthur Grange Brewery banner and, while there were competition golds for the latter two, in the second half of 2015 the Macarthur brand was retired and a new Stockade range emerged. It came with a colourful new look – just check out the artwork on the beers' distinctly

different labels – and a brand new list of beers. Some more experimental beers should be out by the time of publication, while there is a small-barrel program operating too.

Given the scale of BrewPack's operation and connections with major retailers, it will be interesting to see what success the 'HND KRTFD IN OZ' Stockade achieves and whether it suffers from any confusion caused by its different lives to date.

ALSO TRY Chop Shop Pale Ale Peachy Keen Peach Gose

BREWER'S FOOD MATCH
A fresh summer salad, oysters and light seafood. The Sesh also compliments Thai or Indian dishes.

AVAILABILITY
Year-round

BREWERY LOCATION
Smeaton Grange, NSW

BREWERY WEBSITE
www.stockadebrewco.com.au

PACIFIC ALE

STONE & WOOD

 SUMMER ALE 4.4% 3-4°C TULIP OR PINT GLASS

TASTING NOTES Galaxy is the star of the Australian hop breeding program and no beer showcases its distinct passionfruit and citrus character better than this cloudy, pale golden ale that has rapidly become one of the biggest selling craft beers in the country. Best enjoyed fresh, it finishes nice and dry; perfect for the end of a hot day in Byron Bay where it was conceived.

THE STORY The Aussie Dream writ large? Three mates leave the corporate beer world behind, set up a brewery in Byron Bay and take the country by storm. Stone & Wood is possibly the closest thing to a fairytale the local beer industry has seen in recent years – albeit one driven by some very sharp minds and focused characters.

Since opening their first brewery in Byron, Brad Rogers, Jamie Cook and Ross Jurisich have built a far larger second one to the north, where they're continually adding more capacity, not to mention taking measures to make the site as green as possible. Pacific Ale has driven their success, but other limited releases – often in collaboration with artists, sports people and creatives under The Mash Collective banner – have also impressed. New ventures, such as a business incubator and a distribution arm for others' beers

and ciders suggest a desire to leave the industry in a better, fairer shape than when they entered it. Legends of the local beer world. For their full story, see page 64.

ALSO TRY Cloud Catcher | Stone Beer Green Coast Jasper Ale Mash Collective annual releases

BREWER'S FOOD MATCH
Fresh local seafood and salad

AVAILABILITY
Year-round

BREWERY & CELLAR DOOR LOCATION
4 Boronia Place, Byron Bay, NSW 2481

BREWERY WEBSITE
www.stoneandwood.com.au

BRUNSWICK BITTER

THUNDER ROAD

 BITTER   4.6%   5-7°C   **AMERICAN PINT GLASS**

TASTING NOTES From the off, Thunder Road made clear their mission was to try to lure the then 96 per cent of drinkers away from mainstream lager brands. They looked to do so with beers only a few shades away from such brands, albeit using better ingredients and with more character. Brunswick Bitter has been their most successful weapon, adding some fruity Aussie hops to a straightforward, old fashioned, malty bitter.

THE STORY A few years ago, I took an Extra Dry-drinking mate to a Melbourne bar. Thunder Road's Full Steam lager was on tap. It was Thunder Road's launch beer and he was their target audience: a big brand drinker to be lured. He enjoyed it and the next week asked where he could buy some. Now he's into hoppy pale ales: a win for the brewery's mission to win over mainstream drinkers.

Of course, Melbourne's Thunder Road isn't alone in that mission – far from it – but still manages to stand out, and does so without brewing obtuse beers. From the off, they've followed their own determinedly individual path. With one of Australia's most highly specced breweries, complete with a lab that puts most others to shame, they targeted mainstream lager drinkers with beers that weren't a million miles from what they knew. Occasionally,

they've deviated, but mainly it's been lagers and simple ales doing the legwork.

Along the way, they've fought (and lost) a well-publicised trademark battle with CUB, collaborated with American brewers and started brewing beer in Belgium that they ship and sell here. Then, in 2014, they caught the attention of their peers when they entered their first ever beer competition and walked away as an Australian International Beer Awards Champion Brewery. A year later, they retained the crown, meaning they could target a hat-trick in 2016.

ALSO TRY Full Steam Pale Lager
Hop Star Extra Pale Ale
Collingwood Draught
President's Reserve series

BREWER'S FOOD MATCH
Fish tacos

AVAILABILITY
Year-round

BREWERY LOCATION
Brunswick, VIC

BREWERY WEBSITE
www.thunderroadbrewing.com

GOLDEN ALE

VENOM

 GOLDEN ALE 4.8%  4-6°C PILSNER GLASS

TASTING NOTES You don't find many golden ales with as big a character as the first release from Melbourne brewing company Venom. This hazy, pale golden beer brewed with New Zealand hops Nelson Sauvin and Motueka is a riot of kiwi fruit and lime aromas and flavours, with a hefty dose of wheat giving it a refreshing finish.

THE STORY Joel Drysdale grew up around pubs and, perhaps unsurprisingly, ended up in the same industry as his dad. After stints as a rep for Tasmania's Moo Brew then Victoria's Tooborac Hotel & Brewery he decided to launch Venom with wife Janna and his parents. Inspiration for the name came from an incident in which dad John was bitten by a snake and, while waiting for an ambulance, cracked a bottle of macro lager from the fridge. Joel figured that, should it happen again and his dad were to die, he should have a better beer as his last.

The Golden Ale was conceived by Joel's mate, Euan Bayliss, and brewed at Hawkers Beer in Reservoir. It instantly took its place among the very best locally brewed golden ales. It also has one of the most eye-catching and divisive labels I've ever seen; whichever side of the 'love it/ hate it' divide you sit, you'll certainly never forget it.

ALSO TRY Black IPA

☆

BREWER'S FOOD MATCH
Hainanese chicken rice (especially from a little Malaysian restaurant in Strathmore called Mamak Kitchen). Always double up on the chilli sauce – the spice goes well with the Kiwi hops and makes for a very enjoyable meal!

AVAILABILITY
Year-round

BREWERY LOCATION
Reservoir, VIC

BREWERY WEBSITE
www.venombeer.com

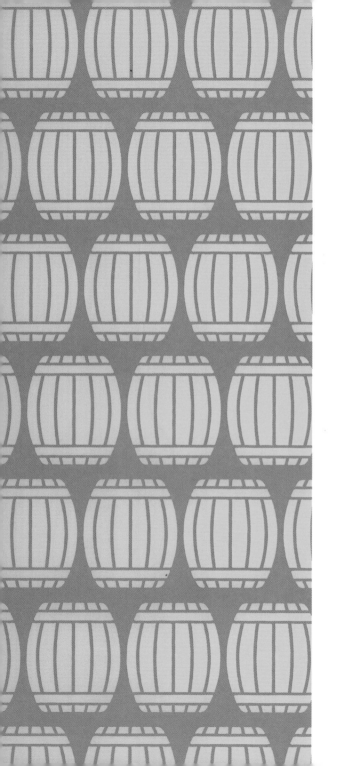

STONE & WOOD

When discussing the selection process for breweries to profile for this book, there was talk of favouring those on the cutting edge: new, innovative or challenging norms. Stone & Wood's mantra of 'take it slow' plus a focus on simple, approachable beers with broad appeal would seem to rule the Byron Bay brewer out.

Yet, when looking for a brewery in New South Wales to profile, could there be any other? There's plenty that are far newer and many that have built a business upon challenging norms. Yet, as much as – if not more than – any other independent brewery in Australia, Stone & Wood is changing the beer landscape across Australia by enticing droves of people away from mainstream lagers via finely conceived beers and an inclusive, loveable persona that belies just how big the business has become in a short space of time.

The story starts with three mates who were working in various roles at CUB decided they'd had enough of the corporate life and set their sights on a change of pace in Byron Bay. The plan was to launch their own brewery, one that would focus on making simple beers they enjoyed and would become very much part of its local community.

Once Stone & Wood Brewing was launched by the trio – brewer Brad Rogers, marketer Jamie Cook and Ross Jurisich overseeing sales – it didn't take long to be embraced by their local community. The first two beers, a lager and what was then called Draught Ale, were perfect for the region's long, hot days.

But it soon became apparent that the rest of Australia wanted to be part of the Stone & Wood community, too.

Most credit for this can be assigned to the Draught Ale, a beer conceived after the trio worked their way through 40-odd diverse beers from all over the world, noted what they liked and disliked from each, and plotted what they thought would be their perfect beer. A few test batches followed and a recipe, which has never been altered, was finalised.

If you're wondering why you've never heard of Draught Ale, don't worry. Once a few sample kegs had been sent around the country and it became apparent they were really onto something, the beer was bottled, thus making 'Draught' something of a misnomer. So, as demand continued to rocket, it became instead Pacific Ale (page 61).

In keeping with their mantra, the beer is simple: a simple malt bill, low in alcohol and only one hop variety. And it's the way it uses this hop, Galaxy, the runaway star of Hop Products Australia's breeding program, that is key. The beer captures its tropical, passionfruit character perfectly; when fresh it's like sniffing a hop cone plucked straight from the bine. And it does so in a delicate and balanced manner too, making the beer approachable to all.

Case in point: the first time my dad was in Australia after Pacific Ale became widely available, I bought him a pint as his first off the plane. After taking his usual, excessively large, first swig, he turned and said: "It's a bloody fruit salad."

It wasn't meant as a compliment. But soon afterwards he ordered a second and still sends messages whenever he comes across an ale in the UK displaying similar characteristics.

The beer's soaraway success has posed significant problems, mostly around meeting demand. Strongly opposed to contract brewing on any grounds, they expanded their Byron Bay brewery to capacity, running it around the clock while building a second site in the Northern Rivers. When they couldn't meet demand, they chose to support their independent customers ahead of major retailers.

They've flown the flag for independence elsewhere, too. When Stone & Wood launched, Little World Beverages, which owned Little Creatures, had a stake in the business. When Little World Beverages was bought by Lion, Brad, Jamie and Ross decided to buy that share back.

Later, when Mountain Goat announced it had sold to Asahi, Stone & Wood took the decision to respond to rumours by making a public statement that they weren't for sale. The cynical claimed it was just a clever marketing ploy, but, given some of the pointed comments directed at others within the statement and taken in conjunction with previous and subsequent decisions, I believe it came from the heart.

Indeed, heart seems a good word with which to associate Stone & Wood. Whether judged by their commitment to their local region, both through employment and supporting causes, their warm embrace of the beer community or bringing in artists, chefs, surfers and writers for their Mash Collective brews in the hope of taking craft beer to new audiences, there's much to admire.

Indeed, at the time of writing they'd just announced a series of parties along the East Coast. No ordinary parties, however. Beforehand guests were invited to bring their families along to help clean up iconic beaches; all profits from beer sales were donated to the environmental group leading the clean-ups. And that, to me, seems like a lot of effort purely for marketing purposes.

PALE
ALES

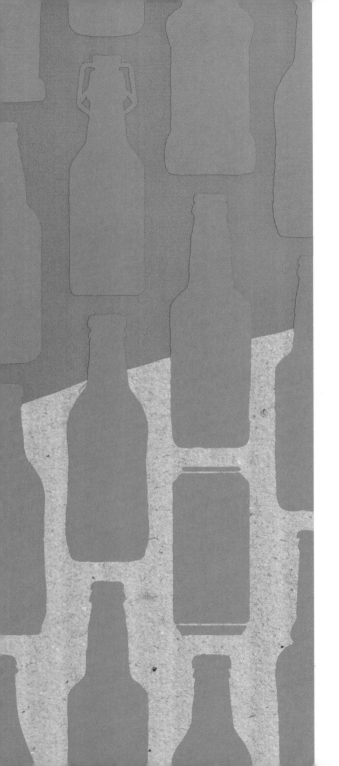

PALE ALES

Take a journey back through beer's history and the first pale ales are generally acknowledged to have come out of breweries in Burton upon Trent in the UK. Yet this chapter could just as easily be entitled American Pale Ales.

As with many traditional styles, the humble English pale ale has been picked up by the brewers of the American craft beer revolution, pumped full of steroids, sent to the gym with its own personal trainer, had its tweed suit, monocle and pipe replaced with sunnies and board shorts, and its soundtrack of Greensleeves replaced by fat beats and an even fatter blunt.

American brewers' bolder, more hop-forward take on the style, embellished by the punchily aromatic hops of the Pacific Northwest, was first introduced in the States in the form of Anchor Steam's Liberty Ale, then popularised further by the Pale Ale from fellow Californians Sierra Nevada.

Later, just as those beers instigated a change in a generation's drinking habits, so did Little Creatures Pale Ale for Australia. The beer that brought American hops and the American pale ale style to Australia around the turn of the millennium has sparked countless imitators; with good reason: for almost every Australian microbrewery that has an American-inspired pale ale on its roster it is their best-selling beer.

That said, you can find a handful of English-style pales in Australia (there are some in the chapter on British and Irish Styles, page 114) and a tiny number of Belgian-style pales (less hops, more yeast-derived fruitiness). Then there is the Australian pale ale.

Essentially created by Coopers Sparkling and the brewery's Original Pale Ale, it shares more in common with the English pale ales upon which it was modelled in early colonial days, due to its fruity yeast characteristics and relatively subdued hop aroma. There are beers of a more recent vintage that follow in Coopers' footsteps, notably Nail Brewing's multiple trophy-winning Nail Ale, but, more often than not, contemporary Australian pale ales tend to share more in common with those from America. Indeed, the Coopers-inspired pales are few and far between, with 'Australian pale ale' these days more likely to indicate an American-style pale that uses Australian grown hops.

What all of this means in practice is beers that are typically golden, copper or, occasionally, amber in colour. Often they are hazy or cloudy too. This can be due to craft brewers leaving their beer unfiltered as a nod to tradition, or even as a visible point of difference from the crystal clear beers from their multinational counterparts. Often microbreweries will bottle-condition their beers too – in other words, with active yeast still in the bottled product – and this too adds a hazy appearance due to the presence of yeast.

Depending on the origin of the hops, in contemporary American-inspired pales you should expect citrus, stone fruit, pine, tropical or grassy aromas. It is worth remembering that these hop aromas and flavours disappear fastest from a beer, hence why these beers should be enjoyed as fresh as possible. If you can, find them on tap at a venue you know handles beer well and turns kegs over fast. If buying bottles, check for a brewed on or best-before date; they're not on every beer yet but more small breweries are realising the value in adding this information.

While hop characteristics are key with these beers, they are nothing without balance. Typically, malt flavours will be of a biscuity, toasty or caramel nature, but generally they are there to play a supporting role to the fruity hop flavours in beers that finish relatively dry with a firm bitterness.

It's also worth noting that, as with IPAs, there is something of an upwards shift in what people expect from modern pale ales –

both brewers and drinkers. Little Creatures Pale Ale remains a fine, beautifully balanced example of the style but there are beers it has spawned that explode with more prominent hop aroma and flavour. Not all do it with finesse, sadly, but those that do are becoming those that many discerning beer drinkers chase down now. Indeed, you'll find beers elsewhere in the book now tagged as golden or summer ales that possess the sort of hop character that once would have been deemed high for a pale.

American brewer Vinnie Cilurzo, of Russian River, coined a phrase 'lupulin threshold shift' to describe how, over time, a drinker's tolerance of hops and bitterness can rise so the exact same beer they found hoppy in the past may not have the same impact for them anymore. This, as well as the market becoming steadily more adventurous over time, may be playing a role in such a change, one that saw Feral Brewing cross out the India of India Pale Ale on the labels of its Hop Hog to acknowledge that, even at 5.8 per cent ABV, it shared more in common with American pales than their bigger, IPA counterparts. And it's why you'll find beers tagged as XPA (Extra Pale Ale) or Session IPA in this chapter, too.

A DOZEN MORE TO TRY

HAWKERS BEER Pale Ale	**GRIFTER BREWING COMPANY** Pale Ale	**SMILING SAMOYED** 12 Paws
PIRATE LIFE Pale Ale	**MORNINGTON PENINSULA BREWERY** Pale Ale	**COOPERS** Original Pale Ale
BRIDGE ROAD BREWERS Beechworth Pale Ale	**HARGREAVES HILL** Pale Ale	**MOO BREW** Pale Ale
THE LITTLE BREWING COMPANY Wicked Elf Pale Ale	**TEMPLE BREWING** Anytime IPA	**EAGLE BAY BREWING** Pale Ale

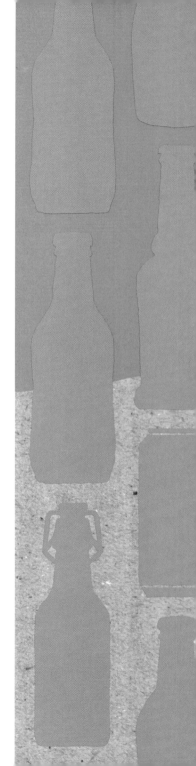

HOP HEAVEN EASY IPA

BAROSSA VALLEY BREWING

 **PALE ALE**   **4.8%**   **7°C**   **TULIP GLASS**

TASTING NOTES The beer formerly known as Organic Ale is one of the mainstays of Barossa Valley Brewing's range that's been given a reworking as well as a new name in recent years. Inspired by West Coast USA pales, it's a lively drop: sherbet-like hop flavours recall candied oranges and lemons, while there's a touch of pine needles in a beer that's sprightly on the palate too.

THE STORY Barossa Valley Brewing is one of the elder statesmen of the South Australian microbrewing scene. Originally opened in 2005 at the Chateau Yaldara winery, it later moved into its own home in a former restaurant in Tanunda. The restaurant acts as the bar and cellar door, with guests able to sample beers shaded by trees in the adjacent garden and brewing taking place in a shed to the rear.

The man behind the business is Denham D'Silva, formerly a merchant banker who'd fallen for craft beer while working in the States only to return to Australia and discover there was hardly any around. So he took matters into his own hands and started brewing his own.

As the brewery's decade approached, the range was overhauled, with this beer beefed up and others, such as the sweetly smoky Barossa Smoke, added. The brewers also take advantage of their location in wine country, most notably in 2015 when they joined forces with David Franz Wines and Maverick Wines to create Threesome, a beer that combined a German-style wheat beer base with Semillon and Reisling wines.

ALSO TRY Double IPA | Bee Sting Barossa Smoke | 3some

BREWER'S FOOD MATCH
Rib-eye with chimichurri sauce

AVAILABILITY
Year-round

BREWERY & CELLAR DOOR LOCATION
2A Murray Street, Tanunda, SA 5352

BREWERY WEBSITE
www.bvbeer.com.au

RYE PALE ALE

BOSTON BREWING

 RYE PALE ALE | 5.0% | 8-10°C | STANDARD ALE GLASS

TASTING NOTES When I called into Boston Brewery, this beer was pouring as a special and was the pick of a solid lineup on offer at the time. It's proved popular enough that it's making ever more regular appearances. The use of rye adds bite and a touch of spiciness to what's a highly hopped, fruity pale ale with a hefty bitter finish.

THE STORY It was during a family holiday that I first visited Boston Brewery in Denmark on WA's south coast. I'll be honest and admit hopes weren't sky high. Due to its remote location and a small brewery that meant little beer ever left Denmark, I'd heard next to nothing about the beers and, what with it sharing a home with a winery on the tourist trail, figured there would be a simple lineup of unchallenging ales.

So it was a pleasant surprise to sit down with a tasting paddle and find – among a number of unchallenging beers designed for mass appeal (understandable given the huge number of families packing the place inside and out) – a feisty IPA, a tasty dark lager and this punchy Rye Pale Ale. What's more, the beers at the softer end – a wheat beer and lager – were clean, refreshing and well made, too.

The brewer was on site so I popped in for a chat. Turned out Tyson Addy was an American who'd flitted back and forth between commercial brewing (initially in Salt Lake City) and mining before landing in Denmark. He'd found some decent beers there and was working to improve them and add more. Since then, he's overseen the installation of a larger brewery and, by the time you read this, should be packaging them to send out to a wider audience.

ALSO TRY Lager | Hefeweizen | Mild Nut Brown Ale | India Black Ale

BREWER'S FOOD MATCH
Barbecued marron

AVAILABILITY
Seasonal: summer

BREWERY & CELLAR DOOR LOCATION
678 South Coast Highway, Hay, WA 6333

BREWERY WEBSITE
www.bostonbrewery.com.au

BLOWHARD PALE ALE

BRIGHT BREWERY

 PALE ALE   5.0%   5°C   TULIP GLASS

TASTING NOTES On a visit to Bright's wonderful High Country home, then brewer Jon Seltin told me he'd just kegged off the first batch of a new recipe, Blowhard Pale. A couple of mouthfuls later and my mind was scrambling to think of a better beer of its kind in Australia. It's best sampled at source, where you'll find a wealth of citrus hop characters and a pleasing, cleansing bitterness.

THE STORY Over the years, Bright has grown from a shed with barely enough room to fit its brewery and bar, to one of the most impressive venues anywhere in Australia. Significant investment – much from grants they've managed to secure over the years – has created a multi-faceted home on the banks of the Ovens River featuring brewery, bar/restaurant and multiple outdoor areas, including a welcoming terrace where you'll often catch live music.

    The beers didn't always live up to the location in the early years, but former home brewer Jon Seltin sorted that with real panache during his stint at the brewery before catching the eye of Hawkers Beer and being whisked off to Melbourne. Into his shoes stepped former BrewDog brewer Ryan Tyack who has been putting his stamp (usually more hops and booze) on things, as well as sporting the most impressive beard you'll find on someone of his relatively tender years.

ALSO TRY MIA IPA | Staircase Porter Stubborn Russian Imperial Stout Fainters Dubbel

BREWER'S FOOD MATCH
Angus beef burger with a side of salad and chips, or gourmet pizza

AVAILABILITY
Year-round

BREWERY & CELLAR DOOR LOCATION
121 Great Alpine Road, Bright, VIC 3741

BREWERY WEBSITE
www.brightbrewery.com.au

BRISBANE BREWING CO

 PALE ALE   **4.2%**   **0°C**   **TULIP GLASS**

TASTING NOTES The BPA (or Brisbane Pale Ale, to give it its full name) is the Brisbane Brewing Co's flagship beer, one of a few beers you should almost always find on tap at their impressive West End brewpub. It's the archetypal Aussie pale ale using the popular Galaxy hop to deliver a tropical hit atop a pale malt base that's there to do little more than let the hops shine.

THE STORY The Brisbane Brewing Co started out brewing beers for the Brisbane Brewhouse in Woolloongabba before its owners opened a second venue in the increasingly crafty suburb of West End. There, at the end of a little laneway you'll find the impressive Brisbane Brewing Co venue, combining bar, restaurant, deli, courtyard and, to one side, the busy brewery.

It's one of the most appealing of all metropolitan brewery venues I've visited in Australia, the sort of place that's ideal for enticing newcomers into the world of craft beer. It has plenty to offer existing beer lovers too, not least that they crank out so much beer to supply their two venues that there's almost always action on the brewing side of the fence (and a brewer who's more than happy to chat).

They brew an extensive array of beers throughout the year too, often in collaboration with fellow brewers. There are staples, such as this BPA plus a golden ale, pilsner, wheat and IPA, but many of the taps are in constant rotation meaning you're as likely to find a Belgian-style ale pouring as you would a barley wine. Time it right and you can work your way along the bar while enjoying live music, too.

ALSO TRY Walker IPA | Saison 88 Gnarly Wine | Up Yer Kilt

BREWER'S FOOD MATCH
Cheese platter or spicy pizza

AVAILABILITY
Year-round

BREWERY & CELLAR DOOR LOCATION
124 Boundary Street, West End, QLD 4101

BREWERY WEBSITE
www.brisbanebrewing.com.au

28 PALE ALE

BURLEIGH BREWING COMPANY

 PALE ALE   4.8%   4-6°C   **SCHOONER GLASS**

TASTING NOTES A tight, humble Aussie version of the American pale ale style popularised by Sierra Nevada Pale, this beer from the Gold Coast's original craft brewers might look like a throwback to another era but is anything but. Floral and citrus aromas lead into the bitter tang of orange marmalade, grapefruit and lychee hop flavours, balanced by caramel malts.

THE STORY By the time this book hits the shelves, there should be three – maybe more – breweries calling the Gold Coast home. Burleigh has been pioneering the brewing of quality beers there for many moons, however, since being set up in Burleigh Heads by Peta Fielding and brewer husband Brennan, who learnt his brewing skills in his home state of Hawaii.

They're one of the biggest microbreweries in Australia, steadily and relatively unobtrusively building a mini-empire in South East Queensland while winning acclaim for many of their beers: from the Bavarian-inspired Hef to the Black Giraffe coffee lager, hoppy drops Hassle Hop and Figjam IPA that represent steps up in size from the popular 28 Pale.

In March 2016, they moved a short distance from their original base to an impressive new home. It's larger, allowing them to increase capacity, while a new pilot brewery will see more small run, experimental beers appear. Perhaps most excitingly for beer lovers, however, is that the new home contains a spacious Tap House open several days a week and offering all of their beers, poured from taps that have miniature surfboards for handles.

For their full story, see page 84.

ALSO TRY Black Giraffe | Figjam IPA Duke Helles Mid Strength Hassle Hop Pale Ale

BREWER'S FOOD MATCH
Red meat with the heat of Morroccan spice

AVAILABILITY
Year-round

BREWERY & CELLAR DOOR LOCATION
2 Ern Harley Drive, Burleigh Heads, QLD 4220

BREWERY WEBSITE
www.burleighbrewing.com.au

GROWERS PALE

ENDEAVOUR VINTAGE BEER CO

 PALE ALE   4.5%   8–12°C **TUMBLER-SHAPED PINT GLASS**

TASTING NOTES The pick of Endeavour's 2015 lineup of approachable ales was their Growers Pale, a hazy light golden drop featuring Tasmanian Enigma and Galaxy hops. They deliver fruity and floral aromas, while the beer achieves a good balance between malt sweetness and hop bitterness.

THE STORY Endeavour is one of a small number of contract brewing companies – businesses that have their beers brewed for them at other facilities – that has achieved longevity and steady success. The trio behind the business are Ben Kooyman, Dan Hastings and Andy Stewart, who is a winemaker.

And there are echoes of winemaking at the heart of Endeavour's schtick: as well as making beers he thought were more interesting than most on the market at the time, Ben wanted to make a feature of visiting Aussie farmers and hop growers each harvest to pick the barley and hops they'd use in their beers that year. Hence the use of tags such as 'Vintage' and 'Reserve'.

The beers have tended towards the more approachable end of the spectrum: pale, golden and amber ales, and are a little different each year depending on which ingredients they select. They've enjoyed some awards success, most notably a silver at the prestigious World Beer Cup, while there is growing talk of a brewery and bar around Sydney – even a 'beer estate' in Tasmania near the growers – if they can find the right spot to join the dozen or more that have opened since Endeavour launched in 2010.

ALSO TRY Growers Bright Ale
Reserve Pale Ale | Reserve Amber Ale

BREWER'S FOOD MATCH
Roast chicken or fish and chips

AVAILABILITY
Year-round

BREWERY LOCATION
Sydney, NSW

BREWERY WEBSITE
www.endeavourbeer.com

PALE ALE

LITTLE CREATURES

 PALE ALE 5.2% 8°C  PINT GLASS

TASTING NOTES The beer that probably inspired more Aussies to become brewers than any other and paved the way for bigger, hoppy American-style beers. Some claim it's changed since the Lion takeover and blind tastings we've held suggests it may pale compared to some peers that have come later. But what remains is a finely balanced combination of fruity, floral hops, light caramel malts and a tight bitterness.

THE STORY What's left to say about this beer? More than any other in Australia, since it was first released as Little Creatures Live on the day that the brewery's HQ on the Fremantle waterfront was opened in 2000, it has done more than any other to change Australia's beer-drinking habits. Inspired by the aromatic pale ales of the USA, such as Sierra Nevada's classic, and the first local brew to use whole hop flowers from the Pacific Northwest to achieve its goal, the moment when it won Champion Beer at the Australian International Beer Awards in 2002, is regarded by many as a watershed moment.

These days, most of it is brewed at Little Creatures' second – and larger – home in Geelong, where the new owners have created quite a wonderful visitor experience. One of several large, red-brick,

former industrial buildings houses the brewery, another a typically colourful (and regularly heaving) Creatures bar and dining area. More recently, a third has become home to sibling brewery White Rabbit, uplifted from its original home in the Yarra Valley and turned into its own unique brewing-cum-hospitality venture.

ALSO TRY Rogers | Furphy | Pilsner Bright Ale | IPA | Seasonal specials

---

BREWER'S FOOD MATCH
Barbecued chilli-lime chicken

AVAILABILITY
Year-round

BREWERY & CELLAR DOOR LOCATION
40 Mews Road, Fremantle, WA 6160 and
Swanston Street, Geelong, VIC 3220

BREWERY WEBSITE
www.littlecreatures.com.au

ALPHA PALE ALE

MATILDA BAY

 AMERICAN PALE ALE   5.2%   4-8°C   GLASS

TASTING NOTES Given the uncertainty that surrounds possibly the most storied of all contemporary Australian beer brands, this is included as much in hope as in the joy it can bring. I say 'can' as it's not proven that easy to find fresh bottles of late. When Alpha does crop up fresh, it's a delight: a punchily aromatic – predominantly orange citrus – US-style pale, with the hops balanced by a touch of sweet caramel and adding a firm bitterness, too.

THE STORY Oh, Matilda Bay, what's going on? The brewery originally spawned by the team that launched the modern Australian craft beer scene at the Sail & Anchor in Fremantle (before the term 'craft' appeared) has been adrift in recent years, lost amid corporate takeovers and the ever-shifting sands of the contemporary beer world.

It took several months and various routes to get an answer as to whether the brand would still be around six months after this book is published; even then, it was a response along the lines of, "Yes, in some form. Alpha, Dogbolter and Redback will survive and it could be used as an incubator for new releases." This didn't fully convince, so apologies if this entry is little more than a sorrowful 'what might have been'.

First Phil Sexton (later to help launch Little Creatures) and then, following the

brewery's move from WA to Victoria, Brad Rogers (who then founded Stone & Wood with two other Matilda Bay alumni), created some of the finest, most flavoursome beers in Australia – many of them Australian commercial firsts, too. A subsequent move to Port Melbourne proved short-lived, as that was closed at the start of 2015 with brewing moved elsewhere.

The success of Fat Yak, initially an approachable baby brother to the Alpha but becoming increasingly insipid as it moved to ever larger breweries, has played a role too; it's now outgrown Matilda Bay and is part of the rather cartoonish Yak Ales brand that may prove the final nail in this pioneer's coffin.

ALSO TRY Redback | Dogbolter

BREWER'S FOOD MATCH
Maple-glazed pork ribs

AVAILABILITY
Year-round

BREWERY & CELLAR DOOR LOCATION
131 Cascade Road, South Hobart, TAS 7004

BREWERY WEBSITE
www.matildabay.com.au

MT TENNENT PALE ALE

PACT BEER

 PALE ALE   5.2%   8–10°C   **SPIEGELAU IPA GLASS**

TASTING NOTES The first Pact beer to be packaged is a topnotch example of a contemporary pale ale. It manages to be tight and clean yet still exhibit lively tropical and citrus hop aromas and a depth of hop flavours. There's a touch of malt sweetness in a hazy pale yellow beer that wraps up with a pleasant bitterness.

THE STORY Champion home brewer Kevin Hingston gave Canberra another brewing company in 2015 when he launched Pact Beer. While retaining his day job in IT, he started travelling around the country to brew batches at the likes of Prickly Moses in Victoria and Blackrock in Sydney, before having his first bottled beer brewed under license at Hawkers Beer in Melbourne.

The launch of Pact completed a pretty rapid turnaround for the former VB man, who went from his first Fat Yak to home brewer to champion home brewer to Pact in just six years. The plan is to pay tribute to his hometown with his beers; Mt Tennent, for example, takes its name from the mountain named (and misspelled) after famous bushranger John Tennant, while 42.2 Summer Ale is inspired by the hottest recorded temperature in the capital.

ALSO TRY Three Lakes Hefeweizen 42.2 Summer Ale

BREWER'S FOOD MATCH
Pork dumplings with vanilla-infused sriracha sauce

AVAILABILITY
Year-round

BREWERY LOCATION
Fyshwick, ACT

BREWERY WEBSITE
www.pactbeer.com.au

XPA

RIDERS BREW CO

 XPA   5.8%   8°C   **NONIC OR TULIP GLASS**

TASTING NOTES Pitched somewhere between a pale ale and an IPA, Riders XPA is a beer that delivers in terms of hops and malt in equal measure. At first you're taken aback by the punchy American hop aromas, before rich, toffee-like English malts come into play to even things up. It's like a good American-style pale ale, but bigger.

THE STORY Many breweries have added a cider to their lineup; Riders Brew Co saw a cider maker head the other way. Gus Kelly, part of the Kelly family that's been making wine and cider in the Yarra Valley for decades, had become friends with Andrew 'Shandy' Gargan when they were neighbours. The former enjoyed the latter's home brews and joked that one day they should make them commercially.

Now they do, from a warehouse in Moorabbin on the kit once used by Coldstream before they became a contract brand. The brewery name – and that of many of the beers – is inspired by Gus and Shandy's shared love of skateboarding, while the beers, whatever the style, hold little back and are testament to Shandy's many studious hours listening to techno and brewing in his man cave.

ALSO TRY Easy Rider Golden Ale
Loose Trucks Porter

BREWER'S FOOD MATCH
Strong, sharp cheeses such as cheddar and aged parmesan; juicy burgers and just about any spicy food, especially Indian curries

AVAILABILITY
Year-round

BREWERY LOCATION
Moorabbin, VIC

CELLAR DOOR LOCATION
Kellybrook Winery, Fulford Road,
Wonga Park, VIC 3115

BREWERY WEBSITE
www.ridersbrewing.com.au

GUNSLINGERS AMERICAN PALE ALE

TOOBORAC BREWERY

 **AMERICAN PALE ALE** **4.8%** **4–6°C**  **AMERICAN PINT GLASS**

TASTING NOTES One of two pales in Tooborac's core range (the other being a less punchy Australian-style pale ale) is Gunslingers, a bold take on the American pale ale style. Pouring a deep, rusty copper colour, the stars are the punchy West Coast US hops that deliver piny, earthy characters and a solid bitterness amid the dark caramel malts.

THE STORY It was all change at Tooborac in 2015. The brewery to the rear of the striking bluestone Tooborac Hotel on the Northern Highway an hour or so north of Melbourne was upgraded and significantly expanded. Well-travelled head brewer Stu Ritchie went to work tweaking – sometimes significantly – the existing range of beers. And, perhaps most dramatically, they embraced a new look, ditching the old-school English stylings for spectacular new packaging designed by Scott Wilson-Browne of Red Duck, taking off his brewer's hat and donning that of his previous career as a graphic designer.

The core beers were much improved, but Stu wasn't finished there. He embarked on a series of more experimental limited releases that included a sour saison, a brown ale brewed with maple syrup and, best of all, a chocolate chilli stout.

It all points to a promising future for the brewery, opened by James and Val Carlin in 2005 after they'd driven past the then abandoned hotel, spotted a 'For Sale' sign, fallen in love with it and decided – with no prior experience in hospitality – to bring it back to life. Today, they've turned it into a welcoming, multifaceted venue, with Stu's beers at its heart.

ALSO TRY Woodcutter's Amber Ale
Chocolate Sanchez Chocolate Chilli Stout
Blacksmith's Porter | Shearer's Lager

BREWER'S FOOD MATCH
Grilled duck with five-spice rub accompanied by shaved fennel, rocket and blood orange salad (and maybe a side of thick-cut twice-cooked chips if you're hungry)

AVAILABILITY
Year-round

BREWERY & CELLAR DOOR LOCATION
5115 Northern Highway, Tooborac, VIC 3522

BREWERY WEBSITE
www.tooboracbeer.com.au

WOLF OF THE WILLOWS

 XPA   **4.7%**   **8°C**   **TULIP GLASS**

TASTING NOTES Whatever an XPA is supposed to be – extra pale, extra hoppy, extra booze – if they all tasted like this then no one would care. Wolf of the Willows' debut beer wowed all who sampled from the start, a lively melange of tropical, passionfruit and citrus hops all in perfect balance with a soft, biscuity malt character. So drinkable it has to be borderline illegal.

THE STORY Wolf of the Willows is about as craft beer a story as you could wish for. Home-brewing husband and wife Scott and Renae McKinnon decided to venture into the world of commercial brewing outside their day jobs, with Scott having been inspired by the American scene while being a ski bum in Colorado. Initially they became one of the brewing companies to take up residence at Cavalier's communal brewery in Melbourne's west and launched with the XPA, a beer whose deliciousness was matched by its beautiful packaging, a reflection of Renae's sales and marketing background.

They've added more beers since, each building their following to the point where they moved in with another friend from the beer world at the end of 2015.

They now brew out of Bad Shepherd's brewpub in Cheltenham, where they own a little under half of the brewery side of the operation, giving them greater capacity and greater control over their brewing, while 2015 also saw the launch of their barrel-ageing program too.

ALSO TRY ISA (India Saison)
JSP (Johnny Smoke Porter

BREWER'S FOOD MATCH
Vintage cheddar cheese or
Vietnamese salt-and-pepper quail

AVAILABILITY
Year-round

BREWERY & CELLAR DOOR LOCATION
386 Reserve Road, Cheltenham, VIC 3192

BREWERY WEBSITE
www.wolfofthewillows.com.au

NORMAN AUSTRALIAN ALE

YULLI'S BREWS

 PALE ALE   **4.9%**   **2–4°C**   **TULIP GLASS**

TASTING NOTES The first Yulli's beer to be canned is a thoroughly pleasant take on the sort of hoppy pale ales that are far and away the most popular with Aussie beer drinkers. Indeed, just as the name 'Norman' was chosen as an everyman Aussie bloke, so is this kind of beer – tropical hops, lively sherbet sweetness and a light, citrusy bitterness – becoming the everyman of the local craft beer world.

THE STORY Much of Sydney is well served by venues pouring a wide array of quality beer these days; indeed, many areas can offer multiple breweries where you can drink at source. But before the craft beer revolution swept through the city and surrounds, choices were few and far between.

One standout was Yulli's, and quite unexpected it was too: a 100 per cent vegetarian bar and restaurant that happened to offer a handful of local craft beers on tap and a wider selection in its well stocked fridges. As its peers and newcomers have caught up, its offering has expanded and, as of 2014, includes beers brewed under the Yulli's Brews banner too.

The brainchild of owner Karl Cooney and home-brewing staff member James Harvey, it operates as a 'gypsy' brewer, pitching up and pitching yeast at the

likes of Wayward, Happy Goblin, HopDog BeerWorks, Blackrock and more, with cans coming from large contract facility Icon. Aside from Norman, they've dabbled in many styles, occasionally in collaboration with fellow brewers, and plan to open their own brewery at some point, too.

ALSO TRY Fat Nerd Vanilla Porter
Slick Rick's Rampaging Red Ale
Bruce Malone IPA

☆

BREWER'S FOOD MATCH
Citrus- or tomato-based marinades and sauces; jalapeño chilli, garlic, basil and black pepper

AVAILABILITY
Year-round

BREWERY & CELLAR DOOR LOCATION
417 Crown Street, Surry Hills, NSW 2010

BREWERY WEBSITE
www.yullis.com.au/beer

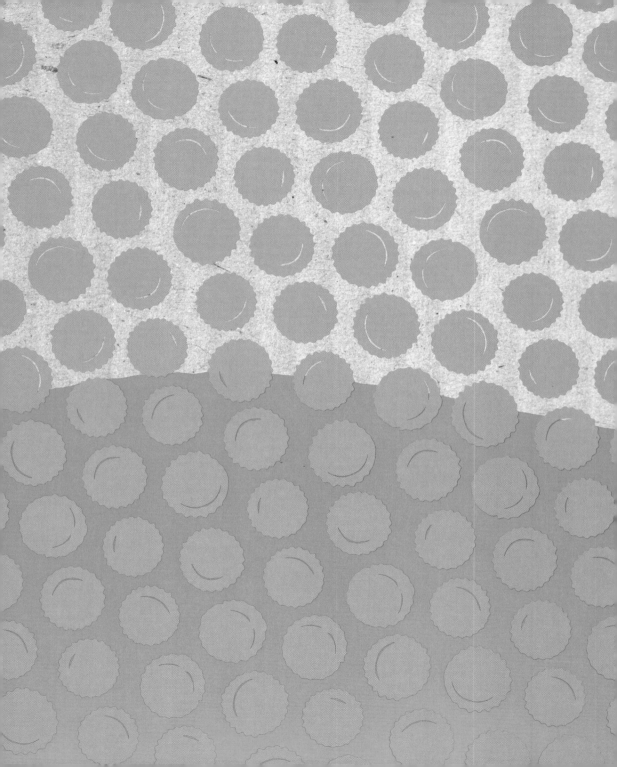

BURLEIGH BREWING COMPANY

Spend time in South East Queensland today and you don't have to look far to find a decent selection of beer. There are dozens of good bars in and around Brisbane, a growing number on the Sunshine and Gold Coasts and in other centres such as Toowoomba and Ipswich.

What's more, you're likely to find offerings from breweries that call the region home. In recent years, the likes of Green Beacon, Newstead Brewing, Brisbane Brewing Co and Catchment have opened brewery venues close to Brisbane's CBD, while there is a lively 'gypsy' brewing scene too, with brewers such as Gavin Croft and Brewtal Brewers using others' equipment to make their beers.

Slightly further out you'll find the likes of All Inn and the utterly unique Bacchus Brewing. Fortitude and Noisy Minor sit atop Mount Tamborine with Beard and Brau occupying a farmhouse at its base. Ipswich has its own in the shape of Pumpyard Brewery & Bar, the home of Four Hearts Brewing, while by the time this book hits shelves there will be three breweries operating on the Gold Coast and at least one more in the wings.

All of which is a rather longwinded way of saying that anyone living in or visiting the region with a penchant for something other than straightforward lager is pretty well served. Certainly, compared to as recently as 2011 or 2012, the picture is unrecognisable. If you were a beer lover who'd left

Brisbane five years ago, returning today would be akin to a lost and parched traveller summoning a last burst of energy to pull themselves over one final sand dune only to tumble down the other side into the most luscious of oases.

Prior to the recent outbreak of good craft beer, there was one significant outpost: Burleigh Brewing, which launched the first beers from its Burleigh Heads brewery in August 2007. There were other, smaller operations in Queensland at the time: typical brewpub-style operations sending little beer outside their premises, but Burleigh was serious, opening with a brewhouse that even today would dwarf pretty much every other microbrewery in Australia.

It was the brainchild of Peta and Brennan Fielding, the former a Queensland native who had always wanted to build her own business, the latter a brewmaster from Hawaii who gave her a product around which to build that business (as well as a family). They met in Hawaii, where Brennan ran the Brew Moon brewpub, then later, after time spent in Japan, bought the brewery where he had worked, selling it two years later for a profit and heading to the Gold Coast to start up their own.

Given the craft beer industry across the whole of Australia was still very much in its infancy, it was a tough market to enter. So it goes without saying that doing so in Queensland, on the Gold Coast no less, was about as tough a challenge as they could have set themselves.

It's one they've achieved with aplomb and with a multifaceted approach. They brewed beers specifically for their local market, with the various iterations of their Premium Lager and mid-strength Helles style lager only available within their region, while brewing 'craftier' beers to be sent further afield. They also chose to brew a 'no carb' beer, Big Head, something I imagine the vast majority of small brewers would sniff at but which is stocked far and wide, including on the shelves of major retailers.

All have been presented with a bright and breezy persona that makes a play of their location close to the surf and, often with humour too, particularly when it comes to the brewery's 'Bit on the Side' seasonal range that includes excellent beers such as the Black Giraffe coffee lager and Hassle Hop pale ale. But, perhaps most crucially, they've been brewed consistently to a high standard, with Brennan's beers among the cleanest in Australia. They seem to win gold every time they enter beer into the World Beer Challenge in Chicago, although their greatest achievement may well be a gold in the hugely prestigious World Beer Cup. Their Hef, a Bavarian-style wheat beer, beat all rivals, including those brewed in Bavaria.

Not one to be left in the shadows, former lawyer Peta's business prowess has been an equal part of Burleigh's

success. The brewery has won multiple business awards on the local and regional level, including Queensland Business of the Year in 2013. She has been lending her talents to the broader industry too, taking up a role as chair of the Craft Beer Industry Association.

The combination of smarts inside and outside the brewery has seen Burleigh grow incessantly, gradually taking over adjacent units in the industrial park where it was initially based. Eventually, growth reached the point where they needed to move and, in March 2016, they threw open the doors of a new site complete with impressive tap house.

With Black Hops and Balter Brewing, the latter a project launched by surfers Mick Fanning, Joel Parkinson, Josh Kerr and Bede Durbidge, opening a short drive down the coast, it appears that what was once unthinkable could well be happening: the Gold Coast is becoming a craft brewing powerhouse.

IPAS

IPAS

Has any beer style captured the imagination of the new wave of brewers – and indeed drinkers – around the world in the same way as the India pale ale, or IPA as it's more commonly known? Sure, within Australia's craft beer industry it's golden and pale ales that are doing the heavy lifting, selling in far greater numbers than anything else right now. But few beers seem to get the more eager beer drinkers excited than a well made, pungent, full-flavoured and firmly bitter IPA.

In the States, where the traditional English IPAs were first supercharged into the modern monster, and where IPAs are, for the most part, higher in alcohol and bitterness than those brewed here, they are now the biggest selling style in their ever-growing craft sector. Given how often the market here follows what happens there, expect to see IPAs making similar inroads here too, eventually picking up traction outside the world of beer geeks.

It is a style that these days tends to act as little more than a showcase for hops, but has a long and storied (and much debated) history. The most commonly told tale is that of the brewers charged with supplying the British colony on the Indian subcontinent realising that their ales had a better chance of arriving in reasonable condition if they were highly hopped and higher in alcohol as both hops and alcohol act as preservatives.

There is a second, less commonly told, tale that accompanies this. The location sometimes changes, but essentially the story is that ships destined for India carrying this hoppy, boozy cargo were shipwrecked not far off the British coastline. This allowed locals to sample such beers for the first time, declare them wonderful and kick-start a market for them in the UK.

Such tales have been picked apart by historians of beer, but there are elements of truth hidden within. What is known for certain is that English ales were sent to the Indian subcontinent and, after weeks at sea in wooden barrels, could arrive in rather poor condition. It is also known that brewers were advised to add extra hops to beers when sending them overseas from England, but this knowledge predates India pale ales and was used by brewers sending beer to countries other than India too.

Either way, by the 1830s, the phrase East India Pale Ale was being used to describe these hoppy, relatively high alcohol pale ales; indeed, according to historian Martyn Cornell, who writes the fantastically researched blog *Zythophile*, the first recorded use of the phrase 'India Pale Ale' was actually in Australia, in the *Sydney Gazette* and *New South Wales Advertiser* of

August 29, 1829. And by the middle of the 19th century the style was growing popular in the UK too.

A century and a half later, it became the perfect conduit for many of the brewers involved in the American craft beer revolution following a mantra of 'bigger is better'. Using the wonderfully pungent, typically citrusy and piney, hop varieties developed in the Pacific Northwest, they took IPA to another plane. Since then, the sky has been the limit when it comes to experimentation and taking hopping levels and indeed alcohol levels to extremes with the IPA style.

There have been double IPAs, imperial IPAs, black IPAs (something of an oxymoron given it means creating a black pale ale), white IPAs (usually featuring Belgian yeasts) and much more besides.

The love of such beers has been taken up by Australian brewers and drinkers alike. Indeed, since 2013, more than a quarter of beers voted for by the public in the annual Hottest 100 Aussie Craft Beers poll founded by The Local Taphouse have been IPAs of one form or another.

A recent trend, both here and overseas, has been the rise of session IPAs. There's debate over exactly what this means and whether it should even be considered a style. But, at its heart, the aim is to create beers with the hop character and, potentially, bitterness of a full strength at a much lower alcohol.

With such beers, which are always best drunk fresh, drinkers should be expecting big hop aromatics and similarly hop-dominated flavours, but balanced with enough malt sweetness to stop the bitterness from getting out of control. Most brewed in Australia are inspired by the American approach, although you will occasionally find a locally brewed English IPA.

A DOZEN MORE TO TRY

MODUS OPERANDI
Zoo Feeder

BRIDGE ROAD BREWERS
Bling Bling Imperial IPA

THE LITTLE BREWING COMPANY
Fastidious Bastard

MURRAY'S CRAFT BREWERY
Icon 2IPA

LOBETHAL BIERHAUS
Double Hopped IPA

HOPDOG BEERWORKS
Horns Up Rye IPA

NOISY MINOR
ANZUS IPA

NEW ENGLAND BREWING CO
Hop Cannon IPA

MORNINGTON PENINSULA BREWERY
IPA

LORD NELSON
Double Nelson

EXIT BREWING
IPA

BRIGHT BREWERY
M.I.A. IPA

WEST COAST IPA

BATCH BREWING CO

 WEST COAST IPA **5.8%**  **4°C** **SPIEGELAU IPA GLASS**

TASTING NOTES When I asked a panel of industry experts to come up with the ten best new releases out of New South Wales in 2015, there was one slightly odd entry. So impressed were they by several of the IPAs from Marrickville's Batch Brewing that they nominated them en masse. The West Coast variant is probably their most iconic, a tautly constructed lean machine with grapefruit dominating and a supremely dry finish.

THE STORY Sydney's Inner West is the place to go if you fancy a spot of brewery and brewpub hopping. Even ignoring the very many fine bars, restaurants and hotels which make quality beer part of their offering, you could satisfy your every beery desire drinking in the company of the stainless steel within which your drink was brewed.

Such has been the rapid proliferation in the area, with Young Henrys' arrival in Newtown setting off a chain reaction, despite only opening in late 2013, Marrickville's Batch Brewing can count themselves as elder statesman. Founded by American expats Andrew Fineran and Chris Sidwa, the aim – as the name puts front and centre – was to focus on single batch releases, and to support and become very much part of their local community.

They've stayed true to that for the most part, with nothing too much in the way of a core range (even if certain beers are found more often than others) and even less beer travelling more than a few kilometres from the cellar door. Indeed, it's to their frequently pumping and recently expanded brewery bar that you're best to head to enjoy the broadest selection of their beers, including the frequent collaborations carried out with friends – brewers and otherwise.

ALSO TRY American Pale Ale
Other IPAs | Whatever else might be on tap

BREWER'S FOOD MATCH
A big, juicy steak

AVAILABILITY
Year-round

BREWERY & CELLAR DOOR LOCATION
44 Sydenham Road, Marrickville, NSW 2204

BREWERY WEBSITE
www.batchbrewingco.com.au

SPROCKET

BENTSPOKE BREWING CO

 IPA 6.6% 4°C **TULIP OR IPA GLASS**

TASTING NOTES Tagged as the younger sister to the brewery's flagship IPA Crankshaft, in typical BentSpoke fashion Sprocket is actually bigger, at least in terms of alcohol content. Amid a vast array of fine drops from the Canberra brewpub, this earned its guernsey by means of delivering one of the biggest tropical fruit hits we've experienced from within a wonderfully balanced, bright yellow beer.

THE STORY Few brewpub openings have been as eagerly awaited among Australia's more ardent beer fanciers than that of BentSpoke in 2014. The Canberra venue was the new venture from double Champion Brewer of Australia Richard Watkins and partner Tracy Margrain. With support from friends in the industry, they built a truly spectacular brewery–bar–restaurant in a new development in the burgeoning suburb of Braddon.

It wasn't just Richard's past double triumph that had people excited, it was also the fact that he'd won the titles at the Wig & Pen, the Canberra institution at which, tucked away with a tiny brewery surrounded by all manner of barrels, he had created a dazzling and diverse lineup of cask ales, imperial stouts, fruit and spice beers and blended sours.

BentSpoke didn't disappoint. Across 18 taps (each with a custom-made handle designed by a regular), he and Tracy pour excellent examples of contemporary craft beer styles – IPAs and pales – alongside more traditional ales and lagers, ciders, historical recreations and those brewed with unlikely ingredients. In the first 12 months alone, 160,000 litres flew through the taps. In more good news, at the end of 2015 they announced plans for a second venue with a bigger production brewery and a canning line. The initial intention is to still focus on the local market but, hopefully, once that is sated, people outside ACT will be able to discover what the fuss is all about.

For their full story, see page 186.

ALSO TRY Crankshaft IPA | Big Nut Braddon Bitter | PSI Imperial Saison Cluster (various versions) | Derailleur

BREWER'S FOOD MATCH
Fish tacos

AVAILABILITY
Year-round

BREWERY & CELLAR DOOR LOCATION
38 Mort Street, Braddon, ACT 2612

BREWERY WEBSITE
www.bentspokebrewing.com.au

HOP HOG

FERAL BREWING COMPANY

 IPA / PALE ALE   **5.8%**   **4–8°C**   **IPA GLASS**

TASTING NOTES Is it an IPA? Is it a pale ale? In recognition of changing tastes (and perhaps just how easily it goes down) Feral Brewing have put a cross through the word 'India' on labels of their all-conquering Hop Hog. Indeed, it's entered as a pale ale category at beer awards too. Still, it's most widely known as an IPA so it's here, in all its impeccably balanced orange citrus and pine, subtly sweet malt and perfectly judged bitterness glory.

THE STORY The best Australian brewery of the contemporary craft beer era? WA's Feral Brewing certainly has as strong a shout as anyone. Since launching with a brewery tucked into one corner of a log cabin-style brewpub in Swan Valley, Feral has blazed a trail for many beer styles, particularly the American-inspired hop forward ales that now dominate much of the craft beer world.

These days, Feral's brewpub kit is used to create its more esoteric beers as well as new experiments, both of which cover a vast spectrum of flavours and textures. On a visit, you could expect to enjoy everything from a 10 per cent ABV imperial stout or barley wine to a soft, barrel-fermented take on the Hop Hog, from Belgian hybrids to fruity sours. Feral's most popular beers, however, now come from the BrewCorp brewery set up with

co-founder Brendan Varis and his old mate John Stallwood of Nail Brewing.

Well into its second decade, Feral continues to innovate, pushing the importance of refrigeration more than any other brewer, and trialling new styles and techniques. Case in point: as Australian brewers and drinkers started to fall in love with sour styles such as Berliner Weisse, Feral was busy collecting Champion Craft Beer for its Watermelon Warhead – a beer debuted in 2012, long before the majority of those brewers or drinkers would even have known such beers existed.

For their full story, see page 112.

ALSO TRY Watermelon Warhead Boris | Razorback | White | Karma Citra Raging Flem | Smoked Porter | Tusk

---

✰

BREWER'S FOOD MATCH
Lamb kofta on a freshly baked flatbread, served with eggplant, feta, tomato, pomegranate, mint and a dollop of yoghurt

AVAILABILITY
Year-round at all good bottleshops, pubs and bars

BREWERY & CELLAR DOOR LOCATION
152 Haddrill Road, Baskerville, WA 6056

BREWERY WEBSITE
www.feralbrewing.com.au

FIXATION BREWING COMPANY

 IPA   6.4%   8°C   **IPA OR TULIP GLASS**

TASTING NOTES The launch IPA from a brewing company that pledges to brew nothing but IPAs takes its inspiration fair and square from those of West Coast USA. Punchy citrus and pine aromas meet you well before the glass gets to your mouth, with those big American hop flavours balanced nicely by biscuity, caramel malts that ensure the bitterness does its job, but nothing more.

THE STORY Fixation could just as easily be called Serendipity. Towards the end of 2015, West Coast IPA fanatic Tom Delmont – then Mountain Goat's longest serving and best known sales rep – visited Byron Bay's Stone & Wood unannounced, chatted about the beer world with its owners, grabbed some beers and continued on his family holiday. Two weeks later, he took a call from his boss at Goat telling him the business had been sold, 100 per cent, to Asahi Premium Beverages. Devastated, Tom pondered his future as offers flooded in from independent breweries all over Australia. Among the requests for a chat was one from Stone & Wood, who had Tom fresh in their minds after his surprise visit. The brewery's owners had been chatting about launching an IPA offshoot since a trip to the States early in 2015 during which it had been glaringly apparent just how popular the style was; Australia tended to follow American trends and they knew just how passionate Tom was about such beers.

Thus Fixation was born, stating it would only ever brew variations on IPA, and with Tom and his family flying to Byron to brew the first batch. From a chance encounter via a devastating phone call to the launch of a new business backed by one of the best breweries in the country and fronted by a man who loves IPA (almost) more than life itself: serendipity, indeed.

ALSO TRY More IPAs

BREWER'S FOOD MATCH
Thai chicken and kaffir lime leaf sausage rolls with a spicy sriracha dipping sauce

AVAILABILITY
Year-round

BREWERY & CELLAR DOOR LOCATION
8 Boronia Place, Byron Bay, NSW 2481

BREWERY WEBSITE
www.fixationbrewing.com.au

BIG SUR

THE GRIFTER BREWING CO.

 WEST COAST IPA   6.7%   7°C PINT GLASS

TASTING NOTES Big Sur is one of California's most iconic spots. And when it comes to iconic beers from the States, there's little that can hold a candle these days to West Coast IPAs – lean, pale ales that overflow with hop aromatics. They're becoming increasingly popular with Aussie brewers, with Sydney's Grifter an early adopter. Their Big Sur ticks all the boxes: heaps of citrus and pine character and just enough malt to keep things in balance.

THE STORY The Grifter Brewing Co. is, more or less, a happy accident. Three home-brewing mates, Matt King, Trent Evans and Glenn Wignall, chanced upon an opportunity to brew a commercial batch of their beer at newly opened Young Henrys in Newtown. The beer was well received, they enjoyed the experience, Young Henrys had spare capacity at the time, so they came back and did it again. And again.

They started out by hand-delivering growlers (two-litre glass bottles) of their pale ale (then called Edward) to venues, doing it with such frequency that some people thought growlers – then relatively new to Australia – were actually called Grifters. Subsequent beers were just as well received and, as both they and Young Henrys expanded, it became apparent they would have to go their own way.

So they did, buying their hosts' old gear, finding a warehouse that formerly housed a laundromat in Marrickville and installing it there, alongside more tanks and a bar and pool room. Not only has it given them a home for their beers (and Sydney's inner west yet another awesome brewery venue) but also the freedom to create even more specialties alongside their fine core range.

ALSO TRY Pale Ale | Marnie's Majority
The Omen

BREWER'S FOOD MATCH
American BBQ

AVAILABILITY
Year-round

BREWERY & CELLAR DOOR LOCATION
1/391 Enmore Road, Marrickville, NSW 2204

BREWERY WEBSITE
www.thegrifter.com.au

HAWKERS BEER

 IPA    6.5%   6°C   PINT GLASS

TASTING NOTES It's a sign of how consistently good Hawkers has been since the off that I could have put any of their four core beers in here and few would have grounds for complaint. As it is, their IPA features as its impeccable balance of juicy American hops and balancing malts, complete with finely judged bitterness, make it so damned drinkable it will surely become one of the country's favourite beers of the style.

THE STORY Renowned Melbourne restaurateur Joseph Abboud – a man who didn't drink beer as all he'd tried previously was mainstream lager – went to his mother country, Lebanon, in the search of new flavours, ideas and ingredients for his restaurants Rumi and Moor's Head. While there, he was introduced to Mazen Hajjar, a man who counted war photographer, banking CFO and international airline founder among his past lives, but was by then founder and head of 961 Beer, the Middle East's first microbrewery.

The former became caught up in the latter's whirling maelstrom, found he'd become an importer of 961 Beer to Australia and soon embarked on a rapid journey of discovery in the beer world. A few months later, after visiting Australia to launch his beer here, Mazen and Joseph started chatting about launching their own brewery.

Less than two years later, Hawkers Beer opened in Melbourne's northern suburbs, won an award for its Pale Ale two days later, and a year later was among the biggest independent microbreweries in Australia. With former Bright Brewery head brewer Jon Seltin at the helm and a sales team headed by one of Melbourne's best known reps, they exploded onto the scene with great beers and fierce determination to make a difference. It would be a surprise if they aren't a major force nationally by the time they turn two.

ALSO TRY Pale Ale | Saison | Pilsner

BREWER'S FOOD MATCH
Salty fried food, grilled meats,
Indian curries and Mexican

AVAILABILITY
Year-round

BREWERY & CELLAR DOOR LOCATION
167 Henty Street, Reservoir, VIC 3073

BREWERY WEBSITE
hawkers.beer

AUSTRALIAN IPA

HAWTHORN BREWING CO.

 IPA 5.8% 4–6°C IPA GLASS

TASTING NOTES The Hawthorn team has known from day one who its audience is: people looking for something a little different and more flavoursome than mainstream beers, but without being challenged too much. Thus, their entire range delivers approachable takes on popular craft beer styles. The Australian IPA is their biggest, but remains restrained, delivering Juicy Fruit-like tropical hops without much in the way of bitterness.

THE STORY The trio of mates that would launch Hawthorn Brewing Co. originally met via family friend connections while growing up in the same suburb, in Melbourne's east. Hamish Reed would bring samples of his home brew to share with Darren Milo and Peter Willis, beers that over time went from pretty bad to better to, "You should release these commercially."

When they did so in 2009, it was as a contract brewer, with Hamish travelling to breweries around Victoria and then further afield to have his recipes for approachable beers – American-style pale ale, pilsner, amber ale – brewed for them. There has been talk of opening their own brewery but, as the years pass and the business grows successfully without one, is there any need?

Their success can be measured in more than just growth too. In recent years, their beers have enjoyed success at the International Beer Challenge in the UK, a prestigious competition judging packaged beer from the world over. Trophies for several beers, including this IPA, and for the brewing company itself saw them launch into the UK market in 2015.

ALSO TRY Pale Ale | Golden Ale
Amber Ale | Pilsner

BREWER'S FOOD MATCH
Spicy Asian food

AVAILABILITY
Year-round

BREWERY LOCATION
Smeaton Grange, NSW

BREWERY WEBSITE
www.hawthornbrewing.com.au

ILLAWARRA BREWING COMPANY

 IPA 6.3% 3-4°C **WHATEVER YOU CAN FIND**

TASTING NOTES Illawarra's entry in *150 Great Australian Beers* was their IPA and it still is now, albeit a slightly different one. The new brewer at the helm was unable to source enough of the Calypso hop that gave Apocalypso its name and much of its extravagant hop character, so he designed a new beer with new hops, a new name but, thankfully, just as much hop character: citrus and strawberry on the nose, joined by peach and pine to taste.

THE STORY Much has changed at Illawarra Brewing Company since the publication of *150 Great Australian Beers*. One of its former pair of head brewers joined Sydney's Wayward Brewing Co, while the other was snapped up by the (at the time of writing) yet-to-open Stomping Ground project from The Local Taphouse team.

Into their shoes stepped Chris Sewell, a home brewer who had been honing his recipes with a best mate who was well established as a commercial brewer (while Chris was also my daughter's first swimming instructor, fans of totally obscure and pointless facts...). A crash course in learning his way around the brewery, its processes and his predecessors' recipes followed before, very quickly, he set about putting his own mark on the place.

Rather than play it safe and stick simply to the existing beers, he embarked on a single hop series, launched this new IPA, and discovered some gifts left for him in the form of lambic-style sour ales that had been ageing for years in oak. The two releases that ensued: one unblended, one blended with raspberries, were so well received that the barrels were soon refilled in the hope of similarly successful results in the future.

There's been more recent change too, with Chris returning to Melbourne, and Illawarra rebranding and tweaking its lineup.

ALSO TRY Pale Ale | Rust Amber Ale Porter | Smashing Rumpkin

BREWER'S FOOD MATCH
Spicy Asian food

AVAILABILITY
Year-round

BREWERY LOCATION
North Wollongong, NSW

BREWERY WEBSITE
www.illawarrabrewingco.com.au

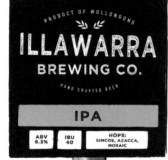

CTHULHU BLACK IPA

KAIJU! BEER

 BLACK IPA   6.5%   6-8°C   **SPIEGELAU IPA GLASS**

TASTING NOTES Maybe I'm getting soft in my old age – or perhaps being unwittingly perverse – but in selecting Cthulhu as KAIJU!'s feature beer I've plumped for the least hoppy beer from a brewery that's built its brand upon using monstrous amounts of hops. But there you go. It's my favourite of their range, one in which predominantly herbaceous hops are very much present but balanced by layers of dark cocoa, roast malt and coffee.

THE STORY It's fair to say the KAIJU! crew has enjoyed a colourful start to life in beer. Part of that is down to their approach. The business conceived by brothers Callum and Nat Reeves and the former's wife Clara launched (as Monster Mash until Monster energy drinks bullied them into changing their name) with boisterously eye-catching artwork by Texan Mikey Burton, with whom Clara had always wanted to work in her other career in game design.

And it was also launched with an ethos based around squeezing as many hops into any beer as physically possible – sometimes more. Indeed, the very first Monster Mash beer was quite the statement of intent: a nigh on 10 per cent ABV double IPA that brewer Nat followed with a hoppy red ale that promptly took out a trophy at the Australian International Beer Awards. It announced them to a

wider audience as not just hopheads, but hopheads who knew a thing or two about brewing.

Further huge beers have followed, almost all featuring a different Kaiju (Japanese monster) as well as a relatively tame beer by their standards, Robohop, which was the first beer to feature a hero rather than monster on its label. As of late 2015, they'd opened their own brewery in Melbourne's southeast, so look out for far more rampaging hop monsters on the loose. And maybe the odd hero, too.

ALSO TRY Metamorphosis IPA Hopped Out Red | Robohop Golden IPA Where Strides The Behemoth Aftermath Double IPA

BREWER'S FOOD MATCH
Gooey, smelly cheese, ribs in sticky sauce, or even chocolate mousse. But really, the best match is a well-aged Japanese whisky.

AVAILABILITY
Year-round

BREWERY LOCATION
Dandenong South, VIC

BREWERY WEBSITE
www.kaijubeer.com.au

STOMPBOX

KICK | SNARE

 WEST COAST IPA 6.1% 7°C  PINT GLASS

TASTING NOTES Stompbox announced to the discerning drinkers of Andrew Swift's hometown of Lonny that here was a new brewing company worth watching out for. This West Coast IPA blew people away: a rusty amber treat awash with herbaceous, stone fruit and orange hop flavours and aromas. The hops are supported by a solid malt backbone that helps Swifty achieve great balance and deliver a seriously smooth beer.

THE STORY Beer is all well and good. But is there anything that gives greater joy and comfort to more people in more ways than music? I'm in the no camp on this one, but perhaps a better answer is that together they can be greater than the sum of their parts.

And while there's few breweries that don't vibrate to the sound of their favourite bands on brew day, and brewery-musician collaborations have been many, there is no Australian brewing company combining the two like kick|snare. The fledgling Tassie brewery takes its name from one of jazz-playing, arts-teaching brewer Andrew Swift's instruments and his beers all take inspiration from music, too.

The Fifty-Eight is named after Shure's classic microphone (so they sent him a load to convert into tap handles);

Stompbox after the guitarist's effects pedal of the same name. Others come with tap handles made lovingly from cassettes. Since graduating from home brewing, Swifty's approach has been slow and hands-on, with bottles labelled by hand. At the time of writing, there were concerns over the lease of the unit he shares with a forthcoming craft maltings but, having come this far, he made it clear he'll still be brewing somewhere come what may.

ALSO TRY The Fifty-Eight Pale Ella Brown of Motown

BREWER'S FOOD MATCH
Fish and Chips

AVAILABILITY
Year-round

BREWERY AND CELLAR DOOR LOCATION
27 Montagu Street, Invermay, TAS 7248

BREWERY WEBSITE
www.kicksnarebrewing.com

BLACK IPA

KOOINDA

 **BLACK IPA**   **7.0%**   **4–6°C**   **IPA OR TULIP GLASS**

TASTING NOTES After Kooinda's first release, the ballsy-for-its-day American Pale Ale, it was the Black IPA (née Full Nelson) that got beer geeks excited more than any other. A fierce collision of potent Kiwi hop Nelson Sauvin and black malts, on song it was a uniquely powerful and impressive beer. It's a different beast now, featuring a blend of hops and a different malt bill: less smack-you-around-the-chops; more nuanced and in tune with the times.

THE STORY The Kooinda story has always been one of the best in the contemporary Australian beer world. Built very slowly by a bunch of mates, including a number of home brewers, in a shed in a Rosanna backyard, using water pumped from the swimming pool to chill tanks, their beers were punchy and their presence always livened up any event.

Over the years, the original group dwindled once they'd moved to a bigger brewery in Heidelberg in Melbourne's north, sometimes from fallouts, sometimes for family reasons, sometimes to pursue other opportunities. In 2015, the last of the founders left, having sold to new owners. Then the guy brought in to run the show ran into unforeseen visa issues, went to New Zealand to sort them out and got stuck there for four months.

Thankfully, what was in danger of turning into some sort of dark farce had righted itself by 2016. The new team is back together, much needed upgrades have been made to the brewery and the beers have been streamlined – both in terms of number and character, while Friday nights at the breweries continue to pull crowds. No doubt more will have changed by the time you read this but, presumably, for the better.

ALSO TRY American Pale Ale
Range still being finalised at time of printing

BREWER'S FOOD MATCH
Steak, barbecued meats, creamy chesses, or blue cheese with prosciutto

AVAILABILITY
Year-round

BREWERY AND CELLAR DOOR LOCATION
28 Culverlands Street, Heidelberg West, VIC 3081

BREWERY WEBSITE
www.kooinda.com.au

DEAD MAN'S REVENGE

LAST RITES BREWING COMPANY

 BLACK IPA **6.5%** **8-10°C** **SPIEGELAU IPA GLASS**

TASTING NOTES Up until recently, Tasmania's small number of microbreweries tended to eschew hoppier American-style beers. Now, as the number of brewing companies expands, those sort of beers are on the menu, too. They're the house specialty of newcomer Last Rites, with this black IPA the pick on my first visit: it's their hoppiest drop, with plenty of piny and forest floor-like hops backed with a touch of chocolate and roast.

THE STORY It's fair to say the team behind Last Rites Brewing Company doesn't take itself too seriously. Not only do they have beers with names such as Cloudy With A Chance Of Awesome and She's No Bette Midler, but on the evening they welcomed Tasmanian Premier Will Hodgman to their official brewery opening in October 2015 they announced the beer brewed to mark the occasion was to be called the Premier's Horn.

The brewing company was launched by five mates with diverse backgrounds, albeit including experience in various areas of the state's liquor industry: those with involvement in Hobart craft beer pub Preachers and the Abbey bottleshop; a vineyard manager; and a beer distributor too. Most importantly, they counted home brewers among their number and cut their teeth commercially brewing a few batches at Morrison Brewery in Launceston before setting up their own joint in Cambridge, just a few hundred metres away from fellow newcomers Doublehead.

Their intention, as much as anything, was to indulge their love of hoppy American-style ales. Now, with a bar at their warehouse brewery open every week, with food trucks parked outside, you can, too.

ALSO TRY Horn of Diligence Pale Ale
She's No Bette Midler Red Ale
Georgie Ella Summer Ale

BREWER'S FOOD MATCH
Slow-cooked venison

AVAILABILITY
Year-round

BREWERY & CELLAR DOOR LOCATION
Unit 3, 18 Kennedy Drive, Cambridge, TAS 7170

BREWERY WEBSITE
www.facebook.com/lastritesbrewing

HEL

EKIM BREWING

 BLACK IPA 9.2% 4-8°C TULIP GLASS

TASTING NOTES Ekim Brewing's Mike Jorgensen loves hops. Lots of them. Particularly American ones. They're a feature of pretty much everything he releases, including this beer that, from a distance, might have you thinking it's a big stout. Black as night and very full of body, it's also awash with tropical, citrus and piny hops. There are some roasted, dark sugar and toffee characters in there too, adding balance and a surprising smoothness to a seriously big beer.

THE STORY Were you to try to summarise Sydney brewery Ekim in two words, you'd probably plump for 'hops' and 'Vikings'. As stated in the tasting notes, founder and head brewer Mike is a huge fan of the former, filling his beers with them and often decorating his eye-catchingly cartoonish bottle labels and tap decals with them; one, for his Berserker amber IPA, has a bearded Viking warrior holding a 'decapitated' hop flower in his hand like a spoil of war.

The Viking side of things comes from Mike's heritage, even if the rather Norse-sounding Ekim is nothing more than his name backwards. Viking touches are found in the names and images for his beers; most feature bearded, horn-helmeted men of some description, although for the beer featured here inspiration was taken from the Nordic goddess of the underworld.

Mike's brewing started out on a 100-litre kit at home before he realised he'd rather be doing it full time rather than around his former job as a landscape gardener. That led him to share a brewery with Happy Goblin and, soon after, into the affections of beer lovers looking for American-style hopped-up ales.

His beers continue to grow in popularity, requiring significant brewery expansion and a decision to stop bottling most of them in order to focus on satisfying venues' demand for kegs. A grapefruit twist on his Viking IPA went nuts, while late 2015 saw Ekim open a cellar door so fans can head to Mount Kuring-gai and drink at source.

ALSO TRY After Battle Pale Ale | Viking IPA
Grapefruit Viking IPA | Berserker Amber IPA
Vinlander Porter | Rök Double IPA

BREWER'S FOOD MATCH
Rich chocolate mud cake

AVAILABILITY
Year-round

BREWERY & CELLAR DOOR LOCATION
11/1 Marina Close, Mount Kuring-Gai, NSW 2080

BREWERY WEBSITE
www.ekimbrewing.com.au

COPY CAT AIPA

MASH BREWING

 AMERICAN IPA **6.8%** **5°C** **PINT GLASS**

TASTING NOTES For a beer that started out – or at least turned into – something of a running joke with fellow Swan Valley brewery Feral, Mash's Copy Cat has done pretty damn well for itself. The beautifully judged take on big American IPAs leaves nothing in the locker room, creating a hop-driven yet balanced beer of real depth and subtle complexity that's collected pretty much every major gong for which it's been entered.

THE STORY In *150 Great Australian Beers*, I wrote that Mash Brewing, in its earlier days, was a fine brewpub that had been crying out for a good brewer to give it the beers it deserved prior to Charlie Hodgson joining them from Gage Roads. At that time, he'd already done a fine job of steering Mash in the right direction; since then, things have gone from strength to strength.

The Copy Cat was named Champion Beer of Australia at the Australian International Beer Awards in 2014 – the most prestigious title a beer can achieve locally – and has continued to hoover up medals and trophies since. And, aided by its eastern outpost in Melbourne – at the 3 Ravens brewery it saved in 2013 – the brewery itself has been honoured, with Berliner Weisse expert Brendan O'Sullivan swapping his Ravens for a Mash one when creating a series of flavoured takes on the sour German style and subsequently collecting more shiny baubles.

That said, while Mash beers are more widely available than in the past, it remains a predominantly WA operation. As well as its Swan Valley brewpub home, it operates two other venues (in Bunbury and Rockingham) which are the best places to sample a wide selection of Charlie's beers, many of which appear in short, keg-only runs.

ALSO TRY Challenger English IPA Berliner Weisse Series | Grasscutter Russell American Amber

BREWER'S FOOD MATCH
Good pub grub or a burger and chips

AVAILABILITY
Year-round

BREWERY & CELLAR DOOR LOCATION
10250 West Swan Road, Henley Brook, WA 6055

BREWERY WEBSITE
www.mashbrewing.com.au

TWO TO THE VALLEY IPA

NEWSTEAD BREWING CO

 IPA   5.9%   4-6°C   **SPIEGELAU IPA GLASS**

TASTING NOTES Work your way through Newstead's range and one of the most striking characteristics you'll find in common is just how neatly constructed the beers are. That's certainly the case with their American-style IPA, which delivers everything you could want – piny, citrusy hops, subtle caramel malts and a clean bitterness – all within a tightly wound package. A damn fine drop.

THE STORY It's not uncommon when a home brewer steps up for the first time into the commercial world for them to take a little while to find their feet. They need to scale up their recipes and learn their way around new gear, while there could be challenges with packaging and getting beer to customers. So it was a pleasant surprise when I first visited Brisbane's Newstead shortly after it opened to find a consistently good and well-made range across all of their brewpub's taps.

Having since delved a little deeper into the Newstead story, it seems less surprising. Head brewer and co-owner Mark Howes comes from a science background (cellular biology to be specific) and his approach to brewing – home or otherwise – can safely be described as fastidious; in the 12 months leading to the brewery opening he brewed 96 batches at home in his spare time.

The venue itself was opened with Michael Conrad, a man with a lengthy career in high-end hospitality. As such, its restaurant offering, which overlooks the brewery upon which Mark often brews alongside fellow brewers from Brisbane and further afield, is of a rather finer standard than most Aussie breweries. All being well, they'll open a second venue and production facility near the Suncorp Stadium in 2016, allowing them to bring all brewing back in-house.

ALSO TRY 3 Quarter Time Session Ale
21 Feet 7 Inches Porter
Liquidambar Amber Ale
The Mayne Thing Golden Ale
Its many collaborations

BREWER'S FOOD MATCH
Newstead buffalo wings or green mango and chicken curry

AVAILABILITY
Year-round

BREWERY & CELLAR DOOR LOCATION
85 Doggett Street, Newstead, QLD 4006

BREWERY WEBSITE
www.newsteadbrewing.com.au

IIPA

PIRATE LIFE BREWING

 **IMPERIAL IPA**   **8.8%**    **COLD** (LET IT WARM AS YOU GET THROUGH IT)   **NONIC PINT GLASS OR SHIRAZ GLASS** (FROM THE CAN IS GOOD TOO)

TASTING NOTES   The biggest (to date) of the hoppy beers released by Adelaide's Pirate Life is as excellent as it is large. The IIPA (imperial India pale ale) crams a monstrous amount of juicy tropical and citrusy American hops into an 8.8 per cent ABV beer with enough malt to keep the bitterness in check but not enough to distract from the hops. Destined to become an Aussie cult classic.

THE STORY   Red Proudfoot and Jack Cameron are two young Aussie brewers who met while working at Scotland's noisily trailblazing BrewDog. Upon returning to Australia, they continued to hone their brewing skills in WA – Red at Margaret River start-up Cheeky Monkey, Jack at Little Creatures in Freo – before setting off on their own adventure in Adelaide with Jack's dad Michael the third piece of the Pirate Life jigsaw.

They hit the ground not so much running as sprinting, with a trio of hop forward beers that had beer lovers drooling from the off. Their Throwback 'session' IPA delivered a serious hoppy, bitter kick in mid-strength form, while their West Coast American-style Pale Ale is a true marvel. Indeed, it's possibly even better than this IIPA, but misses out on being the feature beer for one reason: while the Throwback and Pale come in standard size cans, the IIPA, despite being by far the highest in alcohol, got the 500 ml tallboy treatment. And it comes in black – as bold a '$%^& you!' statement of intent as we've seen.

The trio has worked (and partied) hard in support of the brand, hosting countless events across the country in their first year in business, while also significantly expanding the brewery and adding a tasting room where you can sample the beers as fresh as humanly possible.

For their full story, see page 46.

ALSO TRY   Pale Ale | Throwback IPA And an IPA expected in 2016

BREWER'S FOOD MATCH
Real Texan chilli con carne and a side of corn bread

AVAILABILITY
Year-round

BREWERY & CELLAR DOOR LOCATION
89 South Road, Hirdmarsh, SA 5007

BREWERY WEBSITE
www.piratelife.com.au

BENGAL IPA

RED DUCK

 IPA 7.0% 5–6°C PINT GLASS

TASTING NOTES Picking one beer from Red Duck's range to feature is as hard as with any brewery. After all, the Ballarat brewery has released more than 100 in its time. In the end, an old favourite that's survived the test of time gets the nod. Bengal is an IPA inspired by the earthier styles of the UK but given a citrusy, piney boost from the use of US Centennial and Cascade hops. It's no hop bomb, however, more a hearty, malty, full-bodied affair.

THE STORY Red Duck celebrated 10 years of brewing in 2015 and it's fair to say Scott and Vanessa Wilson-Browne's decade in beer has been unlike any other. From early days brewing in a converted dairy on the grounds of Purrumbete to the barrel-heavy current setup in Ballarat, with time spent running a provedore in Camperdown along the way, the graphic designer-turned-brewer (and occasional graphic designer) and his wife have carved a niche as owners of one of the most adventurous breweries in the land.

Before celebrating 10 years (with a suitably big 10 hop, 10 per cent ABV version of one of his favourite beers, Golden Dragon), Scott had already passed the 100 different beers mark. Among them were hop-less Medieval-style smoky sours and beers using yeast cultured up from

sourdough inspired by ancient Egyptian brews, imperial stouts and porters, many barrel-aged experiments and plenty of collaborations.

Yet he likes to remind people that his biggest sellers remain beers like his Pale, a straightforward take on American pale ales, and he's equally at home playing around with more approachable hoppy beers. That said, he finds the lure of the other pretty tough to resist and is starting a distillery, called Kilderkin, too.

ALSO TRY The Ox | Golden Dragon Hoppy Amber | Topaz | Hop Shark Various barrel-aged sours

---

☆

BREWER'S FOOD MATCH
Nasi lemak with beef rendang

AVAILABILITY
Limited release, but generally available year-round

BREWERY & CELLAR DOOR LOCATION
11A Michaels Drive, Alfredton, VIC 3350

BREWERY WEBSITE
www.redduckbeer.com.au

---

777 IMPERIAL IPA

RIVERSIDE BREWING COMPANY

 IMPERIAL IPA   9.2%  4°C   IPA GLASS

TASTING NOTES In *150 Great Australian Beers*, I highlighted Riverside's 77 IPA as one of the best India pale ales in Australia. That same year, they launched 777 – an even bigger imperial version. As with the original, the brewery showed a mastery of hops, cramming heaps of piny, citrusy American hop character and no small amount of booze into a lean, clean and dangerously drinkable beer.

THE STORY Paramatta's Riverside Brewing burst onto the NSW beer scene midway through 2012 like few others. Within months, there was a buzz amid Sydney's beer cognoscenti about this new brewery pumping out some of the best American-inspired, hop forward beers anyone had sampled from a local brewery.

Home brewer-turned-pro brewer Dave Padden proved a master of hops, with beers such as his 44 American Amber and 77 IPA in particular becoming mainstays at many of the best bars in the city. Then, at the end of 2014, something of a tremor was sent through the beer world as Dave announced he was leaving Riverside over disagreements with business co-founder Stephen Pan.

Any fears for what this might mean for one of the state's best-loved breweries seem to have been put to rest since,

however. Dave has launched Akasha Brewing (with some fine hoppy beers, of course), while Stephen's new brewing team has taken up the reins, keeping the former's recipes going and adding beers of their own, making quite the statement with their first: a 9 per cent ABV imperial red ale called Tzar.

ALSO TRY 44 American Amber 55 Pale Ale | 77 IPA | 88 Robust Porter Othello's Curse | Tzar

BREWER'S FOOD MATCH
Spicy food

AVAILABILITY
Year-round

BREWERY & CELLAR DOOR LOCATION
Unit 3/2 North Rocks Road, North Parramatta, NSW 2151

BREWERY WEBSITE
www.riversidebrewing.com.au

IPA

SMILING SAMOYED

 IPA   6.8%   5-6°C TULIP GLASS

TASTING NOTES The biggest beer in Smiling Samoyed's core range – 'Big, bold and bitter' according to its label – is an impressively tightly wound take on the IPA style. It opens with prominent pine and citrus aromas before balancing caramel malts with fruity hop flavours and finally delivering a punchy, resinous and clean bitterness at the finish.

THE STORY One imagines Simon Dunstone and Kate Henning have no regrets after deciding to ditch their careers in software development and litigation respectively to take over what had been a less-than-successful brewing operation an hour south of Adelaide in Myponga. They moved into the charmingly ramshackle and rustic shed late in 2012, named it after their beloved pet dogs and set about upgrading every part of it, from brewery to physical structure.

These days, it's regularly fully booked weeks in advance at weekends, as visitors flock to sample their beers while tucking into local produce, taking in views over the neighbouring reservoir and, on occasion, enjoying themed nights or degustation dinners. The first of these have the greatest pull, with the beers in big enough demand across South Australia that the brewery has been in a state of steady expansion since they took over.

Some have snagged trophies too, with the Dark Ale winning Most Outstanding Beer and the 12 Paws Pale Champion Australian Style Pale at the 2015 Royal Adelaide Beer Show. Should you sample them at source you can do so with one of the best tasting paddles I've come across: repurposed 12-inch vinyl records.

ALSO TRY 12 Paws Pale Ale | Dark Ale
Hop Harvest Ale | Seasonal ESB

BREWER'S FOOD MATCH
Fruit chocolate

AVAILABILITY
Year-round

BREWERY & CELLAR DOOR LOCATION
48 Main South Road, Myponga, SA 5202

BREWERY WEBSITE
www.smilingsamoyed.com.au

HOP BAZOOKA

SOUTHERN BAY BREW CO.

 IPA   5.6%   4-6°C **SPIEGELAU IPA GLASS**

TASTING NOTES It's fair to say that Southern Bay's somewhat archaic brewery isn't exactly set up to knock out big or overly adventurous beers. Yet in recent years they've managed to release a fair few of good quality, including the Hop Bazooka IPA. A collection of New World hops added in sizeable amounts deliver a tropical fruit salad of aromas and flavours alongside balancing caramel malts.

THE STORY Geelong's Southern Bay is predominantly a brewery for hire, creating scores of beers for other brewing companies on machinery that, if you take a tour through the brewery, at times feels like a journey into brewing's past. Much of it is repurposed, some dates back to before the Second World War – put simply, it's a far cry from the majority of breweries you'll find around the country.

Yet, instigatedby Steve 'Hendo' Henderson when he was head brewer, then continued by subsequent brewing teams, under the Southern Bay banner they've occasionally attempted to push the old girl to her limits. Back in Hendo's time, they launched this IPA and a well-received porter; more recently, under head brewer Phil Rutjens they've become more ambitious still.

Towards the end of 2015, a White IPA – a Belgian witbier/American IPA hybrid – impressed, while better still was a beer released earlier in the year. The Vanilla Oatmeal Stout wowed all who tried it with its opulent lusciousness. While opportunities to create such beers are few and far between, here's hoping the brewers keep grabbing them with both hands.

ALSO TRY Southern Ocean Ale

BREWER'S FOOD MATCH
Anything spicy. There's usually at least half a dozen different hot sauces on the brewery lunch table!

AVAILABILITY
Year-round

BREWERY LOCATION
Moolap, VIC

BREWERY WEBSITE
www.southernbay.com.au

IPA

WATTS RIVER BREWING

 IPA   6.6%   4-6°C   TULIP GLASS

TASTING NOTES One of two colourfully packaged beers from new Yarra Valley brewing company Watts River, this IPA belies its brewers' past lives at White Rabbit, where they'd have spent their days ensuring that everything that left the brewery was tight as hell. A beer that puts the pale into India pale ale, it boasts grapefruit, pine and sweet citrus aromas and a good depth of hop flavours, all tied up by a pleasant piny bitterness.

THE STORY When it was announced that Lion was to close down the White Rabbit operation in Healesville and move it to Geelong, there were plenty who bemoaned the news. In all likelihood, Ben Hamilton and Aaron Malmborg were among them. And with good reason: they worked for the brewery and lived nearby.

In hindsight, the solution was easy: open their own brewery to step into the void left by the move. So, in the second half of 2015, they did. With their wives as business partners, they launched Watts River, named after the river that runs through Healesville. Initially, they brewed their beers with their mate Gus Kelly at Riders in Moorabbin as their home in a warehouse took shape.

By the time you read this, that home should be open, complete with cellar door and a barrel program with which Ben and Aaron plan to develop a series of wild and mixed fermentation beers. They've also started collecting barley from the farms where Ben and wife Hanna grew up that, in true paddock-to-glass style, they intend to have malted for use in their beers.

ALSO TRY Blonde Ale | Stout | Brett IPA

BREWER'S FOOD MATCH
Anything that complements the fruity hop characters and crisp bitterness

AVAILABILITY
Year-round

BREWERY & CELLAR DOOR LOCATION
7 Hunter Road, Healesville, VIC 3777

BREWERY WEBSITE
www.wattsriverbrewing.com.au

NON CORPS PROMISE

WHEATY BREWING CORPS

 RYE IPA   7.3%   6–10°C   FANCY (TULIP GLASS)

TASTING NOTES When they launched the brewing arm of their iconic Adelaide pub, the Wheaty crew said only one recipe would never be tweaked: that of their Corps Promise, a rye pale ale. Yet, soon afterwards, Non Corps Promise, a souped-up IPA version, appeared. And it's great, featuring wonderfully tropical and piny hop aromas melding with spicy rye and a cracking bitterness. Never say never indeed.

THE STORY In well over a decade at the Wheatsheaf Hotel (better known as The Wheaty), co-owner Jade Flavell collaborated with many of the finest brewers from Australia and overseas. The keen home brewer sometimes did this at the pub on her 50-litre home-brew kit, and sometimes by travelling with her partners to brew at friends' breweries.

The beers were frequently daft in conception – an anchovy beer brewed with Italy's Birra del Borgo because brewer Leo di Vicenzo had previously released My Antonio with America's Dogfish Head and it sounded a bit like anchovy, for example. Each collaboration – or spooning, as regular co-conspirators Yeastie Boys call them – would be accompanied by well-attended and uproarious events, too.

Thus it seemed almost inevitable when Jade announced they'd be adding a brewery to the back of the pub. Wheaty Brewing Corps launched in 2014 and within its first year had brewed 61 batches of 44 beers, many of them collaborations with brewers from interstate, Europe and the States. They now fill one font of the pub's bar and allow Jade and her team to line up face-offs when visiting brewers take over the other font so drinkers can sample like-for-like styles alongside each other.

It's a fun and welcome addition to what was already arguably the country's best beer venue.

ALSO TRY Corps Promise | Wheaty-Bix Blood Oats | Sir Bob

BREWER'S FOOD MATCH
Anything big and spicy

AVAILABILITY
Year-round

BREWERY & CELLAR DOOR LOCATION
Wheatsheaf Hotel, 39 George Street,
Thebarton, SA 5031

BREWERY WEBSITE
www.wheatybrewingcorps.com

FERAL BREWING COMPANY

They may not be the oldest, biggest or newest microbrewery in Western Australia, but few in the beer world would underestimate the importance of Feral Brewing.

Matilda Bay started the contemporary craft beer scene rolling in Fremantle in the 80s (before being sidelined into irrelevance by CUB and SABMiller), while Little Creatures (now owned by Lion/Kirin and producing most of its beer in Geelong) has turned on more craft beer drinkers and brewers to flavoursome ales via its Pale Ale than any other in the past 15 years.

Yet, from humble beginnings at the log cabin-like brewpub in the Swan Valley that is still its spiritual home, Feral has spent the past decade or so turning out groundbreaking beer after groundbreaking beer, all the while maintaining a focus on quality and consistency that every other small brewery in Australia would do well to mirror. Its Hop Hog (see page 92) was for years the best locally brewed, American-style IPA on the market before being reclassified as an American Pale Ale in recognition of a changing landscape that has seen IPAs head higher than its 5.8 per cent ABV. Yet elsewhere the brewery's lineup is full of equally fine beers in myriad styles: sours; big stouts; Belgian-inspired ales; hybrids; barrel-aged beers.

The brewery started out as a joint venture between schoolmates Brendan Varis and Alistair Carragher, both of whom had been inspired by trips through the USA. At their

Swan Valley home, they wasted little time in foisting innovative beers onto an unsuspecting public, most of whom would have experienced nothing like it before. Over time, word began to spread among the early adopters within Australia's nascent craft beer culture, while the trophies began to flood in too; in 2009 alone, they took home five of 15 major trophies, including Champion Exhibitor, at the prestigious Australian International Beer Awards.

Yet, a limited capacity on one hand and a determination never to send beer across the Nullarbor until they could guarantee refrigeration from source to pub on the other, meant you still had to visit WA to have any chance of finding out what the buzz was about. Those that made the journey would be met with the most diverse sampling tray in Australia and return to their mates with stories to bolster the burgeoning Feral myth.

Finally, having dabbled with a couple of taps at Alistair's Melbourne pub, the Great Northern Hotel, and special events, such as a total 20-tap takeover with 20 different Feral beers at The Local Taphouses in Sydney and Melbourne at a time when no other brewery could have supplied that many different beers, a steady stream of kegs and bottles started making their way – refrigerated, of course – across the Nullarbor to the East Coast's best beer venues.

That trickle has started to resemble something of a flood – at least by independent craft beer standards – enabled by the opening of Brewcorp in 2012, a 50-hectolitre brewery joint venture with one of Brendan's oldest buddies in the beer world, John Stallwood of Nail Brewing. Meanwhile, following a breakup with the Carraghers that made the pages of the press, Feral is now under the Varis family's sole guidance, with special mention to Will Irving, Brendan's long-standing head brewer and source of many of the brewery's beers and even more of its quirky, humorous and sometimes close-to-the-bone beer names.

The increased size has done nothing to dampen innovation or ambition. Under its Brewpub Series of bottled releases and a never-ending stream of draught-only beer, Feral continues to push the envelope. Its Watermelon Warhead Berliner Weisse style beer has won trophies and helped nudge sour beers out of the shadows, while pick pretty much any style and Feral has a great example to call its own.

The focus on quality and freshness continues too. Twice a year they hold 'Tusk Day', sending kegs of a ridiculously hoppy, high alcohol imperial IPA from brewery straight to venues refrigerated with a demand that the venue must tap their keg immediately so that drinkers can experience the beer in the best condition possible. And, as their range expands, it has

allowed to them to keep setting and breaking their own records for the biggest single brewery tap takeover in Australia; at time of writing, their record was 33 different Feral beers pouring at the same venue at the same time.

Yet, while such things – out there beers, daft names, 'How big is yours?' type events – might say gimmick to some people, one only has to pick up a Feral beer (or 33 of them) to realise the quality of what's in your glass comes first.

BRITISH & IRISH ALES

BRITISH & IRISH ALES

Gathering together this collection of beers under the heading 'British & Irish Ales' makes for a pretty broad church. What's more, as you'll read in the introductions to many of the other chapters in this book, there are plenty of other beers in these pages that can trace their lineage back to the British Isles.

But, as is also made clear in those chapters, over the past few decades many such styles, some of which had been practically lost and were rarely brewed, have been revived, reinvigorated and reinvented as something shiny and new. This chapter features beers created by Australian brewers that, for the most part, aim to stay true to the more traditional ales brewed in the UK and Ireland.

Such beers are in the minority when compared to those that take their lead from the US, but still make for a pretty eclectic collection. Furthermore, even when setting out to create a beer that is, to all intents and purposes, an interpretation of an Old World beer, many brewers struggle to resist the temptation to add a New World flourish, typically decorating them with tropical hops.

Thus here you will find low alcohol English Bitters featuring Australian and New Zealand hops alongside more authentic recreations: pale ales or darker, richer malt-led ales that feature more subdued, earthy or gently floral hop varieties that originate in the UK.

Alongside such beers are some higher alcohol ales. Generally, these are based on English Strong or Old Ales: typically sweet and malty, with distinct fruity esters and complex, warming, multi-layered flavours. There is also a strong Scotch ale, the Seeing Double, that adds smoky peated distilling malt to the mix, while smoked malts also feature in The Monk's delicious Vintage.

With so many different styles gathered in one place it is impossible, in fact it would be dangerous, to draw much in the way of commonality between them. What can be said is that English hops, of which East Kent Goldings and Fuggles are the two most frequently used in Australia, share similarities with the noble hops of Europe, in that they possess a subtlety and elegance, and generally lend a softer, broader bitterness on the palate.

Hop usage in these beers also tends to be at a lower level than those favoured by many brewers of New World beer styles, who will add them in greater volumes and at many more stages in the brewing process than in traditional British and Irish beers. Equally, they are sometimes used to add complexity or depth to some of the American or Australian pales and IPAs found elsewhere in the book.

Current circumstances may well lead to a renaissance for such hops too. The rise of craft beer and, in particular, highly hopped pale ales and IPAs has led to occasional hop shortages. In 2016, this reached a critical juncture. Not only did the country's major grower lose a significant chunk of its annual harvest after storms ravaged its farm in the Victorian High Country, but supplies of popular New World varieties from overseas, particularly the States, fell well short of demand. Every crisis presents opportunities and that may include a chance for brewers to not only look for new varieties on the market but to rediscover the merits of existing, less fashionable ones.

Returning to British and Irish ales, another common characteristic can be the fullness imparted on beers by British malts – a fullness both in terms of flavour and mouthfeel. Yeast strains from the old country, particularly those typically used in English ales, often impart fruity characteristics upon the beer during fermentation too, distinct from the generally cleaner impact of American ale yeasts.

A DOZEN MORE TO TRY

BENTSPOKE BREWING	**HOLGATE BREWHOUSE**
Braddon Bitter	ESB
REDOAK	**3 RAVENS BREWERY**
Bitter	English Ale
COOPERS	**NAPOLEONE BREWERS**
Sparkling and Vintage Ales	ESB
BACCHUS BREWING	**VAN DIEMAN**
Moreton Bay Bitter	Ragged Jack
MASH BREWING	**7 CENT WHAPPING BREWERY**
Crafty Challenger	Whapping Wharf ESB
MORRISON BREWERY	**RED DUCK BREWERY**
English Bitter	Crafty Burton

ESB

4 PINES

 **EXTRA SPECIAL BITTER** **5.6%**  **5–8°C**  **TRADITIONAL PINT GLASS**

TASTING NOTES A beer that instantly transported me back to a corner of an old English boozer at first sniff and sip, and which has gone on to win all manner of medals and trophies since. It's a rich, multilayered toffee and raisin treat that backs up its malty lusciousness with a hefty dose of earthy English hops to ensure a dry, bitter finish.

THE STORY 4 Pines is one of the major success stories of Australia's craft beer revolution. Originally opened as a brewpub overlooking the ferry terminal in Manly as a means of giving its founders somewhere to drink that had beer as good as that which they'd grown up drinking in WA, it has since grown to be one of the largest independent Australian breweries.

Powered by a heady mix of good beer, business smarts and *joie de vivre*, demand soon outstripped the capacity of the tiny brewpub setup, requiring them to contract out the brewing of their most popular beers as they built a 50-hectolitre second site in Brookvale – at the time of opening, the largest of any small Aussie micro. Even when it opened, they couldn't meet fast-growing demand and perhaps one of the most remarkable things about 4 Pines is how well they have managed brewing at multiple other breweries as they've awaited completion of each stage

of expansion. Proof of this is found in the multiple champion brewery titles they've collected in recent years.

Between their two sites, they release dozens of beers each year – some in tiny runs only available at their Manly brewpub and new Brookvale Truck Bar – and do so with impressive results. Despite their size and constant need to expand, a sense of playfulness is never far away, whether exhibited through their venues, their quirky mixed-pack releases or the colourful – occasionally controversial – labels that adorn their beers.

ALSO TRY Pale Ale | Stout | Kolsch Keller Door Series Beers

BREWER'S FOOD MATCH
Gamey meats such as duck, venison, moose or free-range bison, or simply with a good summer cheese board

AVAILABILITY
Year-round

BREWERY & CELLAR DOOR LOCATION
3B 19–13 Winbourne Road, Brookvale, NSW 2100

BREWERY WEBSITE
www.4pinesbeer.com.au

RAGING BULL

BOOTLEG BREWERY

 STRONG ALE | 7.1% | 7°C | BRANDY BALLOON

TASTING NOTES From the Margaret River region's longest established microbrewery, this is one of its oldest beers. Because, while Bootleg has rebranded, reworked its range, and been brewing many hoppier and more experimental releases, Raging Bull remains its most iconic beer. When first released, this warming strong ale – all raisins, chocolate, berries, treacle and dark sugar – was unlike much else in Australia and, today, it remains a delicious drop.

THE STORY Today, the Margaret River region of WA is home to more microbreweries than any other part of Australia, with more opening each year. Yet, up until 1994, when school teacher Tom Reynolds decided to open Bootleg in the heart of wine country, there was none.

His vision set a template that many have followed: a large building housing a brewery, bar and restaurant surrounded by acres of lawn; live music on a regular basis; and room for the kids to play while their parents quench their thirst. Tom lends his name to one of the brewery's oldest beers, Tom's Amber (and a newer, oak-aged version), which is one of a handful to survive a reworking of the brewery's offering since it turned 20 years old.

In its third decade, Bootleg shows no signs of slowing, as head brewer Michael Brookes (who's been there since 1998) and sidekick Ryan Nilsson-Linne brew more limited release beers than ever before. Among them is an ongoing single hop series showcasing different hop varieties, while, like many of their fellow local brewers, they're not averse to collaborating – their intense rye IPA Ryezilla brewed with Mane Liquor, in particular, has found much love in WA beer circles.

In early 2016, they were chosen by San Diego legends Stone Brewing as one of a tiny number of breweries woldwide to brew a version of the iconic Arrogant Bastard Ale.

ALSO TRY Speakeasy IPA | Ryezilla Black Market Black IPA | Tom's Amber Ale

BREWER'S FOOD MATCH
Red meat, or a Raging Bull and beef pie

AVAILABILITY
Year-round

BREWERY & CELLAR DOOR LOCATION
Puzey Road, Wilyabrup, WA 6285

BREWERY WEBSITE
www.bootlegbrewery.com.au

SEEING DOUBLE

BREWBOYS

 SCOTCH ALE 8% 10-15°C BRANDY BALLOON

TASTING NOTES Brewboys' highly hopped Hoppapotamus tends to get the beer geeks chatting about the SA brewery most these days, but the Seeing Double remains, for me, their most eye-catching beer. A strong Scotch ale with a higher than usual percentage of peated malt. Alongside the smokiness from the peated malt you'll find rich caramel and toffee flavours and fruity esters inside a thick, hearty body.

THE STORY When referring to the Adelaide beer scene while writing *150 Great Australian Beers* two years ago, there was an acknowledgement that it was a sleepy landscape that was finally coming to life. Since 2014, it has done just that – and then some – with dozens of pubs and bars finally embracing craft beer and new breweries opening across the state, including some with onsite bars.

Brewboys has been offering just that for years at its home across the road from Coopers, where head brewer Simon Sellick produces a range of typically souped-up beers, from German style lager to Motörhead-referencing stout to massively hopped IPA. Many come with more than a nod to his other passion, motorsport, too.

Just as the SA beer scene has grown in the past couple of years, so has Brewboys, with Simon installing a larger brewery at the back of the Croydon Park venue. Head along and you can try the beers fresh, sometimes blended with each other or with ingredients added through the 'Hopinator' on the bar. And, depending on when you call in, you might get to tuck into smoked food or catch a band playing on stage in the tasting room itself, too.

ALSO TRY Ace of Spades | King Brown Hoppapotamus | Maiden Ale

BREWER'S FOOD MATCH
Goes extremely well with an after-dinner cheese board – especially one featuring strong blue cheeses and dried fruit

AVAILABILITY
Year-round

BREWERY & CELLAR DOOR LOCATION
151 Regency Road, Croydon Park, SA 5008

BREWERY WEBSITE
www.brewboys.com.au

OLD ADMIRAL

LORD NELSON BREWERY

 STRONG, DARK ALE   **6.1%**    **4–6°C**   **PINT GLASS**

TASTING NOTES This English-inspired strong, dark ale is my pick of the permanent lineup at the Lord Nelson. It pours a deep brown and offers up a wealth of predominantly malt-derived flavours and aromas. There is sweetness of the chocolate, caramel and treacle variety and plenty of dark fruits too – plums, raisins and rich fruit pudding – all backed up by its gently warming alcohol.

THE STORY These are heady days for the Lord Nelson, with 2016 seeing the brewery hotel in The Rocks celebrate 30 years of brewing since its colourful owner Blair Hayden returned from living and working in the UK, took over the oldest licensed venue in Sydney and started brewing beers based on the real ales he'd fallen for overseas.

Some of the beers – and indeed some of the regulars at one of the most iconic old pubs in the country – have been there from day dot, although the brewers haven't been afraid to spread their wings. In recent years, there's been a highly enjoyable Belgian ale brewed for a prior anniversary, while the Double Nelson, an American style IPA, very nearly made the pages of this book. But the Old Admiral perhaps captures the essence of the Lord best, with its old-fashioned, warming and welcoming charms.

The beers you can enjoy on tap among a bustling collection of locals and tourists at the long, wooden bar are brewed on one of the most incredible setups in the country. Fitted into all manner of nooks and crannies over two floors of the heritage-listed building, pipes wend their way ingeniously from cellar to cellar, while there's a ladder and fireman's pole to help the brewers get around.

It's a wonderful piece of Australian microbrewing heritage; here's to the next 30 years!

ALSO TRY Double Nelson | 2IC Brown Ale Three Sheets Pale Ale | Nelson's Blood Victory Bitter

BREWER'S FOOD MATCH
Australian aged cheddar or Italian parmigiano-reggiano; grass-fed rib eye with truffle butter; flourless chocolate cake; ale-poached pears with King Island cream

AVAILABILITY
Year-round

BREWERY AND CELLAR DOOR LOCATION
19 Kent Street, The Rocks, NSW 2000

BREWERY WEBSITE
www.lordnelsonbrewery.com

OLD RELIABLE PALE ALE

CHEEKY MONKEY

 **PALE ALE** **5.0%** **6°C** **NONIC GLASS**

TASTING NOTES Hagenbeck Belgian IPA remains the brewery's official flagship beer, but when it came to launching their first cans in 2015 they opted for a cider and two beers: the fruity summer ale Blonde Capuchin and this English-inspired pale ale. Centennial hops from America add a New World citrusy touch, but otherwise it's a punchy take on ales from the mother country, featuring bold biscuity, nutty malts and a full, earthy bitter finish.

THE STORY It's common for new breweries to endure painful births as they navigate red tape or bump up against issues with utilities or equipment suppliers. Prior to opening in the famed Caves Road in the heart of the Margaret River region, Cheeky Monkey may have endured the most tortuous of all.

Their plan to set up next door to Cullen Wines, one of Australia's leading biodynamic winemakers, didn't sit well with the winery's owners, who feared the impact of brewing yeasts in the air. In the end, after a much-publicised and drawn-out battle, approval was granted and WA welcomed another impressive, family-friendly microbrewery (with a focus on cider, too).

Despite being one of the larger brewery sites in the state (which is no mean feat), during the summer months it attracts crowds in such numbers it's worth parking up as soon as it opens if you're after a table to dine, while head brewer Ross Terlick says you can watch tanks of their most popular beers visibly draining in front of your eyes. It means little beer leaves the site, although the installation of a canning line in 2015 should see that change.

ALSO TRY Hagenbeck Belgian IPA Traveling Monk | Southern Wailer seasonals

BREWER'S FOOD MATCH
Barbecued lamb ribs

AVAILABILITY
Year-round

BREWERY & CELLAR DOOR LOCATION
4259 Caves Road, Wilyabrup, WA 6280

BREWERY WEBSITE
www.cheekymonkeybrewery.com.au

SPECIAL PALE

COWARAMUP BREWING COMPANY

 **EXTRA SPECIAL BITTER**   **5.4%**   **10–13°C**   **TRADITIONAL ALE PINT GLASS**

TASTING NOTES Despite being away from the UK for more years than he lived there, Cowaramup's co-founder and head brewer Jeremy Good has lost none of his passion for the ales he grew with in England. Of all his beers, the Special Pale is his baby, a take on the Extra Special Bitter style that kicks off with floral hop aromas, biscuity malt flavours and a touch of fruitiness before finishing with a soft, earthy and persistent bitterness.

THE STORY There's a belief in much of the Western world that unless you're constantly growing and expanding then you're not succeeding. Then there are those who get to where they want to be and are happy to enjoy it without the need to chase more, more, more.

There are a few brewers around Australia who fit into that latter category, typically those who've set up a brewpub at which they can sell pretty much all of their beer to regulars and tourists. It might not bring untold riches, but keeps a roof over their heads and allows them to enjoy their passion: brewing the beers they love to drink and sharing them with guests.

Jeremy Good, who runs Cowaramup Brewing Company in the Margaret River region, is one such brewer. After learning a few tricks of the trade volunteering as a dogsbody at Feral Brewing, he ditched a career in IT to take his brewing from home to pro and has spent the subsequent years honing a small and predominantly English-inspired lineup of beers. Along the way, he's won a major trophy for his Pilsener – only brewed initially to satisfy locals' tastes – while the venue he set up with co-founder Claire Parker is a delightful spot to while away an afternoon or evening (particularly if you end up in conversation with Jeremy, in which case a designated driver is highly recommended).

ALSO TRY Pilsener | Lightsign Summer Ale India Pale Ale | Porter

BREWER'S FOOD MATCH
Shepherd's pie, roast beef and Yorkshire pudding, or traditional ploughman's lunch with pork pie and Scotch egg

AVAILABILITY
Year-round

BREWERY & CELLAR DOOR LOCATION
229 North Treeton Road, Cowaramup, WA 6284

BREWERY WEBSITE
www.cowaramupbrewing.com.au

ESB

EAGLE BAY BREWING

 **EXTRA SPECIAL BITTER**   **5.4%**   **6–8°C**    **TRADITIONAL PINT GLASS**

TASTING NOTES In *150 Great Australian Beers*, I wrote that were Eagle Bay's ESB bottled it would have made the book (which featured only packaged beer). Soon after publication it was, bringing the glistening auburn brew's mix of creamy caramel malts and floral, earthy hops to a wider audience. Indeed, they've started bottling many more beers now, including some fine seasonals and collaborations.

THE STORY Even in a region where many of the brewery venues have to be seen to be believed – impressive restaurant and cellar door buildings surrounded by sprawling grounds and kids' play areas – Eagle Bay can still take the breath away. Built by the d'Espeissis siblings on their parents' farmland on the northwestern tip of the Margaret River region, it not only boasts a fine restaurant and tasting room (with views into the brewery) but also incredible ocean views.

Since starting out on their own in 2010, head brewer Nick d'Espeissis has refined the core range, designed with approachability in mind (it is on the edge of a popular tourist region, after all) to the point that beers such as the Kolsch and Pale are among the best of their kind.

Outside of those beers, he and his brewers have been having fun, both in the form of seasonal releases, such as

a black IPA and cacao stout, and via collaborations with all and sundry. They've brewed with their Margaret River peers, local venues and chefs visiting the region for the annual Gourmet Escape festival. Perhaps their best collaborations to date, however, have been with Perth bottleshop Mane Liquor with whom two beers using local wine barrels – the Chardonnay/saison hybrid Saisonnay and beautifully packaged black IPA/Cabernet Sauvignon Black and Tannin – have caught the eye.

ALSO TRY Pale Ale | Kolsch | Black IPA Cacao Stout | Mild Ale | Black and Tannin

BREWER'S FOOD MATCH
Beef burger with bacon, mature cheddar, red onion and lettuce

AVAILABILITY
Year-round

BREWERY & CELLAR DOOR LOCATION
252 Eagle Bay Road, Naturaliste, WA 6281

BREWERY WEBSITE
www.eaglebaybrewing.com.au

MOONSHINE

GRAND RIDGE

 STRONG SCOTCH ALE **8.5%**  **6–8°C** **BRANDY BALLOON**

TASTING NOTES Moonshine is one of the longest continually brewed beers in Australia. Originally called 1080 in reference to the hefty beer's original gravity, it was also the name of a brand of poison, forcing a rethink. It's a hearty, dessert-in-a-glass affair, deep russet in hue and awash with mouth-coating toffee, treacle, caramel and plums. Age hasn't dimmed its appeal, however, as in 2014 it took out a trophy at the country's biggest beer awards.

THE STORY In 2015, Grand Ridge celebrated 30 years in business, making it comfortably one of the oldest microbreweries in the country. It's based in farming territory in Gippsland, sitting atop the Strzelecki Ranges, from which arch-raconteur and brewery owner Eric Walters will tell you he obtains the best water you could wish for when brewing.

Over the three decades, he's helped breweries get off the ground (Mountain Goat's first batches were brewed there) and many breweries around the country have brewers who once plied their trade at Grand Ridge running operations. As for the beers, for the most part Eric and his brewers have stayed true to traditions, with a lengthy lineup featuring everything from lagers, pale ales and stouts through to the Moonshine strong Scotch ale and its big barley wine sibling Supershine, while resisting the lure to chase insanely high hopping regimes or dabble with sour styles.

That said, in late 2015, there were signs of a change as two new beers appeared with a vastly different look to the old-school English vibe the Mirboo North brewery had been rocking for so long. The beers themselves – a golden ale and pale ale – were very much aiming for the middle of the road, but the new look, featuring microscopic images of the beer in crystallised form, suggested Victoria's oldest microbrewery was preparing to don new clothes.

ALSO TRY Gippsland Gold | Supershine Hatlifter Stout | Mirboo Madness

BREWER'S FOOD MATCH
Dark chocolate or sticky date pudding

AVAILABILITY
Limited batch releases year-round

BREWERY & CELLAR DOOR LOCATION
1 Baromi Road, Mirboo North, VIC 3871

BREWERY WEBSITE
www.grand-ridge.com.au

ESB

HARGREAVES HILL

 EXTRA SPECIAL BITTER   **5.2%** ❄ **6–8°C**   **NONIC GLASS**

TASTING NOTES An Australian craft beer classic, Hargreaves Hill's ESB was one of the first Victorian beers to combine the traditional malty backbone of an English Extra Special Bitter with New World hops. The result was a sort of American pale ale–English bitter hybrid that was judged to perfection, with the tropical, passionfruit hops working harmoniously in tandem with the toffee malts.

THE STORY It's been quite the ride for Hargreaves Hill. Founded by a classically trained pianist and his opera singer wife in a shed on the latter's parents' land in the Yarra Valley – with a beautiful cellar door and restaurant in the former National Bank building in Yarra Glen – Hargreaves Hill quickly garnered a reputation around Melbourne for well made, British and European-inspired ales. Then, during the Black Saturday fires, the brewery was destroyed, although, thankfully for them and many others, the wind changed direction just metres before the front reached Yarra Glen.

After a few months brewing with friends, Simon Walkenhorst opened a new brewery in an industrial unit in nearby Lilydale and set about re-establishing the business, while Beth oversaw the restaurant. The rebirth was marked with the brewing of a special beer, the Phoenix

imperial red ale, one of many big beers Hargreaves Hill brews on occasion, among them the R.I.S. (Russian Imperial Stout) and AD (Abbey Dubbel), that are always worth hunting down.

Since then, the business has steadily grown, with existing beers refined and joined by a wide array of new releases, including a series of IPAs inspired by Simon's regular research trips to the States and experiments with barrel-aged sours. Like its founder, much about Hargreaves Hill is understated but should never be underestimated.

ALSO TRY Pale Ale | Hefeweizen | Stout Phoenix | R.I.S. | AD

BREWER'S FOOD MATCH
Charcuterie, rillettes and pickles

AVAILABILITY
Year-round

BREWERY LOCATION
60/64–86 Beresford Road, Lilydale, VIC 3140

CELLAR DOOR LOCATION
25 Bell Street, Yarra Glen, VIC 3775

BREWERY WEBSITE
www.hargreaveshill.com.au

BRUCE

LOBETHAL BIERHAUS

 BITTER   **3.5%**   **8°C**    **TRADITIONAL PINT GLASS**

TASTING NOTES   The first of many collaborations between Lobethal Bierhaus and New Zealand's Yeastie Boys is a simple affair: a relatively low alcohol yet boldly hopped take on the traditional English bitter. Named, as all their collaborations have been, after one of their dogs, Bruce is a hazy copper drop featuring floral, spicy hops and nutty, woody malts that's a favourite at Adelaide's leading beer venue, The Wheaty, too.

THE STORY   Despite being around since May 2007 and regularly packed to the rafters since then, and despite having collaborated on beers with SA's big hitters Coopers and high profile Kiwis, the Yeastie Boys, it still feels like Lobethal Bierhaus is one of the Australian beer world's hidden secrets.

It probably comes down to the unassuming nature of Al Turnbull, the head brewer who opened the brewery in the Adelaide Hills with a mate and now runs it with his partner Rosie. Since 2007, he's focused on brewing a steadily expanded lineup of mostly traditional beer styles and brewing them as well as he can without ever shouting about it. The capacity has expanded, the number of taps and hand pumps on the brewery bar has grown, crowds have continued to fill the venue, he's collaborated with Coopers and started

doing a spot of malting in-house; yet it's not a name known broadly outside SA.

And that's probably how Al likes it, especially as he's still able to sell most of his beer within state lines, even after the last – significant – expansion, which also saw a high quality bottling line installed. It makes any visit to the former tweed factory (adorned with much motor racing memorabilia) a joy, where the range is so consistently good across the board that I considered half a dozen beers to feature here before plumping for Bruce.

ALSO TRY   Chocolate Oatmeal Stout Pale Ale | Double Hopped IPA (the straight IPA is good too) | Red Truck Porter Little Devil | Bohemian Philsner

BREWER'S FOOD MATCH
A mild curry accompanied by plenty of friendly banter

AVAILABILITY
Year-round

BREWERY & CELLAR DOOR LOCATION
3A Main Street, Lobethal, SA 5241

BREWERY WEBSITE
www.bierhaus.com.au

VINTAGE

MONK CRAFT BREWERY KITCHEN

 SCOTCH ALE 5.2% 5°C BRANDY GOBLET

TASTING NOTES Upon first sampling the Vintage, my notes concluded: 'Feels like a Northern Hemisphere Christmas'. By this, I wasn't thinking of the festive beers layered with spices that appear at that time of year. Instead, it felt like what you'd cradle in your hands by the roaring fire of a cosy old pub. This deep brown beer is a subtly layered treat, with a touch of smokiness atop a body of toffee, treacle, chocolate and drying earthy, twiggy hops.

THE STORY Fremantle's Monk has a history of punching above its weight. Even following a recent expansion, the brewpub's brewers are limited by the space in which they operate behind the bar, yet no matter how limited their workspace and no matter who has been at the helm, Monk beers have collected trophies on a local and national level with amazing regularity. Indeed, the lively brewpub has an impressive alumni now plying its trade successfully throughout the beer world (not to mention Australia's foremost beer food chef, Mitch 'Beersine' Mitchell, in the kitchen).

Given this track record, it took some balls for Craig Eulenstein (since departed for a new challenge at Fury & Sons in Melbourne) to arrive from Mountain Goat, tear up the beer list and start again. What's more, he told me that part of his reason for taking a head brewer role was to try to become Champion Brewer of Australia.

His new beers came with an unusual naming approach that eschewed the tried and tested methods of naming by style or choosing colourful titles. Instead, Common, Reserved, Extra, Vintage were chosen to indicate colour, strength and flavour. Whatever his thinking, he proved he had the skills to back up his bold move when he collected the 2015 CBA Champion Small Brewery trophy.

ALSO TRY Extra | Common
And look out for their always interesting Specialty brews

☆

BREWER'S FOOD MATCH
Blackwood Valley rump steak,
roast potatoes, chimichurri sauce

AVAILABILITY
Year-round

BREWERY & CELLAR DOOR LOCATION
33 South Terrace, Fremantle, WA 6160

BREWERY WEBSITE
www.themonk.com.au

KENTISH ALE

SEVEN SHEDS

 PALE ALE   **5.2%**   **6–8°C**   **STRAIGHT-SID PINT GLASS**

TASTING NOTES   Beer writer-turned-brewer Willie Simpson brews so many interesting beers it's almost a shame to focus on his flagship. But the Kentish Ale, named with a nod to the council area in which Seven Sheds is based and the English ales it's inspired by, is a cracker. Brewed with English malts and hops (plus some local hops), it's a subtle blend of floral and peachy hop aromas, sweet biscuit and caramel malts and a soft, earthy bitterness.

THE STORY   Today, there are plenty of people writing about beer in Australia, professionally and amateurishly (sometimes both at the same time), and far more with an interest in reading about beer and brewers than ever before. For a long time, however, there was a paucity of writers looking to stoke an interest in what was happening in the beer world; of those that were, Willie, a well-travelled Kiwi who'd ended up in Australia, led the way, most notably via a column for the Sydney Morning Herald which he finally retired in 2013.

While his decision to stop writing was a loss, particularly given the ill-informed content that passes for beer writing in much of the media today, it was a boon for beer lovers. By then, the brewery and cellar door he'd set up with partner Catherine Stark in Railton, was well established. There, they grow hops, occasionally smoke their own malt, and combine fine regular releases with fascinating experiments.

Recent years have seen beers in barrels traverse Bass Strait for weeks on end to recreate the journeys of the original IPAs and the first porters to come to Australia, beers brewed with ingredients such as ginseng and chocolate from northwest Tasmanian producers, and a superb pilsner brewed with Cape Grim water, allegedly the purest on the planet. The only downside: they brew so little that it's almost entirely sold in Tasmania or via the cellar door.

ALSO TRY   Stark Raven Oatmeal Stout Elephant's Trunk | Willie Warmer | Black Inca

BREWER'S FOOD MATCH
Rabbit pie and chips

AVAILABILITY
Year-round

BREWERY & CELLAR DOOR LOCATION
22 Crockers Street, Railton, TAS 7305

BREWERY WEBSITE
www.sevensheds.com

REAL ALE

YOUNG HENRYS

 ENGLISH BITTER   **4.0%**   **6–8°C**   **PINT GLASS**

TASTING NOTES For all the outré ingredients Young Henrys have thrown at beers over the years, all the leftfield collaborations they've carried out, and all the partying they've done at their Newtown home and events around the country, their core range is surprisingly sensible. The Real Ale is their take on co-owner Richard Adamson's beloved English ales, adding a citrusy New World hop twist to a smooth toffee malt base.

THE STORY If ever a brewery can be said to own its territory in Australia, it's Young Henrys. Within months of opening in Sydney's inner west, you could find at least one tap pouring a Young Henrys beer in pretty much every bar and pub worth its salt in their home suburb of Newtown and those that surround it. Today, their brewery and associated venue has expanded to swallow up a little corner of the suburb and, armed with a beer called The Newtowner, has become something of a community hub.

As much as anything, it's a success born of an attitude. Sure, they've released a huge array of beers – some brewed with bands including You Am I, others with radio stations, chefs, coffee roasters, government bodies, art galleries and more besides – but the wild spirit that infuses the brewery and those who work

for it tapped into the spirit of their home turf and has been heartily embraced. On the subject of spirits, they have started making their own, the first of which was the Noble Cut gin.

Late in 2014, they joined the growing ranks of Aussie brewers putting their beers into cans to make them more widely available. But, for the full Young Henrys experience, nothing beats a trip to their Newtown home, where an ever-changing lineup awaits on tap – plus as much facial hair, tatts and rock 'n' roll as you can possibly handle.

ALSO TRY Hop Ale | Their many, many one-offs and collaborations, which are always interesting and often launched in the unlikeliest of spots

---

BREWER'S FOOD MATCH
Roast duck with braised onions

AVAILABILITY
Year-round

BREWERY & CELLAR DOOR LOCATION
76 Wilford Street, Newtown, NSW 2042

BREWERY WEBSITE
www.younghenrys.com.au

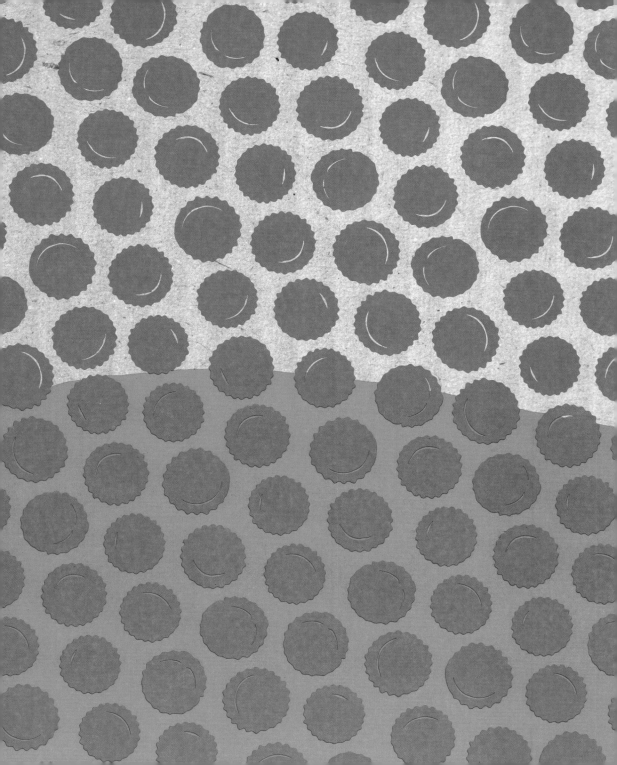

REDS & AMBER ALES

REDS &
AMBER ALES

As the title suggests, the beers gathered together in this chapter are united more by their hue than any other characteristic. And, for the most part, there is no great historical heritage attached to the terms red ale or amber ale.

There are exceptions, such as the Flanders Red style (see the French and Belgian Ales chapter, page 188), a unique sour and fruity ale that originates in Belgium but which is practically non-existent within the entire output of Australia's brewers. Also, the Irish red ale is often touted as its own style. However, there is debate as to whether it is anything more than a tag applied to English-style bitters brewed in Ireland. That said, brewers calling beers Irish red ales in Australia today, including those in this book, typically use malt bills that give them a ruddy hue and richer, sweeter characters than paler English bitters.

More recently, American Amber Ales have become acknowledged as a category. In many ways, these beers are simply a step up from American Pale Ales. Usually, they share those beers' citrusy hop aromas, but are, of course, darker in colour and possess a more strident malt character, typically sweeter and of a caramel nature.

It is these American influences that have proved increasingly popular with Australian brewers. The majority of beers contained in this section would fall under the American Amber banner through their combination of upfront hop aromas, rich malt flavours and distinct bitterness.

There are others, however, that reflect contemporary brewers' affection for experimentation and creativity, for the merging of traditional beer styles. A growing number are tagging their beers as 'India Red Ale', 'Red IPA' or even 'Amber IPA'. In many ways, it's like a code that can be easily deciphered. Whenever you see the word 'India' attached to a beer style, it's likely to be a brewer's shorthand that refers back to India pale ales so you can expect higher levels of hop aroma, hop flavour and hop-derived bitterness.

Similarly, you can usually work out what to expect from your glass or bottle from the colour accompanying the IPA tag. When used in conjunction with a colour, such as red, amber, black or white, it is describing the colour of the beer; from that, deductions can usually be made as to the flavour as well. In red or amber beers, the drinker can expect richer, sweeter malt flavours – caramel, toffee, chocolate, nutty, biscuity.

Black IPAs, which are covered elsewhere, are typically something of a con trick, using dark malts that don't impose the usual roast or coffee characteristics you expect from black beers, but instead attempt to deliver the aromas and flavours of a more 'normal' IPA but black. Meanwhile, white IPAs usually describe a hybrid: a combination of the spicy, softly fruity yeasts of a Belgian witbier yeast with the aggressive hopping regime of an American-style IPA.

With the red and amber ales that follow, however, their colouring is achieved purely through the brewer's choice of malt. Malts that have been kilned until they are of a darker hue than the pale malts used as the basis for the vast majority of beers can deliver red, amber and ruddy colouring as well as the aforementioned sweeter flavours, even when used as a small percentage of the overall grain bill.

A DOZEN MORE TO TRY

2 BROTHERS
Grizz

MOUNTAIN GOAT
Hightail and India Red Ale
(occasional release)

FERAL BREWING
Fantapants

TWO BIRDS
Sunset Ale

STONE & WOOD
Jasper Ale

RED DUCK
Amber

FLAT ROCK BREW CAFÉ
Red Rye IPA

BOOTLEG BREWING
Tom's Amber

KAIJU! BEER
Hopped Out Red

NEWSTEAD
Liquidambar

BARROW BOYS
India Amber Ale

WIG & PEN
Sequoia

FIRE WITHIN

AKASHA BREWING COMPANY

 **AMERICAN AMBER**   **5.8%**   **8–10°C**   **TULIP GLASS**

TASTING NOTES In his former life at Riverside, Dave Padden's favourite drop was the 44 American Amber, a bold beer that also found broad favour within craft beer circles. The style returns at his new home, Akasha, albeit bolder still, with the familiar collision of rich and roasty malts and pungent US hops turned up a further notch or three without abandoning his balancing touch.

THE STORY After sniffing around breweries for advice and spare bits of stainless steel for a year or two, Dave Padden abandoned a career in IT to launch Riverside Brewing in Parramatta. His typically hop forward, US-inspired beers quickly won over Sydney's beer enthusiasts as he proved himself a master of extracting clean aromas and flavours from his hops – something not that many local brewers can yet claim.

At the end of 2014, a fallout with his business partner led him to leave, the announcement shocking people for whom Riverside was Dave and his beers. He soon reappeared with a man who is enthusiasm-for-life made flesh – brother-in-law Wesley 'Two Guns' White – at his side under the Akasha banner. After launching with beers brewed with his mates at Rocks Brewing, the pair opened

their own brewery in Five Dock and set about creating another roster of fine, hoppy beers.

As for the name, Akasha is the unseen fifth element of legend, alongside earth, water, wind and fire. The idea is that, in the brewery, that's Dave: the fifth element breathing life into his water, malt, hops and yeast. It might sound corny, but anyone who's sampled his brews knows he has something of a magic touch.

ALSO TRY Freshwater Pale Ale Hopsmith IPA | Tradewinds Lager

BREWER'S FOOD MATCH
Pairs beautifully with American-style barbecue – try a classic smoked brisket. Also matches well with a nice, strong aged cheddar.

AVAILABILITY
Year-round

BREWERY & CELLAR DOOR LOCATION
10A Spencer Street, Five Dock, NSW 2046

BREWERY WEBSITE
www.akashabrewing.com.au

HERON'S CRAIC

BLACK DUCK BREWERY

 IRISH RED **4%** **4°C**  **TULIP GLASS**

TASTING NOTES With all the Black Duck beers I've tried, there's a common thread: brewer Al Owen likes to pack plenty in, whether it's his intense Phoenix stout or resinous, tropically hopped IPA. That said, this Irish Red is a standout, with a mere 4 per cent ABV concealing lovely, balanced layers of toasted nuts, caramel and milk chocolate. There's a soft, earthy bitterness that helps it finish drier than those flavours would have you believe.

THE STORY For Al and Kate Owen it was a trip to the UK, visiting the country's real ale pubs and breweries, that inspired the decision to take up brewing. After learning the ropes on a small setup in his garage, Black Duck launched in 2010 on the property the couple had bought in Heron's Creek with a single beer, the English Bitter, on tap.

A move to nearby Port Macquarie followed, with the couple building a bar that also houses the brewery. Double the size of the Heron's Creek setup, Al now operates an 800-litre brewhouse that had been part of the first wave of microbreweries in the 1980s before the Ballarat brewery it served closed, and which had spent the subsequent two decades in storage until the Owens snapped it up.

The beer offering has expanded significantly since the days of the lone Bitter. At the time of writing, Al was brewing 13 different beers that are available at the brewery to drink there or take home. With almost everything sold locally, little escapes, but you can also find Black Duck in a very small number of outlets south to Sydney and north to Coffs Harbour.

ALSO TRY Phoenix Migration Stout Golden Goose APA | Indian Runner IPA

BREWER'S FOOD MATCH
Curried goat pita pocket

AVAILABILITY
Year-round

BREWERY & CELLAR DOOR LOCATION
6B Acacia Avenue, Port Macquarie, NSW 2444

BREWERY WEBSITE
www.blackduckbrewery.com.au

CASTLEMAINE BREWING

 CELTIC RED ALE **5.2%** **2°C** **CONICAL PINT GLASS**

TASTING NOTES While most contemporary small-scale brewers are chasing new techniques or flavours, Michael 'Wolfey' Wolfe is happier looking to the past. As he brings brewing back to Castlemaine, it's with more traditionally minded beers. His Red is a tribute to the first Wolfe to leave Ireland for the Goldfields in the 1850s, adding some citrusy, piney flourishes to the more traditional toffee and caramel malts of the Irish Red style.

THE STORY By the time you read this, Wolfey should be well established in his brewery and taproom in Castlemaine, as the Central Victorian town becomes the latest in the state to welcome back small-scale brewing. Indeed, he's been helped along the way by another brewery that has done just that: Brookes Beer in Bendigo. There, Wolfey stepped up from home brewing to become founder Doug Brooke's assistant while brewing the first batches of his Castlemaine beers.

They are beers that put a more old-school Aussie beer culture front and centre. Wolfey says inspiration for his first release, Gold, was 'misty-eyed nostalgia' for the beers he recalls from the 1970s – albeit brought up to date – while joining it on the roster is this Red and a simple lager given the faintest of twists with the addition of New World hops.

Where his project is very much of its time is in its role helping to revitalise part of the Goldfields town. The brewery and taproom have been built within the former Old Woollen Mill, a home it shares with a range of artisanal producers – a baker, a winemaker, a metalsmith and so on – including roaster Coffee Basics, whose beans appear in the brewery's Black lager.

ALSO TRY Gold | Pils | Black

BREWER'S FOOD MATCH
Wood-fired margherita pizza

AVAILABILITY
Year-round

BREWERY & CELLAR DOOR LOCATION
Old Woollen Mills, 5A/9 Walker Street,
Castlemaine, VIC 3450

BREWERY WEBSITE
www.castlemainebrewing.com

RED EYE RYE

DAINTON FAMILY BREWERY

 RED   **5.0%**   **5-7°C**   **TULIP GLASS**

TASTING NOTES The first beer Dan Dainton released under his own brand set out his stall: why use a handful of ingredients when you can use four handfuls. Here, the multiple hops and malts combine wonderfully to create a layered, glistening red beer that offers up citrus and tropical fruits, toasty caramel flavours, spiciness from his beloved rye and a punchy bitterness.

THE STORY Where to start? Dan Dainton is, quite simply, a character. A shiny pated, frequently moustachioed, occasionally opera singing (usually when inappropriate) character with a mind that's sharp and twisted in equal measure. Unsurprisingly, his beers tend to reflect this: they may be of a style in essence, but they probably take a few detours along the way.

He launched the brewing company with family support and promptly started naming beers after family members, then adorning the bottles with less-than-flattering images and stories that may have also been about family members. In 2015, he brought in graphic designer God Awful who turned his odd fantasies into some of the best label designs in Australia, inspiring Dan to new levels of bizarreness with each beer's accompanying 'poem'.

By the time you read this, he'll have opened his own shiny brewery, complete with cellar door and bar in Melbourne's southeast.

ALSO TRY Samurye Lager
Insane Uncle IPA | Manhattan Ale

BREWER'S FOOD MATCH
Skittles

AVAILABILITY
Year-round

BREWERY & CELLAR DOOR LOCATION
560 Frankston–Dandenong Road, Carrum
Downs, VIC 3201

BREWERY WEBSITE
www.daintonbrewing.com.au

3 SONS

GRAINFED BREWING COMPANY

 RED IPA   **6.0%**   **2–4°C** **IPA GLASS**

TASTING NOTES While tagged a red IPA, the fourth beer from Grainfed feels more at home here. The combination of Aussie and American hops contributes citrus and berry aromas and a firm, drying bitterness, but the malts (seven different varieties) take centre stage. They supply its lovely, deep auburn colour, dark toffee and nutty aromas and layers of creamy malt flavours encompassing dark fruits, burnt treacle and much else besides.

THE STORY At Newcastle Craft Beer Week in 2012, I spent a day with BentSpoke brewer Richard Watkins, during which we called in to the home of Lachlan MacBean, a much-loved member of the Australian brewing community. There, he showed off the first beer from Grainfed Brewing Company while screen printing a Grainfed t-shirt for each of us on an ironing board.

There was one thing missing from the picture. Despite much talk, planning and recipe development, Lachie hadn't actually launched Grainfed commercially. Later that evening, unbeknownst to each other, both Richard and I said to him something along the lines of: "Look mate, you've got a good beer, you've got the brand ready to go, you've just got to put yourself out there!" Albeit possibly in less delicate language.

So he did, commencing brewing his beers under license and quickly finding favour for Sneaky One, his 'Newcastle Summer Ale'. That was followed by a richly multilayered brown ale, a bold, fruity pale ale and, at the start of 2016, this robust red ale dedicated to his kids. Never have I felt less guilt about getting pushy after a few beers!

ALSO TRY Sneaky One | Quiet One | Pale

BREWER'S FOOD MATCH
Beef vindaloo

AVAILABILITY
Year-round

BREWERY LOCATION
Hamilton, NSW

BREWERY WEBSITE
www.grainfedbrewing.com.au

THE BUZZ

HOP NATION

 RED ALE   **6.5%**   **9–10°C**  **IPA OR SNIFTER GLASS**

TASTING NOTES Kiwi winemakers Sam Hambour and Duncan Gibson launched Hop Nation with the intention of bringing an element of terroir via three beers showcasing the hop characters of three key New World hop growing regions: America, Australia and New Zealand. The pick of the three was The Buzz, a hoppy blood orange coloured ale that blends citrus and pine hop characters with toasted sweet biscuity malts.

THE STORY There are plenty of winemakers who've crossed over to become brewers – including some of the very best brewers in the land – and many wineries who've ventured into beer to varying degrees. Yet the tale of Kiwis Sam Harbour and Duncan Gibson still stands out, being that of two mates who met while making wine in Central Otago. They've since made wine the world over and were still doing so in Victoria when they found time to transition some of their home-brewing recipes into commercial releases.

At the time of writing, they'd just completed the trio of releases that will form their core range, each of which is designed to showcase the hops they love from three parts of the world. First up was The Fiend, a restrained Australian IPA, followed by The Buzz, then finally The Damned, a pilsner showcasing hops from across The Ditch. All three come with some of my favourite artwork to adorn local beers recently: The Fiend features tattooed arms in handcuffs, with the tatts hinting at the beer inside; while The Buzz is based around a spaceman's helmet with a hop cone inside.

By the time you read this, they should have opened their own venue in Footscray, too, adding to the burgeoning beer culture developing throughout Melbourne's west.

ALSO TRY The Fiend | The Damned

BREWER'S FOOD MATCH
Smoked fish pie with manuka-smoked hoki

AVAILABILITY
Year-round

BREWERY & CELLAR DOOR LOCATION
6/107 Whitehall Street, Footscray, VIC 3011

BREWERY WEBSITE
www.hopnation.com.au

AMBER ALE

KILLER SPROCKET

 AMBER ALE 4.8% 4-8°C PINT SHAKER

TASTING NOTES Killer Sprocket's first and still, to my mind, best beer, despite some fine and creative follow-ups. It's an American-style amber ale – in other words it doesn't skimp on the hops or the malt, yet judges the input of each nicely while leaving the latter to take centre stage, where you'll find lashings of chocolate, toffee, dark fruit and nuts.

THE STORY Killer Sprocket is a brewing company started by a stand-up comedian and his brewing-partner wife that's named after a database the former worked on while employed by an insurance company. Sean and Anthea Ryan stepped from home brewing to the commercial world in 2012 with their fine Amber Ale and have continued to operate as one of Australia's growing band of brewers-without-a-home.

Not having their own set of stainless steel, at least outside their house, hasn't hampered their creativity. Seemingly once a year they add a new beer to their roster – while also collaborating with friends around the beer world on one-off releases – with their own beers typically marked by a quirk in the recipe. Beer number two was the smoky Bandit, featuring a far higher percentage of peated distilling malt

than most brewers would contemplate. This was followed by a pale ale with liberal additions of juniper berries, and a rye IPA that, like the Bandit, goes big on its key ingredient: the notoriously full-bodied and spicy rye malt.

ALSO TRY Bandit | Hey Juniper | Rye IPA

☆

BREWER'S FOOD MATCH
Smoky barbecue or Mexican food

AVAILABILITY
Year-round

BREWERY LOCATION
Forest Hill, VIC

BREWERY WEBSITE
www.killersprocket.com.au

ARCHIE'S RED ALE

MISMATCH BREWING COMPANY

 RED ALE **5.0%** **4°C** **TULIP GLASS**

TASTING NOTES The first beer released by Adelaide's Mismatch Brewing Co was named after a mate of theirs who'd just beaten cancer, and was a beer designed to fill a gap in SA's just-about-to-explode beer scene. A tightly packaged red ale, it balances aromatic, citrusy hops with dark caramel and biscuity malts. As with most things Mismatch, all the elements are kept in check, favouring approachability over showiness.

THE STORY Mismatch is one of many small brewing companies to launch in South Australia in the past few years and one I expect will be seen more widely than most of their SA peers. There's various reasons to make such an assumption: the mismatch of mates that formed the business have an extensive collection of skills, contacts and experience inside and outside the beverage and hospo industries; they're more ambitious than most; and they're focused on making beers that value wide appeal as much as flavour.

Thankfully, the former beer rep who is now their head brewer, Ewan Brewerton, has proven adept at creating such beers: clean, balanced and approachable but with enough appeal for craft beer drinkers too. And such has been their success since launching in 2013 as the first brewery and tank tenants at Big Shed Brewing Concern that they've had to move to bigger facilities to contract brew their beer while they close in on their own Adelaide brewery.

Their Session Ale has been taking their home state by storm since its launch, while a collaboration with Paddy's Lantern café – an Irish stout brewed with coffee and aged in Hellyers Road whisky barrels – was ridiculously luscious for a beer of just 5.5 per cent ABV, hinting at what might come when their brewery arrives.

ALSO TRY Session Ale | XPA

BREWER'S FOOD MATCH
Lamb korma or any spicy or rich food

AVAILABILITY
Year-round

BREWERY LOCATION
'Gypsy' brewers

BREWERY WEBSITE
www.mismatchbrewing.com.au

FORMER TENANT RED IPA

MODUS OPERANDI

 RED IPA   **7.8%**   **4-6°C** **IPA GLASS**

TASTING NOTES You could pick any number of hoppy beers from this young Sydney brewery – indeed, their Zoo Feeder IPA has won more trophies – but for sheer impact, there are few beers that will blow you away at first whiff like this one. Named after the brewery site's former tenant – a dope dealer – it's as aromatic as the marijuana factory would have been, albeit with explosive citrusy hops replacing the scent of weed, atop a glowing, crystalline bed of luscious caramel malts.

THE STORY If you spend time in the company of Grant and Jaz Wearin, the young couple who opened Modus Operandi in Mona Vale in 2014, you know that they're smart people who have done their research before taking the leap from home brewing to the commercial world. Yet, even having snapped up a brewer from one of America's leading craft breweries, Oskar Blues Brewery, to help them get things up and running, even they couldn't have forecast the dream start to life they would enjoy.

Within three months of launching, they swept the board at the inaugural Craft Beer Awards, collecting trophies for Champion Beer, Champion Small Brewery, Best IPA and Best Amber/Dark Ale. A year later, they retained Best IPA, added Best Pale Ale and were upgraded to Champion

Medium Brewery. Their beers are in demand across the country and disappear fast whenever a venue does manage to snag a keg or two.

They also introduced 'CANimals' to Australia – Oskar Blues' reworking of old canning machines that allows them to fill and securely seal one-litre cans of beer straight from the tap. And, perhaps best of all, they're seriously lovely people too.

ALSO TRY Pale Ale | Silent Knight Porter Zoo Feeder IPA | Kite Flyer Cream Ale Anything hop forward they release

BREWER'S FOOD MATCH
Delicious with the MO Burger: a thick Black Angus brisket patty, bacon jam, baby cos, pickles, mustard mayo, oozing American cheddar and streaky bacon, sandwiched between a soft milk bun. Available at the MO Brewery...

AVAILABILITY
Year-round

BREWERY & CELLAR DOOR LOCATION
14 Harkeith Street, Mona Vale, NSW 2103

BREWERY WEBSITE
www.mobrewing.com.au

IRISH RED

MORRISON BREWERY

 IRISH RED   **5.1%**   **10°C**    **TULIP OR PINT GLASS**

TASTING NOTES Paul Morrison has ventured outside the very traditional and predominantly British- and Irish-inspired world with which he made his name in recent years, but this Irish red remains a standout. A soft and full-bodied ale, it lets the blend of specialty malts take centre stage, layering on the creamy toffee and rich biscuit flavours with a hint of roast at the end ensuring that its sweetness doesn't become cloying.

THE STORY After showing promise at a series of home-brew competitions, Paul Morrison's family backed him financially so he could follow his brewing dream and set up a commercial operation in his hometown of Launceston. Initially, the young brewer continued working his day job at an orchard while sending his traditionally minded British- and Irish-style ales into the world, but soon he'd won over enough followers for the brewery to become his full-time employer.

In the ensuing years, without venturing outside Tasmania except for special occasions such as the Pint of Origin showcase at Good Beer Week, he's continued to build his following, while adding beers that look to Europe and, occasionally, the US for inspiration.

Paul has also been able to lend a helping hand to others looking to make the move from home brewer to pro brewer, inviting the likes of Devil's Brewery, kick | snare and Last Rites to brew at his steadily expanding brewery in Invermay. In turn, his family is still very much part of the Morrison story too.

ALSO TRY English Bitter | Irish Stout Saison

BREWER'S FOOD MATCH
Roasted or barbecued meats

AVAILABILITY
Year-round

BREWERY & CELLAR DOOR LOCATION
1/10 Mowbraw Street, Invermay, TAS 7248

BREWERY WEBSITE
www.morrisonbrewery.com.au

FANCY PANTS

MOUNTAIN GOAT

 **AMERICAN AMBER** **5.2%** **4°C** **TULIP GLASS**

TASTING NOTES Upon its first appearance in 2010, Fancy Pants was tagged the beer Mountain Goat's Hightail would be if money were no object. Subsequent releases of this hoppy amber proved popular enough for it to become the second beer they popped inside cans. There's a touch of fruity hops but mainly it's about the layers of rich caramel malts, balanced by a bitterness that ensures you can go back for another.

THE STORY What now for Mountain Goat? For 17 years and 11 months, the story of Melbourne's longest-established microbrewery was one of Australia's best loved. Two mates, Cam Hines and Dave Bonighton, inspired by time spent in North America, decided to take Dave's home brew (even then called Mountain Goat) and test it on an Australian market that had no idea there was anything other than lager.

From the early days of taking their mates to pubs to drink their first beer, Hightail Ale, so the publicans would buy more, through legendary parties in Richmond and years of struggling to stay afloat; to a position as Melbourne's craft beer legends with an iconic brewery venue and collaborations with some of the biggest names in beer – it was the tale that inspired others to follow their dreams.

Then, following months of rumour, in October 2015, they sent shockwaves through the local industry by selling the company in its entirety to Japanese behemoth Asahi. Cam and Dave stayed on as employees, many others left within weeks. The Goat brand will no doubt thrive and sell more beer than ever under Asahi, but it feels like the much-loved Goat story entered a new, rather different chapter, just short of its 18th birthday.

ALSO TRY Summer Ale (the beer that really launched craft in cans in Australia) Hightail Ale | Rare Breed and Barrel Breed limited releases

---

☆

BREWER'S FOOD MATCH
Barbecued T-bone steak

AVAILABILITY
Year-round

BREWERY & CELLAR DOOR LOCATION
80 North Street, Richmond, VIC 3121

BREWERY WEBSITE
www.goatbeer.com.au

RED

NAIL BREWING

 RED ALE　 **6.0%**　 **6–9°C**　 **PINT OR TULIP GLASS**

TASTING NOTES　There may be rumblings at Nail's epic Clout Stout not being the brewery's featured beer in this book. But, while it is one of Australia's most decadent drops, it's up against tough competition within Nail's stable and I'll wager you'll drink far more of this wonderfully flavoursome, impeccably balanced blend of lively citrus and tropical hops and deep, palate-caressing caramel malts that started out as a one-off but soon was promoted to the core range.

THE STORY　You could dedicate a chapter, if not an entire book, to the story of Nail Brewing and, in particular, its founder John Stallwood. He's been making beer for around two decades, more than 15 of those years commercially, having launched with Nail Ale around the turn of the millennium – five years after he'd registered the trademark for the beer while still a home brewer. In that time, he's played a key role throughout WA's brewing industry beyond merely making beer.

His career, indeed his life, was almost cut short in 2004, when he was punched trying to stop a fight in Freemantle. He ended up in a coma for weeks, had part of his brain removed and now lives with a skull partly made of titanium. He slowly rebuilt his life, then Nail, supported by family, friends and the beer community and

is now back in business, recognised as one of the country's best brewers and, sharing an impressive brewery with Feral, looking to make an imprint from coast to coast.

On the beer front, he's been steadily spreading his wings beyond the more straightforward ales and stouts with which he made his name (and won countless trophies), with some of his limited releases, like the aforementioned Clout Stout – costing $70 a bottle – among the most eagerly anticipated in Australia.

ALSO TRY　Stout | Clout Stout
Huge Dunn Imperial Brown Ale | Golden

BREWER'S FOOD MATCH
Perfect with any roasted or barbecued meats, particularly oven-roasted Aussie lamb, slow-cooked osso bucco, or an aged porterhouse or sirloin steak

AVAILABILITY
Year-round

BREWERY LOCATION
Bassendean, WA

BREWERY WEBSITE
www.nailbrewing.com.au

ADMIRAL ACKBAR

NOISY MINOR

 IMPERIAL RED ALE   **8.2%**   **8-10°C**   **BALLOON OR SNIFTER GLASS**

TASTING NOTES When a beer is this size – 8.5 per cent ABV – and designed to showcase both an array of bold specialty malts and bolshy hops, there's a danger you could end up with an unholy mess. Yet in the hands of brewer Ian Watson, this remarkably popular beer combines its rich toffee, treacle and sweet nutty malts and citrusy hops so well it's nigh-on impossible to tell where one ends and the other begins.

THE STORY The crazy little sibling to Fortitude Brewing, Noisy Minor was launched by the team that calls both the former Eagle Heights and Mt Tamborine breweries home as the label under which they would allow their brewer to go wild. Clearly, former Murray's man Ian Watson needed no second invitation, as he soon set about creating beers that mimicked cocktails, exploring higher levels of alcohol via imperial stouts and this dangerously smooth 'anti-imperial' red ale, all the while doing so with the control seen in the more straight-down-the-line Fortitude beers.

Noisy Minor is perhaps best known for its ANZUS IPA, one of the leaner, drier takes on the IPA style you'll find in Australia; one that showcases American, Kiwi and Aussie hops. Elsewhere, there have been literary-referencing beers, such as the Dorian Gray Baltic Porter,

experiments with oak and spices and even a beer conceived as the sort monks would drink with dinner.

If you fancy tasting them, the best option is to navigate through the dreamcatchers and patchouli until you hit the top of Mt Tamborine and line up a tasting paddle or two at the cellar door, ideally paired with a platter from the fine Witches Chase cheesemakers with whom the brewery shares a site.

ALSO TRY Bad Wolf Imperial IPA Yastrebov Imperial Stout | ANZUS IPA

BREWER'S FOOD MATCH
Hickory-smoked, reverse-seared rib on the bone, or a cheeseburger and fries

AVAILABILITY
Seasonal: early winter

BREWERY & CELLAR DOOR LOCATION
165 Long Road, North Tamborine, QLD 4271

BREWERY WEBSITE
www.fortitudebrewing.com.au

INDIA RED ALE

PRANCING PONY BREWERY

 INDIA RED ALE   **7.9%**   **6-8°C**   **IPA GLASS**

TASTING NOTES Everything about SA's Prancing Pony is colourful: their labels; their venue; their 'fire brewing' story; their branding. Of their beers, however, none is as colourful as the India Red Ale. The first of their 'Thoroughbred' releases – occasional releases in a 500 ml format – it's a deep red beer that marries tropical and herbal hops with a base of caramel, toasted and biscuity malts that keeps the bitterness in check.

THE STORY For many years, the craft beer scene in South Australia was pretty stagnant. It wasn't without interest or good beers by any means, but while other cities and states exploded into beery life it felt like SA was doing a rather good interpretation of the sleepy nature assigned to its capital city.

But, since late 2013 or so, things have come alive. Heaps of new breweries have launched and Adelaide's pubs and bars, who – with notable exceptions – seemed to feel a bank of Coopers taps was crafty enough, have made the switch too.

The rise of the state's industry has been mirrored by Prancing Pony, the microbrewery in the Adelaide Hills opened by expat German couple Corinna Steeb and Frank Samson and friends. In the short time since launching with a scaled-up version of Frank's flame-fired home brew kit, they've had to move to a bigger venue, expanded their capacity multiple times, bought a brand-new brewery, found a spot on the beer lists of some of Adelaide's most refined restaurants and even started sending beer to the UK and Europe.

There's a playfulness in the look and feel of the place, and the venture is a big change of direction for Corinna and Frank after lengthy careers in other fields, but don't let that fool you as there's formidable determination driving this pony.

ALSO TRY Black Ale | Pale Ale | Amber Ale Thoroughbred Copper Ale

BREWER'S FOOD MATCH
Perfect with Asian cuisine, curry dishes or blue cheeses and smoked meats

AVAILABILITY
Year-round

BREWERY LOCATION
Littlehampton, SA

CELLAR DOOR LOCATION
42 Mt Barker Road, Totness, SA 5250

BREWERY WEBSITE
www.prancingponybrewery.com.au

DARK RED IPA

SIX STRING BREWING CO

 RED IPA **6.0%** **6°C** **SPIEGELAU IPA GLASS**

TASTING NOTES A red IPA so dark red it borders on the opaque, like almost congealed blood. Despite being a formidable beer, it's become something of a flagship for the Central Coast's Six String. As well as the dense, chewy, fruity dark malt flavours there's heaps of intense dank and piny hops, all of which makes for a suitably bold beer for a brewery using the tag line 'Amplified Ales'.

THE STORY A genuine rock'n'roll brewery, Six String offers nods to its founders' love of music in its name and its logo. It even has a stage in front of its plectrum-adorned tanks where live music features regularly.

It took three years of battling red tape and four potential sites before they opened their doors in Erina but they soon found a place in the hearts of locals, serving up a selection of traditional ales usually at the bigger end for their style, and ambitious limited releases that have included collaborations with a local coffee roaster and a fine IPA brewed with traditional Thai spices.

For the most part, their beers are found around the Central Coast and Sydney but the installation of a canning line – one of the first local micros to do so – has seen their beers crop up at a handful of specialist bottleshops further afield.

ALSO TRY Hefeweizen | Pale Ale Specialty releases

BREWER'S FOOD MATCH
Something sweet with chocolate

AVAILABILITY
Year-round

BREWERY & CELLAR DOOR LOCATION
4/5 Chiltern Road, Erina, NSW 2250

BREWERY WEBSITE
www.sixstringbrewwing.com.au

CHARMER INDIA RED ALE

WAYWARD BREWING COMPANY

 INDIA RED ALE **5.0%** **6°C** **TULIP GLASS**

TASTING NOTES The very first release from Wayward back when it was a 'gypsy' brewing bit-on-the-side for successful Canadian businessman Peter Philip now finds itself among the permanent pours at one of the most impressive brewery venues in Australia. The smooth red coloured ale melds floral, fruity hops with toffee and toasted malts and, since Wayward's brewery opened, has spawned a bigger sibling, Fat Charmer.

THE STORY Initially, Wayward Brewing Company operated as a 'gypsy' brewer, with expat Canadian Peter Philip using other people's breweries to bring to life home brew recipes honed over 14 years. The Charmer was first to catch people's attentions in Sydney beer circles, soon joined by a series of never-less-than-interesting brews: an unfiltered lager; a high ABV farmhouse style Biere de Garde; an eisbock; and a spiced saison.

There was always talk of opening a Wayward brewery and venue, talk that took a little longer than perhaps originally planned as Peter found it harder than expected to extract himself from the successful e-commerce business he'd founded. Nevertheless, in 2015, and following an unexpected but ultimately successful trademark battle with SABMiller India, the talk became

the walk as Wayward's home opened in Camperdown.

And what a home it is, easily one of the most lavish of any urban microbrewery in Australia, combining brewery, giant murals, the odd motorcycle and a 14-tap bar and tasting room decked out in retro furniture inside a former winery. Those taps pour mostly Wayward's beers, brewed in the main by Shaun Blissett, the highly regarded young brewer who Peter snaffled from Illawarra Brewing Company, alongside a few from other 'gypsy' brewers, as Peter offers a nod to the wayward route that brought him here.

ALSO TRY Keller Instinct | Raconteur Fusami Victory | Sourpuss

---

☆

BREWER'S FOOD MATCH
Steak or pizza

AVAILABILITY
Year-round

BREWERY & CELLAR DOOR LOCATION
1–3 Gehrig Lane, Camperdown, NSW 2050

BREWERY WEBSITE
www.wayward.com.au

BROWNS, DARKS & PORTERS

BROWNS, DARKS & PORTERS

Over the coming pages you will find beers that fall into two main categories – brown ale and porter – as well as their American-inspired reinterpretations. They are styles that share many common characteristics and, indeed, at the upper, darker end of the brown ale style there is little to distinguish between such beers and many bearing the porter handle. It's more common for porters and stouts to be grouped together, given the latter grew from the former, but with stouts and imperial stouts more popular than browns, darks or porters – and style categories a fairly fluid beast these days – they get their own chapter.

As for beers tagged dark ale, it is a broad-brush term that could cover brown ales, porters, even stouts. In Australia, the few that carry the name, such as Coopers Dark Ale and the White Rabbit beer featured on page 168, could as easily be called brown ales. And, just to muddy the waters a little further, you can find beers, usually in England, described as brown porters.

The origins of both brown ales and porters are found in the UK. Browns come in two main variants: the Northern English Brown and Southern English Brown. Both share many characteristics, however, in that they are brown in colour, with the former usually lighter in hue than the latter. Their flavours and aromas are predominantly derived from the brewer's choice of malt rather than hops. Expect malt sweetness and anything from milk chocolate and vanilla to toffee, cocoa and coffee, sometimes with fruity elements, such as raisins or plums, apparent too.

American brown ales do what you would expect from American brewers: they take the English originals and turn them up to 11. Generally drinkers should expect fuller, richer malt flavours, slightly higher alcohol content and the addition, in many cases, of more noticeable, often citrusy or piney, hop aromas and flavours.

Porters are beers with one of the most colourful histories of all to have come from the British Isles. Theories that it evolved from a drink called 'three-threads', a blend of three old beer styles popular in London in the 18th century – ale (a lightly hopped beverage), beer and two-penny (a stronger pale ale) – have been dismissed, with the truth rather more sedate. Porter became the name given to strong, highly hopped and aged brown ales brewed by London brewers that became popular with the capital's river and street porters.

No matter the porter's genesis, these beers were to prove hugely popular, a popularity that coincided with the Industrial Revolution in the UK. Huge breweries making use of new technologies emerged, signalling a shift to modern, large-scale commercial brewing, and began sending their beers across the UK and Ireland.

Porters became popular in the early United States and were also sent to Britain's other colonies. When Tasmanian brewery Seven Sheds decided to recreate the journey of the first beers sent from the UK to Australia, it was a porter with which head brewer Willie Simpson filled the oak barrels that spent two months traversing Bass Strait.

By the early 20th century, the style had declined dramatically in popularity. Once more, it was left to the new wave of craft brewers in America to bring it back towards the end of the century. They did so with beers that are usually around about 6 per cent in alcohol content and dominated by rich chocolate flavours and aromas, often with hints of vanilla, treacle, dark fruits, a touch of coffee and sometimes even leather or smokiness.

Sometimes New World brewers will ramp up the hopping regime late in the brewing process to add citrusy or tropical fruit aromas, although most porter brewers in Australia resist this temptation. You will also find smoked porters featuring a small percentage of smoked malt, typically a nod to the earliest days of brown ales in the UK when the malts used to create such beers were smoked over beech or oak fires and would impart a distinct smokiness.

A DOZEN MORE TO TRY

MORNINGTON PENINSULA
Porter

THE LITTLE BREWING COMPANY
Wicked Elf Porter

NEWSTEAD BREWING COMPANY
24 Feet 7 Inches Porter

SEVEN SHEDS
Fuggled Porter

BLACKMAN'S BREWERY
Arthur Smoked Porter

NAPOLEONE BREWERS
Breakneck Porter

LOBETHAL BIERHAUS
Red Truck Porter

MURRAY'S BREWING
Angry Man Brown

NAIL BREWING
Huge Dunn Imperial Brown

TOOBORAC BREWERY
Blacksmith's Porter

MOO BREW
Dark Ale

2 BROTHERS
Growler

HAZELNUT BROWN

BAD SHEPHERD BREWING

 HAZELNUT BROWN ALE **5.9%** **6-8°C**  **TULIP GLASS**

TASTING NOTES This brown ale leaps out of the glass in such an intensely decadent manner that you figure it's going to feel like pouring a dessert into your mouth. Yet, despite layering on the chocolate malts, hazelnuts, hazelnut extract, vanilla and a dash of Frangelico, brewer Dereck Hales manages to deliver a beer that delivers chocolate, nuts and creaminess while still managing to wrap up remarkably dry with a woody, earthy bitterness.

THE STORY The first time I met Dereck he was thoroughly enjoying himself at an event I was hosting for Melbourne Food & Wine Festival while his then girlfriend was stuck feeling ill at his place of work nearby. Thankfully, the latter forgave the former and, four years later, not only were they married but they were opening the doors of a mighty fine brewpub in Cheltenham specialising in barbecue-style comfort food paired with Dereck's beers.

Bad Shepherd – so called as the couple enjoy leading friends, and now paying customers, into temptation – completed an impressively rapid rise through the ranks of brewing for the former Kraft employee. He only started home brewing five years ago before opening the brewpub, moving from dodgy early brews to winning statewide competitions within a couple of years.

That gave him the chance to brew a couple of batches at microbreweries as part of his prizes, experiences he built upon by brewing one day a week at Mornington Peninsula Brewery while still working at Kraft. Now, he shares his kit with Wolf of the Willows, with the buzzing brewpub showcasing beers from both of them plus a rotating selection from their mates in the Victorian beer world.

ALSO TRY American Pale Ale | Tiny IPA California Lager

BREWER'S FOOD MATCH
Fantastic with nutty flavours of hard cheeses and stands up to mild cheddars and soft cheese – or, even better, a baked goat's curd cheesecake

AVAILABILITY
Year-round

BREWERY & CELLAR DOOR LOCATION
386 Reserve Road, Cheltenham, VIC 3192

BREWERY WEBSITE
www.badshepherd.com.au

FRANKENBROWN

BIG SHED BREWING CONCERN

 AMERICAN BROWN ALE 5.3% 3–5°C A MAN'S HAT

TASTING NOTES I was present for the very first tapping of this, Big Shed's very first beer. The brewers were rather sheepish as they'd committed to the launch date but didn't think the beer was quite ready. It wasn't but, as with all their beers, since opening their communal brewery it's got better and better and is now as intended: rich, caramel, biscuit and coffee malt characters topped off with fruity American hops.

THE STORY As far as classic craft beer stories go, the tale of Big Shed Brewing Concern is one that ticks plenty of boxes. Two mates who'd spent years brewing together in a farmer's shed decided to take their passion into the commercial realm and thought they'd give others in their position a leg up, too. They did this by taking their brewing into a much bigger shed, installing a decent-sized microbrewery setup, then inviting small brewing companies and home brewers wanting to take the step up to rent brewery time and tank space off them.

Soon the tanks were fully booked and, perhaps more importantly for founders Jason Harris and Craig Basford, they had the time to focus on their own beers. They brought in a head brewer to polish their recipes, added new beers to their lineup

and started packaging in order to hit up interstate markets – doing so with some of the best and most humorous labels in the country.

The final stage (for now at least) was to open their brewery bar, which they built with various bits of reclaimed timber (including some from the Adelaide Oval of which they're rather proud). It's open now, complete with beer garden and kitchen, pouring a mix of their beers (including pilot batch experiments) and those of the brewers who use their shed as they continue to share the love.

ALSO TRY F-Yeah APA (and its fresh hop sibling) | Californicator | Golden Stout Time

BREWER'S FOOD MATCH
Roast meat or chocolate

AVAILABILITY
Year-round

BREWERY & CELLAR DOOR LOCATION
13/2 Brandwood Street, Royal Park, SA 5014

BREWERY WEBSITE
www.bigshedbrewing.com.au

BROWN ALE

BROOKES BEER

 BROWN ALE 5.2%  6–8°C NONIC GLASS

TASTING NOTES The Brown Ale from Bendigo's Brookes Beer was always my favourite of their core range from the off. Then brewer Doug switched to malts from popular Kiwi maltsters Gladfield and the beer went to another level. It now has a richness and lushness indicated by the dense, nigh on black colour it possesses when it hits your glass. Heaps of chocolate, a touch of coffee, nuttiness and dark fruits await.

THE STORY With middle age approaching, Doug Brookes was at a crossroads. He'd spent his life in a corporate environment, mostly around the airline industry, and figured that not only was he unsure whether he wanted to keep doing it, but if he was made redundant at any point he was of an age where the next job could prove hard to find.

What's more, Doug is a man whose bow has many strings, so he figured he'd start playing one of them – that of a brewer – rather more seriously. Along with partner Melissa Church, he scoured Melbourne and surrounds for a place to open a brewery and ended up in a former abattoir in Bendigo. As one does.

While keen to become embraced by the city in which they set up shop, Doug and Melissa have also sent their beers further afield, while he has released some fascinating and seriously experimental one-offs along the way too. He's also been offering other local brewers a leg up, inviting the likes of Wolfey at Castlemaine Brewing space to brew at the abattoir while he builds his own brewpub.

ALSO TRY Bohemian Lager | IPA American Pale Ale

BREWER'S FOOD MATCH
Hearty meat dishes, roasts, smoked or barbecued meats, or nut-based desserts

AVAILABILITY
Year-round

BREWERY LOCATION
Bendigo East, VIC

BREWERY WEBSITE
www.brookesbeer.com.au

BROWN ALE

CAVALIER BREWING

 **BROWN ALE**　　 **5.0%**　　 **8°C**　　 **TULIP GLASS**

TASTING NOTES They've brewed all manner of beers since launching early in 2011, but their earliest beers – admittedly refined to various degrees over the years – are reminders of why they caused a stir so early. This is a deeply brown Brown, one that kicks off with a distinctly nutty aroma before unveiling layers of chocolate, mocha and a drying toastiness, with earthy hops lurking in the background.

THE STORY Cavalier by name and cavalier by nature, the story of the three founders of this Melbourne brewing company and the people they've swept into their growing business has had something of the helter-skelter about it.

Within a couple of weeks of registering their business they'd taken home a couple of titles from the Victorian Microbreweries Showcase and found their beers in more demand than a 100-litre brewery in a backyard shed could handle. So they started brewing on other people's gear before securing a site in Melbourne's west where they built a brewery with a difference: they invited others to rent brewery time and buy tank space, ending up with a conveyor belt of brewers coming in and out at all times of the week.

Today, some of those they gave a leg up to have their own breweries, while Cavalier expands its reach nationwide.

It tends to do so via more than beer. They've completed collaborations with brewers and venues across the country, host 'Handcrafted' events featuring street and tattoo artists and other handcrafted businesses and always have plenty to offer when major festivals and beer weeks come around.

They also brew Cavalier Courage, a beer and concept developed with Motor Neurone Disease sufferer and Melbourne doctor Ian Davis that raises awareness and funds for research into the disease.

ALSO TRY Pale Ale | Imperial Stout Cavalier Courage

BREWER'S FOOD MATCH
Roquefort cheese

AVAILABILITY
Year-round

BREWERY LOCATION
Derrimut, VIC

BREWERY WEBSITE
www.cavalierbeer.com.au

BROWN ALE

HIX BEER

 BROWN ALE   **5.0%**  **6–8°C**   **ENGLISH PINT GLASS**

TASTING NOTES The Hix range has expanded significantly since I was compiling *150 Great Australian Beers*, with their clean and fruity Aussie Pale Ale and simple yet pleasant Saison, both being enjoyable drops. But I retain a soft spot for the Brown Ale that looks to the UK for inspiration and delivers well balanced flavours and aromas that are equal parts nut, caramel and chocolate with a gentle bitterness.

THE STORY Hix Beer is a brewery that flies under the radar. Found at the wonderfully idiosyncratic Hickinbotham winery in Dromana on the Mornington Peninsula, where the brewery of the same name and Red Hill are well known, Hix started out as a spin-off from the main business, with vineyard manager Cameron Turner taking his home-brewing skills onto a larger scale – albeit with a brewing setup as ingenious and Heath Robinson-esque as many a home brew setup.

A gold for its pale ale in 2011 brought some attention, while it has continued to collect medals at awards around the country, including for this brown ale. All the while, the brewing has grown as a business and the number of beers has expanded too: while the core range of Pale, Pilsner, Brown and Irish Stout remains, there has been a steady stream of the straightforward and the more esoteric, including a barley wine, farmhouse ales and fruity brews, too.

The winery and brewery themselves are equally esoteric. Founded by Andrew Hickinbotham, whose family has a long history in winemaking that began in SA, much has been built out of reclaimed parts from demolished banks and an old school gym. Meanwhile, the brewery has been built around shampoo and milk vats and a brewing process that involves a forklift and hydraulics, showing where a little ingenuity can take you.

ALSO TRY Aussie Pale Ale | Saison Pilsener | Pale Ale | Irish Stout

BREWER'S FOOD MATCH
Hix Brown Ale–braised Gippsland beef short rib, warm ancient grain salad and Hix kitchen garden tomato and onion relish

AVAILABILITY
Year-round

BREWERY & CELLAR DOOR LOCATION
194 Nepean Highway, Dromana, VIC 3936

BREWERY WEBSITE
www.hixbeer.com.au

IRON POT RYE PORTER

HOBART BREWING COMPANY

 PORTER   **4.8%**   **8–12°C**   **PINT GLASS**

TASTING NOTES The second release from the historically, nautically minded Hobart Brewing Company takes its name from the Iron Pot, the lighthouse that operated in Storm Bay in the 1800s, and its stylistic lead from traditional porters. Rye adds a spicy twist, although the most remarkable aspect of this almost black beer is that it's only 4.8 percent ABV as the bittersweet roasty, chocolatey drop drinks like something much bigger.

THE STORY Hobart has witnessed phenomenal growth in the number of breweries that call it home since 2014. Where once there was old timer Cascade and, a short drive or boat trip up the river, Moo Brew, at the time of writing there were close to ten brewing companies in operation. Of those, Hobart Brewing Company is likely to have as big an impact as any.

For one, its location will help it stand out. It's found inside the 'Red Shed', a previously abandoned warehouse on the other side of Hobart's waterfront from Salamanca Place. Then there's the scale of its owners' ambition. They commissioned architects to turn the shed and the wasteland surrounding it into an impressive indoor–outdoor venue with views – unusually for the area – directed back over the city to Mount Wellington.

The beers should stand them in good stead too. At the time of writing there were just two – this porter and the Harbour Master, a flavoursome copper ale – designed by former Moo Brew brewer Scott Overdorf, who learnt his trade in the craft beer hotbed of Colorado. Expect big things from his partnership with beer-loving lawyer Brendan Parnell – and from the brewing hub that Hobart has become.

ALSO TRY Harbour Master Tasmanian Ale

☆

BREWER'S FOOD MATCH
Low and slow pulled pork – the caramel and roasted malts go well with smoky meats

AVAILABILITY
Year-round

BREWERY & CELLAR DOOR LOCATION
The Red Shed, 16 Evans Street, Hobart, TAS 7000

BREWERY WEBSITE
www.hobartbrewingco.com.au

TEMPTRESS

HOLGATE BREWHOUSE

 **PORTER**   **6.0%**   **8°C**   **GOBLET**

TASTING NOTES The temptation was great to ignore Temptress when picking Holgate's feature brew, as it's the one that's always chosen. Then it collected another major trophy at the 2015 Australian International Beer Awards, seemingly as a reminder of why it's always chosen. Initially a one-off, this luscious porter featuring vanilla beans and Dutch cocoa has proved a popular year-round drop and one that's won over many non beer drinkers.

THE STORY A couple of years after deciding to launch Holgate Brewhouse with a brewery at the back of his house, Paul Holgate was doing it hard. He and wife Natasha had started a family at the same time, he was still working full-time in another job, she was doing deliveries with kegs strapped in the back of their car next to their newborn, and some batches of beer were spoiling, leading Paul to despair and, on occasion, tears.

The audience he'd believed would be there for the more full-flavoured beers he'd enjoyed on overseas trips hadn't yet shown up but, undeterred, they decided to create one and bought an old hotel in their hometown of Woodend. Major renovations were required, not least so they could build a brewery at the back, but driven by stubbornness they soldiered on, continuing to work insane hours while ensuring their kids remained their number one priority.

In 2014, the pair celebrated 15 years of Holgate Brewhouse, thankful – as countless drinkers are – for that stubborn streak. They sell beer across Australia now (although their hotel remains their biggest customer) and continue to explore new styles and techniques. There's no resting on laurels, however: Paul has grand plans to significantly expand the brewery and build a visitor centre showcasing Holgate, beer and brewing on site too. And no one who's met them would doubt him succeeding, however long it takes.

ALSO TRY Mount Macedon Ale | ESB Road Trip IPA | Double Trouble | Pilsner Beelzebub's Jewels | Norton Lager

BREWER'S FOOD MATCH
Your favourite chocolate dessert – for example, hot fudge brownie or tiramisu

AVAILABILITY
Year-round

BREWERY & CELLAR DOOR LOCATION
79 High Street, Woodend, VIC 3442

BREWERY WEBSITE
www.holgatebrewhouse.com

JACK OF SPADES PORTER

JAMES SQUIRE

 PORTER   **5.0%**   **8-10°C** **GOBLET OR STRAIGHT-SIDED ALE GLASS**

TASTING NOTES The best beer in the ever-expanding James Squire range is, to my mind, one of the best porters you'll find in Australia. Certainly, whenever I've featured it in blind tastings it's come up trumps. Like the best beers of the style, it manages to squeeze plenty into a relatively light body: chocolate dominates, with roast coffee and some toasted characters backed by a gentle bitterness.

THE STORY As the local beer world changes beyond all recognition, one of the biggest players in the Aussie beer market has set itself up rather nicely.

Lion, owned by Japanese behemoth Kirin, has both Little Creatures and White Rabbit on its roster, meaning it is able to entice drinkers towards better beer in the welcoming surrounds of the former's iconic home in Freo as well as the superb visitor experience offered by both in Geelong these days. It also owns the Knappstein, Kosciuszko and New Norcia brands, all of which offer something more interesting than the mainstream.

Its heaviest hitter in the craftier realms of the Aussie beer world, however, is James Squire, launched at the Malt Shovel Brewery in 1998 and headed up by Hahn Brewery founder Chuck Hahn after he sold his business to Lion Nathan (as it was then). For years, he's used the brand to push the concept of flavoursome beer onto Australian drinkers, often through beer-pairing dinners long before they became a celebrated part of craft beer culture.

The Squire range continues to grow – often at the more approachable end of the beer spectrum – while their branded Brewhouses in the country's capitals offer a gateway experience for drinkers new to anything other than lager.

ALSO TRY Four 'Wives' Pilsener
Nine Tales Amber Ale | Stowaway IPA
Hop Thief American Pale Ale (Series)
The Constable Copper Ale

✡

BREWER'S FOOD MATCH
Hearty, rich meat dishes or chocolate mud cake

AVAILABILITY
Year-round

BREWERY LOCATION
Camperdown, NSW

BREWERY WEBSITE
www.jamessquire.com.au

BROWN ALE

MORNINGTON PENINSULA BREWERY

 BROWN ALE **5.0%** **8-10°C** **TULIP GLASS**

TASTING NOTES Mornington Peninsula Brewery produces many great beers across a broad array of styles, some that sell far more than this. Yet the Brown gets the nod as, more than any other beer, it made brown ales sexy in Australia. It did this by the tried and tested method of making a wonderfully balanced beer with heaps going on – shades of caramel, coffee, chocolate, nuts and raisins – but in a subtle manner.

THE STORY I imagine there are plenty of fledgling breweries – or people considering the leap into the world of commercial brewing – who look at Mornington Peninsula Brewery and think: "That would do very nicely, thanks." Two mates were inspired to open a brewery while celebrating Hawthorn's victory in the 2008 AFL Grand Final and, two years to the day, they did.

They built a 10-hectolitre brewery inside an industrial unit near Mornington Racecourse that used to manufacture exploding golf balls, put a bar and pizza oven alongside it, crossed their fingers and hoped it wouldn't go up in smoke like said balls.

Less than five years later, they'd built a second brewery two-and-a-half times the size down the road, were upgrading the canning line they'd installed in addition to their original bottling line, and could look back on a job well done.

That they'd enjoyed such success is down as much as anything to plucking head brewer Andrew 'AG' Gow from New South Wales and enticing him back to Victoria. The former Mountain Goat brewer has excelled across a wide spectrum of beer styles, occasionally trialling styles or hop varieties not seen in Australia before and more often than not hitting the bullseye from the off.

ALSO TRY Pale Ale | IPA | Imperial IPA Imperial Stout | Porter

BREWER'S FOOD MATCH
Sticky date pudding or slow-cooked meat

AVAILABILITY
Year-round

BREWERY & CELLAR DOOR LOCATION
72 Watt Road, Mornington, VIC 3931

BREWERY WEBSITE
www.mpbrew.com.au

VANILLA PORTER

QUIET DEEDS

 VANILLA PORTER   **6.2%**  **4–7°C**   **GOBLET**

TASTING NOTES While their first releases were so safe to be bordering on insipid, when it came to their first seasonal release, there was a first appearance for flavour and character for Quiet Deeds; it's hard to brew a porter – a vanilla one at that – without offering drinkers some interest. And that's what Quiet Deeds did, combining chocolate, vanilla and a touch of coffee in a relatively light-bodied beer with a touch of roast to finish.

THE STORY When former Rekorderlig cider importers Red Island launched their Quiet Deeds beer brand, the fanfare and bold packaging seemed to be in direct contrast to what was in the bottles. Owners Patrick Ale and David Milstein were keen to target mainstream rather than pointier end beer drinkers, which resulted in beers totally stripped of character – not that they didn't sell.

The release of this Vanilla Porter as a first seasonal hinted at better things to come. And, when they brought in a brewer who'd been plying his trade in Canada to oversee their contract brewing and develop their recipes, their core beers, such as the Pale and IPA, started displaying the sort of hop flavours and aromas and body one would expect of the style. Soon, other seasonals, including

a well-received, if a little muddled, White IPA and the cake-in-a-bottle Lamington Ale, followed.

Unexpectedly, to me, at least, as I'd expected Red Island to remain a contract brewer, they then announced they were building a brewery. Initially slated for their Port Melbourne warehouse, practicalities have led them to a site in Glen Iris instead. It's a promising move, particularly given the upward curve their beers are on, and should be operating some time in 2016.

ALSO TRY Pale Ale | White IPA Lamington Ale

BREWER'S FOOD MATCH
Quintessential winter dishes, including stews, ribs and cheese, as well as desserts such as chocolate, vanilla ice cream or crème brulée

AVAILABILITY
Seasonal: winter

BREWERY & CELLAR DOOR LOCATION
4 Paran Place, Glen Iris, VIC 3146

BREWERY WEBSITE
www.quietdeeds.com.au

SOLSTICE BALTIC PORTER

ROBE TOWN BREWERY

 BALTIC PORTER   8.0%   10-13°C   CERVOISE OR LARGE TULIP GLASS

TASTING NOTES A suitably old school-looking beer from a brewery using the most old-school of methods, this cola-coloured Baltic porter pours with a low carbonation, emitting woody, earthy aromas that mingle with a rich, chocolatey sweetness. There's a lingering dark fruit character alongside the earthy bitterness, with the 8 per cent booze poking its nose in late on.

THE STORY There are quirky breweries in Australia. And then there's Robe Town. Opened in 2015 by a Latvian couple, Maris and Kristi Biezaite, after a couple of years operating as 'gypsy' brewers, Robe Town is truly unique. Within a disused fish factory, former journalist Maris brews using a setup comprised of oak wine-barrel mash tuns, a wood-fired copper kettle, open fermenters and a filtration system that uses straw and hay.

The aim is to bring some lost brewing techniques back to life, making the brewery part window into the past, part creator of unusual beers. To give an insight into the practices at Robe Town, for the beer featured here the extract was made in three oak-barrel mash tuns full of malt, filtered through a bed of straw and hay, then boiled for three hours on the wood-fired kettle before undergoing three days of open fermentation, leaving the liquid open to the elements. You can see for yourself if you visit the town as the cellar door is open most days.

While Baltic Porters were traditionally brewed with lager yeasts, the Solstice uses an ale yeast, hence its appearance in this chapter.

ALSO TRY Shipwreck Stout | Amber Pale Ale

BREWER'S FOOD MATCH
Dark bread with mature cheeses, almonds and dates

AVAILABILITY
Seasonal: twice a year on the solstice

BREWERY & CELLAR DOOR LOCATION
97 Millicent Road (Southern Ports Highway), Robe, SA 5276

BREWERY WEBSITE
www.robetownbrewery.com

THE BUTCHER PORTER

ROCKS BREWING

 PORTER 6.0% 4°C **BOSTON PINT GLASS**

TASTING NOTES Rocks' Pale is its most popular beer, but it only feels right to feature a beer inspired by 19th century England for a brewing company whose schtick is borrowed from the earliest days of settlement. Opaque and close to black, the Butcher offers subtle roast, burnt nuts and dark cocoa on the nose, with dark chocolate, earthy bitterness, a hint of dark fruits and a roasted barley tang inhabiting its relatively light, yet smooth, body.

THE STORY Somewhat counterintuitively, the Rocks Brewing Company is not in The Rocks – although that was the original idea. When the people that started the business tried to secure a site for a brewery in Sydney's oldest suburb and a designated heritage area, their quest, as you can imagine, proved impossible. But those same people also owned Harts Pub in The Rocks, thus the venue became the symbolic home for Rocks Brewing, which effectively became the house brand and filled most of the taps. To supply the beer, brewer Scotty Morgan would tour the state and use other breweries to create the Rocks range.

Meanwhile the search for a brewery site spread ever wider and spanned several years before they finally found what they were looking for in a large industrial space in Alexandria. In it they installed one of Sydney's bigger breweries adjacent to an

impressive wood and concrete bar and kitchen; outside they cajoled an otherwise faceless outdoor space into a quirkily adorned grassless beer garden.

Having their own home has allowed them to develop and broaden the scope of their own beers, including some experimental all wheat brews, souring and fun with barrels. Brewing capacity at their cavernous home also allows them to give friends a helping hand, with the likes of Doctor's Orders, Shenanigans, Odyssey and many more brewing there – something that would likely never have happended had they followed through on their initial aim of opening in The Rocks.

ALSO TRY Hangman Pale | Convict Lager Boxer Red Ale | The 'Conviction' Series

BREWER'S FOOD MATCH
The sharpness from the roasted malt goes great with sweet flavours like caramel and chocolate, making it a perfect match for rich, creamy desserts

AVAILABILITY
Year-round

BREWERY & CELLAR DOOR LOCATION
Zepplin Building 2, 160 Bourke Road, Alexandria, NSW 2015

BREWERY WEBSITE
www.rocksbrewing.com

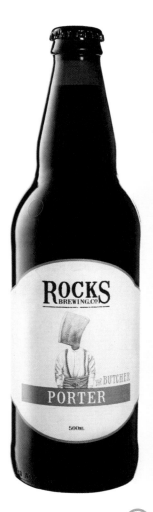

DARK ALE

WHITE RABBIT

 DARK ALE　　 **4.9%**　　 **COLD!**　　 **CERVOISE STEM**

TASTING NOTES　The first ever release from Little Creatures' little sibling has undergone a wealth of tweaks over the years but remains my pick of their core range of three (at the time of writing – a fourth may well appear in 2016). A finely judged balance of darker malts and soft, fruity hops, it's a beer to ease people into the world of darker beers: a little bit caramel, a little bit toasty, a little bit coffee, a little bit fruity, all in balance.

THE STORY　There was concern among many in the beer world when Lion announced that it would be closing White Rabbit's brewery in Healesville. At the same time, they announced that the brewery would continue to operate at the sprawling red-brick industrial site in Geelong that was already partially occupied by its sibling brewery, Little Creatures. Yet many feared this was the bean counters finally bringing their evil whims to bear following the sale of Little World Beverages, the parent company, to Lion in 2012.

As it turns out, White Rabbit has left the Yarra Valley behind (but other breweries continue to open there), but looks set to strive for new heights at its new home. The brewery now has a barrel room to keep it company, with the brewers charged with using the oak to age some

beers, turn others funky and, essentially, take the tiny batch experiments they were carrying out in Healesville on to a much larger scale.

The new site is very much an educational visitor experience, too and should see the launch of new permanent White Rabbit beers as well regular experimental limited run releases.

ALSO TRY　Belgian-style Pale Ale
White Ale | Red Ale

☆

BREWER'S FOOD MATCH
Stands up nicely to rich, bold flavours such as braised lamb or roasted venison

AVAILABILITY
Year-round

BREWERY & CELLAR DOOR LOCATION
221 Swanston Street, South Geelong, VIC 3220

BREWERY WEBSITE
www.whiterabbitbeer.com.au

JUDAS THE DARK

WOOLSHED BREWERY

 DARK ALE   **4.9%**   **COOL**   **TULIP GLASS**

TASTING NOTES Woolshed's beers tend to reference a local creature or landmark. In the case of this one, the Judas in question is the sheep used to entice all others to their fate in a shearing shed or sale truck. Pretty dark, then. As is the beer, which makes use of locally grown and roasted wattleseed to create a beautiful looking dark ale that offers gentle roast, aromatic nuttiness, cocoa and a woody bitterness within a soft body.

THE STORY There aren't too many breweries in Australia that you can cruise up to by boat. But, thanks to its location in a former shearer's shed on the banks of the Murray in regional South Australia, at the Woolshed Brewery you can. Indeed, on busy days, you'll find the banks lined with boats while their occupants indulge themselves on the deck above.

The brewery and cellar door – not to mention associated houseboat hire business – occupy sheds on part of what was once a wheat farm. And while both wheat farming and shearing are a thing of the past, you can wander through the building and get a feel for what was there before.

The present is very much all about beer, however, although even here the Woolshed team tip their hats to their surrounds. Their IPA is called Cherax

Destructor after the yabbies that inhabit the waterways, the Amazon Ale takes its name from a nearby creek, while their AAAMber Ale is a nod to the name given only to the finest quality Merino wool.

ALSO TRY Cherax Destructor IPA
Firehouse Stout | Amazon Ale
AAAMber Ale

BREWER'S FOOD MATCH
Chocolate desserts with ice cream

AVAILABILITY
Year-round

BREWERY & CELLAR DOOR LOCATION
69 Wilkinson Road, Murtho, SA 5340

BREWERY WEBSITE
www.aboverenmark.com.au/micro_brewery.php

STOUTS &
IMPERIAL
STOUTS

STOUTS & IMPERIAL STOUTS

Stouts are the darkest of all beers, typically ranging in colour from dark brown through to opaque, jet black. Most appear seasonally during the colder months, when brewers add them to their bars and drinkers' minds turn towards heavier, heartier beers in much the same way they start craving more comforting and warming meals.

Imperial stouts are, as the name suggests, bigger and bolder versions of these beers: higher in alcohol, thicker in body, usually more complex in aroma and flavour, and sharing some characteristics with fortified wines. Between the two you can find stouts with the prefixes 'foreign' or 'export', even 'foreign export'; originally, these were higher alcohol stouts brewed for export to colonies in the tropics and, while some of those beers survive, today the tag is applied by brewers to stouts that are bigger than a standard stout without reaching the boozy heights of an imperial version.

The stout style evolved from English porters. Originally the term 'stout' was used in England to describe a stronger version of any style of beer but, by the late 19th century, it was most commonly used in conjunction with strong porters, with the phrase stout porter ultimately shortened to simply 'stout', leaving two beer styles with much in common to go their own ways.

As well as being typically stronger, stouts were generally roastier and more bitter as well, with the use of roasted barley lending the beer distinct characteristics they share with roast coffee as well as a bitterness derived from the malt in addition to that obtained from hops.

Stouts have a solid heritage in Australia. While not obviously suited to the country's hot climate, there are brands with a long, unbroken lineage that survived the rationalisation and homogenisation of the beer industry during the 20th century. In many ways, they are anomalies, but welcome anomalies for that.

Their endurance is mirrored across the former British Empire. Various export stouts were transported to the colonies, some proving so popular that many were licensed to be brewed by local brewers on the ground. To this day, you can find variants of Guinness Foreign Extra Stout across the globe and there are other beers, such as the excellent Lion Stout (also known as Sinha Stout) produced by Lion Brewery of Sri Lanka, which was founded in late 19th century colonial times.

Pleasingly, you can peruse the shelves of bottleshops today and see the Southwark Old Stout still bearing its deeply unfashionable livery like a museum relic from another era. Better still, it tastes great and costs very little, making it, like Coopers' fine Best Extra Stout, one of the best value beers in the country. Meanwhile, there are plenty of far smaller and younger breweries for whom their stout is the pick of their range, particularly in South Australia from where Southwark and Coopers originate.

Over time, stout itself has diverged into many variants. Among them are the Dry Irish Stout style made most famous by Guinness, milk or sweet stouts that use lactose to add a creamy sweetness to the finished beer, and oatmeal stouts in which the addition of oats gives a fullness and softness to the mouthfeel.

A quirk of the past couple of years has been the rise of the sweet stout. Most likely it is a side effect of the growth of the GABS festival, which takes place in Melbourne each May during Good Beer Week before touring, at this point in time, Sydney and Auckland. More than 100 brewers create new beers to be launched at the event and the thousands of attendees are invited to vote for a favourite. Given they do so most commonly by sampling just 85 ml of each beer from a tiny plastic cup that doesn't offer much leeway for swirling and sniffing, the big, sweet, rich beers have tended to catch the eye. As such, many brewers have lent

towards beers like sweet stouts, sometimes laced with coffee or vanilla, achieved good results in the popular vote and then continued to brew them after the festival.

The rise in the popularity of 'extreme' beer styles has led to an increase in the number of imperial stouts brewed locally too. Originally an export strength 'stout porter' brewed in England to be sent to the Baltic states and Russia in the 1800s, it is significantly higher in alcohol than normal stouts, often measuring around 10 per cent ABV. Rich, fulsome, hearty and warming, these beers are palate-engulfing delights awash with chocolate, coffee, molasses, treacle, vanilla, dark fruits, leather and much more besides, some possessing vinous qualities too.

Add in American stouts, in which hops are added in greater amounts to become a more prominent feature, Belgian stouts, where the choice of yeast can add a fruitiness, and even summer stouts that might be blended with fruits, and there's plenty of variety to be found in a glass of the black stuff.

Each winter seems to bring forth more from Australian brewers, frequently of an astoundingly high standard. Some are barrel-aged and some are released in rather decadent 750 ml champagne-style bottles, highlighting their suitability for sharing among friends. Ideally with a large chunk of quality blue cheese.

A DOZEN MORE TO TRY

NAIL BREWING
Stout and Clout Stout

HARGREAVES HILL
Stout and RIS

FERAL BREWING
Boris

PRICKLY MOSES
Stout

MORNINGTON PENINSULA BREWERY
Imperial Stout

CAVALIER BREWING
Imperial Stout

MURRAY'S CRAFT BREWING
Wild Thing

LA SIRÈNE
Crafty Praline and Imperial Praline

SEVEN SHEDS
Crafty Stark Raven

TEMPLE BREWING
New World Order

WHEATY BREWING
Corps Wheaty Bix

4 PINES
Stout

DEAD DOG STOUT

BLACK DOG BREWERY

 STOUT 5.4% 4–5°C **SPIEGELAU STOUT OR TULIP GLASS**

TASTING NOTES I featured a dark beer from Black Dog in my last book: the hopped-up Hell Hound, but the Dead Dog Stout has come on so much since then it had to feature. Its dense black body and deep brown head hint at what's to come. And it doesn't disappoint. There's a touch of hops on the nose, but no more, allowing high percentage cacao, burnt nuts, roast, dark treacle, raisins, figs and molasses to caress your palate into submission.

THE STORY James Booth is a glutton for punishment. The fourth generation winemaker who can be found at his family's picturesque winery, at the end of several kilometres of unsealed road outside Glenrowan, decided that making wine wasn't enough of a challenge. So he opted to step his love of home brewing up a notch or two.

He launched Black Dog from a tiny home brew setup, brewing and bottling 70-litre batches, and soon managed to gain a following. Thus emboldened, he installed a brewery almost 30 times bigger in an extension to the winery that allowed him to step up production significantly. Since then, he's continued to upgrade, with a new filler added in 2015 to counter issues with carbonation that had been hampering some of his otherwise fine beers once bottled.

Despite running a winery and brewery pretty much singlehanded (and having a young family to boot), James always seems to have a few new brewing projects on the go. He's collaborated with brewers and other producers from his region, as well as making one beer in conjunction with California's Eel River. And he likes to make use of the winery too, growing hops for some of his brews on his family's land and both ageing and fermenting beers in Taminick Cellars' wine barrels.

ALSO TRY Leader of the Pack IPA
Aussie Terrier IPA | Howling Pale Ale
Hell Hound India Black Ale
Estate Hopped Saison

BREWER'S FOOD MATCH
Confit duck with a rich reduction; chocolate-based desserts

AVAILABILITY
Year-round

BREWERY & CELLAR DOOR LOCATION
339 Booth Road, Taminick, VIC 3675

BREWERY WEBSITE
www.blackdogbrewery.com.au

KING KONG STOUT

CLARE VALLEY BREWING COMPANY

 STOUT   **6.0%**   **6-9°C**   **PINT GLASS**

TASTING NOTES A beer with which Clare Valley Brewing Company hit their straps from the off. It's a bold, big-bodied stout that coats the palate with a welcome, velvety creaminess. Within its luscious black depths, you'll find all manner of treats from the darker end of the beer spectrum: roasted barley, dark chocolate and coffee aromas; burnt treacle and plums, to taste.

THE STORY For a long time, when you saw that a winery had a beer or beers as part of its offering, it was a pretty safe bet that they didn't have a brewery – may not even have been to one – but instead had ordered one off the shelf from a contract facility and stuck their own label and story on it. But in recent years, that has been changing, sometimes with breweries starting up on the site of existing wineries, or wineries adding a brewing wing to their business.

Clare Valley Brewing belongs in the latter category, with a brewery built at Jeanneret Wines in one of South Australia's famed wine regions. The old kit they'd picked up was knocked into shape by SA brewing guru Stephen Nelson and released its first beers, including this fine stout, and a grape cider in 2013. Since then, other beers such as The Fuzz mid-strength and a Mocha Stout have

been added as the growing Clare Valley team has made initial inroads into other markets on the East Coast.

By the start of 2016, they had a new, former Little Creatures brewer overseeing brewing and were hinting at (although not revealing) big plans for the year ahead. These days, they've brought their cellar door back in-house meaning you can add a spot of beer sampling at source on your next visit to Clare.

ALSO TRY Bulls Eye Pale Ale Monkey's Uncle Red Ale

✩

BREWER'S FOOD MATCH
Lamb sausages, beef rib, fruit loaf, dark chocolate

AVAILABILITY
Year-round

BREWERY & CELLAR DOOR LOCATION
22 Jeanneret Road, Sevenhill, SA 5453

BREWERY WEBSITE
www.clarevalleybrewing.com.au

BEST EXTRA STOUT

COOPERS BREWERY

 STOUT   6.3%   8–10°C   **TULIP GLASS OR SNIFTER**

TASTING NOTES Given it was the original brew by Thomas Cooper, has been brewed for more than 160 years and led to the creation of a new style category, perhaps the Sparkling Ale should be here. But the Best Extra Stout remains my pick of Coopers' beers. It's a full-bodied, deeply dark affair (even after slimming down) that offers up an array of milk chocolate, roast coffee, tobacco, dark fruits, molasses and dark cocoa characters.

THE STORY While the beer world watches and, in some cases, frets over the takeover of iconic, much-loved breweries by international behemoths looking to add new brands (and, they hope, associated credibility) to their rosters as tastes change, Adelaide's Coopers family rolls on under the same stewardship. Founded by Thomas Cooper in 1852, his descendants continue to hold key roles in what is the largest (by far) independent Australian brewing company.

A great survivor that struggled through much of the 20th century, sticking (for the most part) to its ale brewing roots while its peers were snapped up only to disappear or go out of business, Coopers now occupies a unique position. To all intents and purposes, it's part of the big boys' world, albeit far smaller than the SABMiller (or maybe AB InBev) -owned

CUB or Kirin-owned Lion, yet retains the affection of craft beer lovers who respect its traditions and, in many cases, would have been weaned off lager by Coopers Pale or Sparkling Ale.

Newish additions to its range – the Thomas Cooper Celebration Ale and Artisan Pilsner – join its fine annual Vintage Ale release in looking to offer something for the craftier drinker, while the announcement that they would brew NYC legend Brooklyn Brewery's Lager for the local market turned heads aplenty in 2015.

ALSO TRY Sparkling Ale | Original Pale Ale Mild | Vintage Ale | Premium Lager

BREWER'S FOOD MATCH
Oysters, pork, beef, soft or hard cheeses, as well as sweet desserts full of apple and cinnamon

AVAILABILITY
Year-round

BREWERY & CELLAR DOOR LOCATION
461 South Road, Regency Park, SA 5010

BREWERY WEBSITE
www.coopers.com.au

SLIGO EXTRA STOUT
FOGHORN BREWHOUSE

 STOUT 8% 5°C PINT SHAKER

TASTING NOTES It took no more than swirling the glass and taking a sniff to know this would be FogHorn's representative. "Ah! That smells like a Sherlock stout!" I thought. It may not mean much to the uninitiated, but if you've had any of the many dark beers he produced at Murray's before starting FogHorn, you know it's a good thing. This trophy winner leaves nothing behind: pronounced earthy hops and dark malts of such depth Jules Verne would be jealous.

THE STORY Having taken up the baton from Murray's original brewer Graeme Mahy, former university history lecturer Shawn Sherlock continued the NSW brewery's arc as one of the most innovative, adventurous and best in Australia. In 2014, he finally set out on his own, founding FogHorn Brewhouse in the heart of his beloved Newcastle alongside American developer James Harvey.

He'd long had his heart set on a brewpub – a venue where he could explore his every beery desire but also have total control over how the beer would reach the customer – and, thanks to James' business network and investment, Shawn has ended up with one of the finest in the country. FogHorn inhabits a large former mechanic's and surfboard shaper's that oozes character from its industrial walls before you even get to the bar.

When you do, you're faced with not only the lineup of nearly 20 taps (most pouring Shawn's beers plus a couple of guests), but also the brewery and fermenters beyond. As he did for his former employer, Shawn has set about creating a dazzling array of beers: subtle Belgian styles, highly aromatic IPAs, beefy stouts and much else besides.

The FogHorn name is a nod to the ships announcing themselves in the port day and night, while many of the beer titles are similarly inspired too, not least the Boganaire IPA for infamous local riches-to-rags billionaire Nathan Tinkler.

ALSO TRY Pivo Bohemian Pilsner Braveheart IPA | Funky Farmhouse Ale

BREWER'S FOOD MATCH
Hickory-smoked, slow-cooked barbecue beef ribs with grilled corn and slaw

AVAILABILITY
Seasonal

BREWERY & CELLAR DOOR LOCATION
218 King Street, Newcastle, NSW 2300

BREWERY WEBSITE
www.foghornbrewhouse.com.au

PHAT MONGREL

FOX HAT

 STOUT **6.5%** **8°C** **TULIP GLASS**

TASTING NOTES One of two fine initial releases from Vale Brewing's spin-off, this is a no-holds-barred stout that throws the kitchen sink into the mix. Accompanying the traditional black and roasted malts creating its black body and typical stout characteristics, is a shedload of piny American hops adding aroma, flavour and no little bitterness. The addition of oatmeal fills out the body and softens the blow at the same time.

THE STORY Under the EXP moniker, Vale Brewing's head brewer Jeff Wright already had occasional license to go a little wild with his recipes. Then, in 2015, after some reshuffles and rebranding of the former McLaren Vale Beer company, he got a whole second brand with which to play around and experiment.

The tittersome, punny Fox Hat Brewing ('Where's the Fox Hat?' etc) got off to a flying start with both launch beers, the metric IPA and this big oatmeal stout, finding favour with drinkers and beer judges in equal measure. The former is a ballsy American-style IPA that crams a mountain of citrusy and piny hops into its 7 per cent ABV body. Here, despite being a stout, there's almost as much in the way of aggressive hopping going on, yet all within the realms of serious drinkability.

The EXP series of occasional out-there releases from Vale continues, but with Fox Hat expect nothing other than envelope nudging.

ALSO TRY metric IPA

☆

BREWER'S FOOD MATCH
Chocolate brownies, crumbly blue cheese

AVAILABILITY
Year-round

BREWERY LOCATION
6 Jay Drive, Willunga, SA 5172

CELLAR DOOR LOCATION
187 McMurtrie Road, McLaren Vale, SA 5171

BREWERY WEBSITE
www.foxhatbrewing.com.au

STOUT

MOO BREW

 STOUT   8.0%   10–12°C   GLASS

TASTING NOTES A beer that, in its various barrel-aged vintages has commanded a price tag of $25 per 330ml bottles and the nickname 'Velvet Sledgehammer' is never going to be a shrinking violet. And it's not, with this annual release long held in high esteem by Aussie beer aficionados. Layer upon layer of chocolate, espresso, dark fruits, liquorice, roasted barley and rich caramel make for a delightfully decadent drop.

THE STORY It's seems a little odd to refer to Moo Brew as part of the MONA empire, given the brewery, like the Moorilla Estate winery that predates it, came before the Museum of Old and New Art. But such has been the success – locally and globally – of David Walsh's outrageous art gallery carved into rock underneath the River Derwent like a 60s Bond bad guy's lair, that that's how it has become.

One of the elder statesmen of the Australian craft beer scene and, for the most part, the only Tasmanian beer outside the big boys (Boag's and Cascade) you'll find with ease on the mainland, Moo Brew specialises in tightly wound beers packaged in sleek, somewhat sensual bottles adorned with artwork by John Kelly.

The core range has something to suit most occasions, from a spicy, European-inspired pilsner and trophy-winning Hefeweizen that sits at the leaner, spicier end of the style, through finely tuned Dark and Pale Ales to the Belgo – an idiosyncratic fruity, spicy, sweet and dry little Belgian-inspired number that's garnered something of a cult following. Their annual wet hop harvest ales featuring hops grown down the road at Bushy Park are also usually bloody fantastic.

ALSO TRY Pilsner | Hefeweizen | Pale Ale
Dark Ale | Belgo | Saison | Harvest Ale

BREWER'S FOOD MATCH
Dark chocolate ganache

AVAILABILITY
Seasonal/special release

BREWERY LOCATION
76A Cove Hill Road, Bridgewater, TAS 7030

CELLAR DOOR LOCATION
Museum of Old and New Art, 655 Main Road, Berriedale, TAS 7011

BREWERY WEBSITE
www.moobrew.com.au

IMPERIAL STOUT

RED HILL BREWERY

 IMPERIAL STOUT **8.0%**  **8°C** **ENGLISH PINT GLASS**

TASTING NOTES Australian drinkers have a wide choice of imperial stouts to pick from these days. A decade ago, the situation was far different, with Red Hill's one of the first. Today, while smaller than many of its peers, it remains one of the finest: a multilayered treat opening with brown sugar, dark fruit and mocha characteristics before turning steadily more roasty and wrapping up with a lingering bitter finish.

THE STORY Inspired by beers and pubs sampled on overseas trips, Karen and Dave Golding decided to jack in corporate careers to open their own brewery complete with venue and hop farm on the Mornington Peninsula. They brewed their first beer in 2005 – just a few months after starting a family – and spent the next decade creating one of Victoria's best loved breweries.

Their beers typically draw inspiration from Europe with a core range of four augmented by a fine range of once-a-year brews that includes this fine imperial stout plus all manner of much sought-after brews, including strong Belgian ales, a Hop Harvest Ale featuring hops from their own farm and, in the past few years, barrel-aged versions of many of them, too.

The brewery is open most weekends and is a great place to visit, tucked under trees on a lush green hillside farm, with special events, such as the Brewer's Secret Stash weekend, seeing them pull out vintage beers, pouring real ale versions of their beers from a hand pump or launching limited release specials.

ALSO TRY Temptation | Scotch Ale Weizenbock | Belgian Blonde | Pilsner The Double Barrel releases

BREWER'S FOOD MATCH
Cashel Irish blue cheese, chocolate

AVAILABILITY
Seasonal: June–July

BREWERY & CELLAR DOOR LOCATION
88 Shoreham Road, Red Hill South, VIC 3937

BREWERY WEBSITE
www.redhillbrewery.com.au

EXTRA STOUT

REHN BIER

 STOUT   6.0%   10-14°C   KELLER GLASS

TASTING NOTES This award-winning beer from tiny Barossa Valley outfit Rehn Bier is an absolute cracker of a stout, comfortably one of the best in Australia. Viscous, almost oily, yet without any lingering cloying finish, it's a gently warming beast of a beer that leans towards sweeter chocolate malts with a touch of coffee sharpness, complemented by a mouthfeel that is rich, full, smooth and long-lasting.

THE STORY I'd never heard of Rehn Bier until brewer Brenton responded to a shout-out for beers when compiling the list for this book's predecessor. With wife Robyn, he runs a tiny operation at their Barossa home, creating traditional, European-inspired brews with a homemade setup, most of which is only available within 100 km of their house, often via the region's farmers' markets.

Having had some bad experiences with a few, similarly homespun 'nano' breweries, the beers were cracked with a little trepidation. All were good, with the Extra Stout being great. It's since gone on to snag a gold medal at the Australian International Beer Awards, while some of its stablemates have fared well at competitions too.

The core range of four is supplemented by occasional limited releases, that have included an even bigger stout as well as a spot of barrel ageing. All are still hand bottled, hand labelled and, in most cases, sold directly to customers by the couple.

ALSO TRY XSB (Extra Special English Bitter) | Tripel | Weizen | Limited releases

---

BREWER'S FOOD MATCH
Slow-cooked red meat and
rich chocolate desserts

AVAILABILITY
Year-round

BREWERY & CELLAR DOOR LOCATION
Gramp Avenue, Angaston, SA 5353
(by appointment only)

BREWERY WEBSITE
www.rehnbier.com.au

SOUTHWARK OLD STOUT

SOUTH AUSTRALIA BREWING COMPANY

 STOUT   7.4%   7–10°C   DIMPLED HANDLE

TASTING NOTES It's reassuring that this past trophy winner has survived – even while other classic beers have been lost to industry consolidation. Light on its feet for a beer at 7.4 per cent ABV, it's a stout with much to discover. Dark brown with a reddish tint and a tan head, it offers up mocha, vanilla and creamy chocolate aromas, flavours dominated by chocolate accompanied by cacao, tar and some saltiness, and a dry, bitter roast sign-off.

THE STORY It may not possess the longevity of some of the beers found in the stable of fellow Adelaide brewer Coopers, but this fine stout from the South Australian Brewing Company, part of the Lion empire since 1993, has legs – both in terms of character and lifespan. Since it was first brewed to a recipe based upon the original London imperial Russian stouts, it's witnessed the rise, fall and rise again of Australia's craft (or boutique, as it once was called) industry as well as much change in the ownership of its brewery.

The beer took out major trophies in the 1980s, 1990s and early 2000s and, despite being no longer available on tap or in longnecks, survives in stubbies. These are packaged with little concern for the evolution of the beer world since the beer was first brewed; indeed, when you spot the beer on a bottleshop shelf you could be forgiven for thinking it's part of a heritage display.

Yet that just adds charm to a beer that, while very much on the fringes of the contemporary Australian beer world – not a key plank of its brewery's plans and not one to cause a buzz among those immersed in the rapidly evolving craft scene – has deservedly garnered something of a cult status.

ALSO TRY N/A

BREWER'S FOOD MATCH
Rich desserts (e.g. chocolate cakes, toffee- or caramel-topped puddings)

AVAILABILITY
Year-round

BREWERY & CELLAR DOOR LOCATION
107 Port Road, Thebarton, SA 5031

VANILLA MILK STOUT

THIRSTY CROW

 VANILLA MILK **5.2%** **8°C** **PINT GLASS**

TASTING NOTES A legend in its lifetime, right from the word go. The first ever batch of this was entered into the country's biggest beer awards a few months after Thirsty Crow opened its doors and promptly snapped up the first of many trophies. It's a beer so luscious it should come with a warning, with lactose creating a smooth creaminess, Madagascan vanilla luring you in and rich chocolate and coffee completing the picture.

THE STORY After learning his trade at breweries in Queensland and New South Wales, Craig Wealands returned to the city where he'd grown up and decided to give its people a brewery to call their own. And, while he did create a couple of beers with tamer local palates in mind, such as the summery Sporting Ale that in 2015 joined the Vanilla Milk Stout as an AIBA trophy winner, he also filled plenty of his taps with far more innovative and adventurous beers – among them a coffee imperial stout, heavily hopped numbers and collaborations with other local breweries.

In early 2016, Thirsty Crow moved from its original colourful brewpub to a new, bigger and better location. There, the same combination of onsite brewery, bar with rotating taps, live music and kitchen serving the frequently crazy pizzas that Craig conceives at home, has been installed. In addition, there's also a hardcore Coffee Bar that showcases Australia's finest roasters and thus allowing its owner to indulge another of his passions without leaving the building.

ALSO TRY Sporting Ale | Red Light 26Fifty Summer Ale | Robust Porter Road to Ruin Imperial Coffee Stout

---

BREWER'S FOOD MATCH
Mocha-chilli mousse

AVAILABILITY
Year-round

BREWERY & CELLAR DOOR LOCATION
153 Fitzmaurice Street, Wagga Wagga, NSW 2650

BREWERY WEBSITE
www.thirstycrow.com.au

VELVET CREAM

WIG & PEN

 STOUT   6.5%   3°C NONIC GLASS

TASTING NOTES A classic among many cult classics from Canberra's semi-mythical Wig & Pen. Velvet Cream is an Irish foreign or export stout, bigger and richer than a straight dry Irish stout, but not reaching imperial levels. It's been tweaked over the years and occasionally appears on hand pump. However you find it, expect to luxuriate in layers of creamy malt characters: bitter roast, coffee, nuts, chocolate, liquorice and a woody bitterness.

THE STORY Many moons ago, during a late night stopover on a bus from Sydney to Melbourne, I popped into an appealing-looking Canberra pub with a giant Norwegian I'd just met. After one delicious pint, he persuaded me we had time for a second. So we did, and missed the bus, resulting in a freeway chase by taxi and a coach full of angry, tired passengers. It was almost a decade later, now no longer a backpacker but an Australian resident, that I realised we'd chanced upon the Wig & Pen Tavern; little wonder we were sucked in...

The brewpub has legendary status among beer aficionados well beyond Australia's shores, for the most part a legacy of Richard Watkins' time there as head brewer before launching BentSpoke. Over a decade and a half, he created a kaleidoscopic array of great beers – real ales, imperial stouts, barrel-aged sours, US-style hoppy ales – and collected two Champion Brewery titles along the way.

For years, rumours swirled that development of Canberra House would force it to close; in the end, owner Lachie McOmish moved it to the nearby ANU, taking the pub frontage and many of the fittings with it. New brewers have kept many of the old beers alive, while allowing the Wig & Pen's spirit of adventure to suffuse their own creations, too.

ALSO TRY Pale Ale | Brewers IPA
Russian Imperial Stout | Sequoia

BREWER'S FOOD MATCH
Huge bowl of wedges

AVAILABILITY
Year-round

BREWERY & CELLAR DOOR LOCATION
William Herbert Place, Canberra, ACT 2601

BREWERY WEBSITE
www.wigandpen.beer

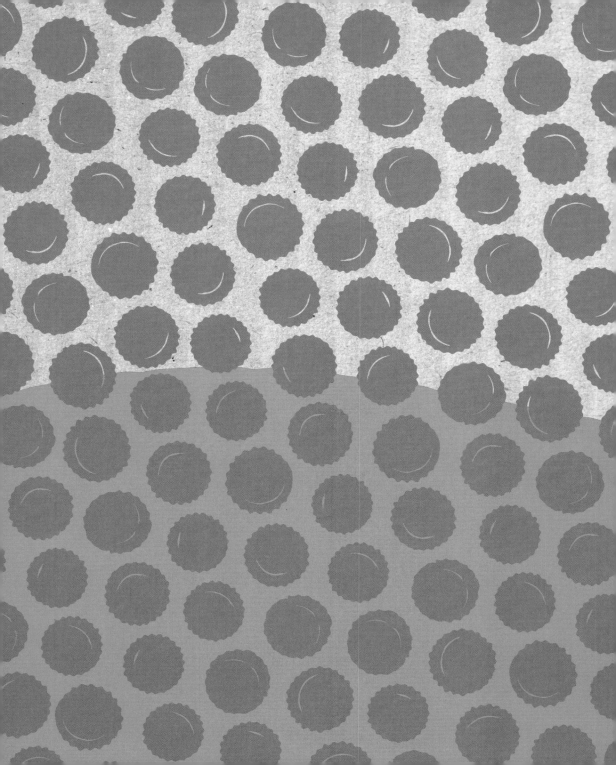

BENTSPOKE BREWING CO

Today's beer landscape in Australia is as colourful as it's ever been. While the most popular styles within the craft beer world are hoppy pale ales, elsewhere experimentation and niche brewing has never been as widespread or innovative.

There are brewers working with barrels for a variety of reasons: those that specialise in Belgian-inspired farmhouse styles; others seeking to take hopping regimes into the stratosphere; others still working to create sour beers by a multitude of methods. There are even some out there who are doing all of the above and more.

Yet, as the sands shift like never before, making this a truly exciting time (as much because, for the most part, standards are improving too), step back in time a decade and you'd have found much of this already happening – in a brewpub in Canberra called the Wig & Pen. There, for over ten years, head brewer Richard Watkins operated as a one-man blue-sky research department.

Visitors to the pub were likely to find everything from genuine cask ales poured from proper beer engines to high-octane imperial stouts, and from hoppy, American-style ales to Belgian-style sours, often created as a blend of three different vintages of beer aged in different barrels. And, aside from the odd keg escaping Canberra to appear at special events, those visitors were the only people who would get to try his beers, beers that saw the Wig & Pen twice take out the Champion Australian Brewery title at the Australian International Beer Awards.

However, you may have noticed that this article is about BentSpoke Brewing Co, not Wig & Pen. That's because in 2014 Richard started up his own brewpub in the capital. With partner (and cider maker) Tracy Margrain at his side, he opened BentSpoke over two floors within a new apartment development in the revitalised Canberra suburb of Braddon. They sold more than 3,000 litres of beer on their opening weekend; by the time the brewery turned one, visitors had made their way through 160,000 litres, all brewed by the pair in the brewhouse on the first floor of the venue.

At the time of writing, some of the more esoteric elements of Richard's time at the Wig & Pen, such as the use of barrels, hadn't carried across to his new venture – little surprise, perhaps, given how frequently he has been brewing to meet demand. Yet, across the venue's 18 taps and hand pumps, he has showcased a veritable smorgasbord of beers: British-style bitters, hoppy American-style ales, faithful recreations of European lagers, spiced dark beers, various farmhouse beers, including one brewed with ancient grain freekeh, beers that have gone well beyond 10 per cent ABV and others fermented with souring yeasts and bacteria.

A 'hopinator' – a glass cylinder through which beer can flow before hitting the tap – allows for the addition of spices, fruits and other ingredients; what's more, Richard was the first brewer to build such an instrument for his bar when at the Wig & Pen and many of those you now find in Australian breweries and bars were built by him.

His beers are showcased within one of the most impressive – and clever – brewery venues in Australia. There's a cycling theme running throughout (hence BentSpoke): tasting paddles are called 'handles' and are made with bike handles; some of the incredible overhead light shades designed by Tracy are made from bike parts; and there are bits of bike decorating the walls, too.

Then there are the tap handles. At the Wig & Pen, one of the regulars, retired cartographer Peter Rogers, used to design and draw the artwork for their decals. Now, he heads to his shed and creates individual tap handles for each BentSpoke beer from hand-carved wood, pieces of metal, salvaged parts of bikes – essentially, whatever it takes to match concept to beer.

Add to that the means by which Richard transfers the liquid from his brewery to the tanks on the ground floor. Take a close look at the bannisters on either side of the stairs and you'll notice that they're actually pipes; looking-glass windows at the top of the stairs allow you to watch the beer as it's being transferred.

Up until 2016, the only way to enjoy BentSpoke beers was to visit the venue itself or find a mate who could and ask them to fill up one of their stylish aluminium growlers and bring it to you. Visiting is still the best way to go about discovering BentSpoke, not least because they do a fine line in food, too. Even that comes a little bent; when I first visited, among the dishes I shared with Richard was a plate of crushed grain-coated lambs' brains.

However, late in 2015, they announced they had secured a second site in the city. This will house a family-friendly venue, a second, larger, production facility and also a canning line, meaning that, for the first time ever, beers from one of the most respected brewers in Australia will finally be packaged for distribution.

As for the Wig & Pen, that moved to a new home at the Australian National University, where young brewers continue to create many of Richard's colourful recipes while keeping his spirit of innovation and adventure alive with new creations of their own.

FRENCH & BELGIAN ALES

FRENCH & BELGIAN ALES

As stated in *150 Great Australian Beers*, it feels somewhat criminal to be lumping all Belgian beers together in one place. It's almost like writing a book on wine and having a separate chapter for every red grape varietal and then one chapter for whites. Yet, this time around, they sit together once more, this time with the addition of French too, as some of the beers within take inspiration from styles with origins in the northern French regions that border Belgium.

The beers that come from this part of Europe, particularly Belgium, encompass many of the most idiosyncratic styles created in beer's millennia-long history. What's more, they are held in the highest of regard in Belgium itself; when the world's greatest beer writer, the late Michael Jackson, recorded an episode on Belgian beer for his classic TV show *Beer Hunter* it was entitled 'The Burgundies of Belgium' in recognition of beer's gilded position there

While Belgian brewers do produce straightforward lagers, including volume shifters like Stella Artois, it is the kaleidoscopic array of fruity, spicy, complex, sour, intense and deeply rewarding ales that originate in Belgium that warrants the admiration of beer aficionados the world over and makes a tour of its classic breweries, some of them found within monasteries, nothing less than a pilgrimage for many. While the grand tour of America's craft breweries and tap-heavy beer bars has become almost a rite of passage for keen Australian beer lovers, I'd suggest a few days in Belgium would prove significantly more rewarding.

The story of Belgian witbiers is covered in the chapter on Wheat Beers (see page 206). Other styles native to the country include Belgian pale and blonde ales, golden ales of varying strength, saisons, dubbels, tripels and quadrupels, plus a range of unique sours: lambics, which when multiple vintages are blended create gueuzes; fruit beers such as Kriek and Framboise that add cherries and raspberries respectively to a base beer; and Flanders Red and Brown ales (or Oud Bruin).

There are entire tracts written about each of these styles, so any summary here can only hope to be the briefest of introductions with which to entice you to explore the region's wonderful and unique heritage. What can be said is that, for the most part, unlike the vast majority of their New World peers, traditional French and Belgian brewers are less interested in showcasing hops than in creating beers of incredible complexity through the use of malt (often in combination with specialty sugars) and a range of idiosyncratic yeasts.

A common thread found through most of these pale ales, golden ales, dubbels, tripels and quadrupels is the fullness of their malt profile and a distinct fruitiness (ranging from raisins and plums to bananas), sometimes enhanced by spicy characteristics, that is obtained from the yeasts used.

Dubbels are potent dark ales typified by characteristics such as chocolate, caramel and dark fruits that are usually around 6–7 per cent ABV. Tripels are lighter in colour, usually stronger in alcohol, and often display citrusy characters alongside peppery spices. Quadrupels, often referred to as Belgian Dark Strong Ales, sit at the top of the chain, regularly greater than 10 per cent in alcohol content and offering incredible depth of flavour, which is again typified by sweet malts, dark fruits and Christmas cake-like spices.

Many of the finest examples are regarded as among the greatest beers on the planet. And many of them are brewed by monks, or at least at breweries operated by or originally built by monasteries. At the time of writing, there are 11 brands that carry the official 'Authentic Trappist Product' label, the majority in Belgium but also two in the Netherlands and one each in Germany, Austria and the United States. They include some of the most iconic names in the world of brewing, such as Chimay, Orval, Westvleteren and Rochefort, although there are other Belgian brewers creating beers of similar styles to the same, occasionally arguably higher, standards too.

When it comes to sours (some of which are listed in the Specialty Beer chapter), you enter another world altogether. At the most basic level, there are two main approaches taken by Belgian brewers. Those creating lambics and gueuzes leave their wort in large, wide, shallow open vats to ferment with wild yeasts native to the area in which the brewery is based. They also pick up bacteria living within the brewery, resulting in uniquely sour ales with characteristics often defined as 'barnyard', 'horse blanket' or 'wet dog'. It is worth noting that brewers of such beers may use hops that are several years old and boil them for up to six hours to ensure that they impart no flavour or aroma upon the finished beer – quite a distinction from most craft brewers.

When it comes to beers such as Flanders Reds and Browns, the process involves creating base beers that are often rich and malty then ageing them within old wooden casks. These casks contain wild bacteria such as *Lactobacillus* and *Pediococcus*, along with wild yeasts such as *Brettanomyces*, which in their own way can add sour, acidic or funky characteristics to the finished beer. More often than not, the brewers will blend various vintages or the contents of different

barrels, often with young, fresh beer, before packaging and releasing their beers. Rodenbach, which is widely available in Australia, is the best known example, its impressive redbrick brewery home to 294 large wooden foudres.

Add saisons and Biere de Garde, farmhouse ales that originate in the Wallonia region of France and Belgium that are typically fruity and spicy (with saisons lighter and zesty, Biere de Gardes stronger and darker), and you have the most wildly varied collection of beers of any country in the world.

In Australia, brewers have attempted to create pretty much all of these styles, with a recent growing interest in sour styles. While some brewers inoculate beers with purchased 'wild' yeast strains and bacteria (something of an oxymoron), there are a few going to extraordinary lengths. Two Metre Tall has spent a decade in the Derwent Valley learning – often the hard way – how to capture the essence of its farm in truly unique beers; La Sirène has constructed a coolship within a factory building by Darebin Creek in Melbourne to capture indigenous airborne yeasts and bacteria with which to ferment its beers; Boatrocker Brewery opened a dedicated Barrel Room in 2015 that is home to around 300 barrels, most of which are intended to create Australia's largest sour beer program; and White Rabbit is amassing several hundred of its own barrels in Geelong.

In this chapter, you will find some fine interpretations of many of the styles listed above. There are also some New World twists upon the styles, usually involving the addition of huge amounts of hops, while you will find many more small batch Belgian beers released as draught-only by local brewers.

———— *A DOZEN MORE TO TRY* ————

THE LITTLE BREWING COMPANY
Mad Abbot range

BOATROCKER BREWERY
They have an evolving range of Belgian-inspired styles, including rare, blended beers

RED HILL BREWERY
Temptation

BRIDGE ROAD BREWERS
Chevalier Saison and India Saison (a collaboration with Nogne Ø)

MOO BREW
Belgo

BENTSPOKE BREWING
PSI Imperial Saison

7 CENT BREWING
B4 Belgian Strong Dark Ale

HOLGATE BREWHOUSE
Double Trouble

SEVEN SHEDS
Elephant's Trunk

HARGREAVES HILL
AD (Abbey Dubbel)

LOBETHAL BIERHAUS
Little Devil

MORRISON BREWERY
Saison

SAISON D'HÉRÉTIQUE

AUSTRALIAN BREWERY

 SAISON   6.2%   ❄ 6°C   TULIP GLASS

TASTING NOTES This fine saison first appeared as a one-off in a fine looking can, bearing medieval script and Joan of Arc. It's a bold take on the style: herbaceous and spicy, with green peppercorn and lemon citrus combining with malt sweetness and a dry finish under a towering, fluffy white head. It collected a gold medal at the country's toughest beer competition and, soon after, to my delight, was added to the Australian's expanded core range.

THE STORY Located in the decidedly un-crafty northwestern Sydney suburb of Rouse Hill, and with a large sports bar as part of its brewery venue, the Australian Brewery isn't exactly typical of a modern Australian microbrewery (whatever 'typical' might mean). Yet, while head brewer Neal Cameron ensures that there are some easily quaffed drops on tap for the local market, the brewery has been something of a pioneer.

In 2012, it became the first Australian microbrewery to install a canning line, and it has been busy exploring overseas markets as diverse as India, Canada and Abu Dhabi since. The core range is made up of tightly wound beers of the sort you'd expect from an experienced beer judge, while they're embellished by frequently appealing one-offs too.

Their entry here was originally going to be for The Pilsner, a lager we've long rated one of the best in Australia – so good Brendan Varis from Feral agreed to make an imperial version with Neal (called Stormtrooper, *Star Wars* fans). Then this delicious saison made the leap from one-off to staple and snatched The Pilsner's guernsey at the last moment.

ALSO TRY The Pilsner | Pale Ale
Extra Hoppy Ale | All Star Session IPA

BREWER'S FOOD MATCH
Grilled Roquefort on sourdough toast

AVAILABILITY
Year-round

BREWERY & CELLAR DOOR LOCATION
350 Annangrove Road, Rouse Hill, NSW 2155

BREWERY WEBSITE
www.australianbrewery.com.au

BELGIAN BOMBSHELL

BANDICOOT BREWING

 ALE   **6%**   **4–8°C**   **TULIP GLASS OR GOBLET**

TASTING NOTES It may not be to everyone's tastes, but Bandicoot's Belgian Bombshell certainly took my fancy when we found it pouring on tap at the Mill in the brewery's hometown of Echuca. The creamy, copper coloured beer could almost act as a dessert beer, with a touch of banana on the nose from the fruity Belgian yeast and flavours that are dominated by rich honey and toffee biscuit flavours.

THE STORY Bandicoot Brewing is the work of successful home brewer Tracey Green and her husband Bruce, established in a warehouse in Echuca while the pair of them continued with their day jobs. They first caught the eye with their decision to package their beers into aluminium bottles (predominantly for protective and environmental reasons) although have since switched to glass to allow them to brew and package a wider variety of beers.

They've set up Echuca's first genuine brewery since the very start of the 20th century yet, aside from a gentle blonde ale, there's been little holding back in terms of flavour for any unprepared local palates. Tracey's pale and dark ales are both as bold as this Belgian.

That this can pose challenges in a region away from Australia's craft beer heartlands can be found in the brewery itself. At a beer festival, a woman approached Bruce at their brewery's stall and asked what the Belgian Bombshell, the one beer his wife makes that he doesn't enjoy, was like.

"Fucking awful," he replied, as Tracey shook her head. With timing suited to an Ealing farce, another woman walked up and asked if she could hand over extra tokens in return for a large glass of the Bombshell as it was her favourite of all beers at the festival. Proof that everyone's tastes are different and that, with Bandicoot, there's a straight-up country honesty: what you see is what you get.

ALSO TRY Rusty Pale Ale | After Dark Ale Barbed Wire Blonde

BREWER'S FOOD MATCH
Sausages, wild game birds, schnitzel, saltimbocca, or prosciutto with ripe brie

AVAILABILITY
Year-round

BREWERY & CELLAR DOOR LOCATION
Factory 2B, 100 Northern Highway, Echuca, VIC 3564

BREWERY WEBSITE
www.bandicootbrewing.com.au

BON CHIENS

BEARD AND BRAU

 FARMHOUSE ALE   7.9%   ❄ 8°C   TULIP GLASS

TASTING NOTES The 'champagne' beer of Beard and Brau's range, Bon Chiens is a farmhouse ale from the now farmhouse brewers. Brewed with a hybrid champagne yeast as well as a special candied sugar made with oranges, orange peel and honey, its dense head tops off a cloudy orange beer that's all about mouth-filling honeyed malts, heaps of floral and citrus aromas and soft, fruity flavours.

THE STORY My first encounter with Beard and Brau was when they were based in Adelaide. There, Chris 'Fish' Herring, who founded the brewery with partner Tanya Harlow in 2008, was good enough to sweat in sympathy as he showed me around the warehouse and shared beers in temperatures in excess of 40°C.

A few months later, the warehouse brewery was no more as the pair (and the Schnauzers after which their brewery and many of their beers are named) headed to Queensland. At their new home in Tamborine, they're creating an environmentally conscious farmhouse brewery inspired by the traditional farmhouse breweries found in parts of France and Belgium.

What this means in practice is making a focus of local ingredients, capturing their own water with which to brew (then using the waste water to spray the local pasture) and looking to minimise impact on their land. Longstanding beers in their lineup, such as Golden Paw, Red Tail and Black Snout, have thus been joined by specials featuring locally harvested ingredients, including elderflower, mulberries and even nettles.

ALSO TRY Golden Paw | Red Tail
Black Snout

☆

BREWER'S FOOD MATCH
Soft cheeses

AVAILABILITY
Year-round

BREWERY LOCATION
Tamborine, QLD

BREWERY WEBSITE
www.beardandbrau.com.au

BEACH HOUSE SAISON

BLACK HOPS

 SAISON   **4.8%**   **4°C**    **TULIP GLASS**

TASTING NOTES At the time of writing, the only Black Hops beer available to sample in bottles was the Beach House. To borrow from the old Lilt soft drink ads in the UK, it's a 'totally tropical taste' – appropriate for their Gold Coast location. Tagged an 'Australian saison' it piles heaps of fruit – pineapple, lime, lemon curd – into its lively, pale yellow body, with a touch of soft spice to taste and a drying finish.

THE STORY For a brewing company so young and small, Black Hops sure displayed a mastery of capturing people's attention from the off. Their first release was an Eggnog Stout that caused a buzz around Brisbane's beer scene and they've since, among other things, hooked up with the makers of one of the world's biggest computer games, Call of Duty, to brew an official beer for its Australian release, the 'Black Pale Ale', Black Hops III.

Formed by three home-brewing mates, one of whom was already brewing at Fortitude when they launched in 2014, they built a reputation with a series of beers brewed at the likes of Beard and Brau and a smart online presence. They documented every step of their journey via a blog, going into great detail about everything from how they brew their beer to how they raised money to get things rolling.

By the time you read this, Dan and partners Eddie Oldfield and Michael McGovern should have opened their own brewery on the Gold Coast, one that they invited beer lovers to be part of: a successful Pozible campaign was the final piece in the jigsaw, raising $10,000 to help them bottle beers such as this saison.

ALSO TRY   Gold Coast Pale Ale | 30 Cal Eggnog Stout | Code Red

BREWER'S FOOD MATCH
Eating's cheating! (Fish and chips at the beach.)

AVAILABILITY
Year-round

BREWERY & CELLAR DOOR LOCATION
15 Gardenia Grove, Burleigh Heads, QLD 4220

BREWERY WEBSITE
www.blackhops.com.au

SAISON GRENADE

CROFT BREWING

 SAISON 4.3% 4-8°C **TULIP GLASS OR CHAMPAGNE FLUTE**

TASTING NOTES Of all the beers to launch a business with, there would be few guidebooks encouraging a brewer to opt for a pink one brewed with pomegranate and hibiscus flowers. Yet that's how Gavin Croft took his first steps from home to pro brewer and what a delightful beer it is, too. A soft, floral delicate twist on the French/Belgian saison style, you'll find some delicate berry flavours in a beer that's refreshingly, gently tart.

THE STORY When first notified that another brewer was set to release beers in Brisbane, Gavin was described as a 'man about town' – someone everyone on the beer scene knew and loved. Indeed, by the time he released the first Croft Brewing beer, this saison brewed, according to the label, not just with water, malt, hops, yeast, hibiscus and pomegranate but also 'love, of course', he had brewed or spent time at multiple breweries across South East Queensland and further afield, honing his knowledge and making friends along the way.

It's a habit that's proved useful as the business has grown since 2014: without a brewery of his own, he's been reliant on others allowing him to use their equipment. Initially this was at All Inn Brewing, Bacchus, and Beard and Brau, but most often he's brewed at Newstead alongside head brewer Mark Howes. There between them they've knocked out a series of collaborations, most recently a series of kettle soured beers named after iconically druggy books or movies.

It's not just the beers – Belgian styles, fruit sours, a smoked lager – that are colourful either. They have all come with vivid labels featuring an array of comic book-style characters, hinting at the man about town behind the beer's broader interests; interests that have seen him host comedy and film nights around Brisbane, too.

ALSO TRY Wolf Scratch Pale Ale Light Stalker | Golden IPA All manner of collaborations

BREWER'S FOOD MATCH
Grilled or fried seafood canapes, or mild cheese; haloumi, pomegranate and rocket salad, sprinkled with walnuts and dressed with a sweet and sour vinaigrette

AVAILABILITY
Year-round in South East Queensland

BREWERY LOCATION
'Gypsy' brewers

BREWERY WEBSITE
www.facebook.com/CroftBrewing

SAISON

EXIT BREWING

 SAISON 6.2% 10°C SAISON DUPONT GLASS

TASTING NOTES The first and sixth releases in Exit's numbered and stylishly packaged releases – #001 and #006, to be precise – were both saisons and damn fine ones, too. The second version refined their eye-catching debut, making it leaner but no less enticing, switching hops but still creating a spicy, peppery, dry and tart drop with a touch of lemon and citrus as well as hint of the barnyard.

THE STORY While they grew up not far from each other in Melbourne, it was while working (or, mostly working) on the other side of the planet that Fraser 'Frase' Rettie and Craig 'Grum' Knight discovered the joys of great beer and brewing. The former had moved to the UK to work on major IT projects; the latter headed over later, visiting family at first and then also working in IT.

A trip to Belgium opened their eyes to what they'd been missing out on within Australia's predominantly mono-beer culture (hence launching with a beer inspired by Belgium) and soon afterwards they were home brewing. Various beer-themed trips followed as they sought further inspiration while investing in a swish home-brew kit that they later brought back to Australia (after Frase lived in Belgium for three months to soak up yet more inspiration) and used for tiny batch

releases even after starting to 'gypsy' brew, initially with Cavalier in Melbourne's west, then at KAIJU!'s Dandenong site.

Two of the most amiable chaps in what's an amiable business, their brews have often leaned towards those heavy in American hops but also taking in stouts smoky and sweet, rich ales and even a gluten-reduced beer, too. Throughout, they've maintained a consistency that should stand them in good stead as they attempt to live up to their brewery name: Ex-IT.

They've now added a core range too. At the time of going to print, this consisted of a punchy IPA and the delicious Amber; fingers crossed they're joined by a saison on a permanent basis.

ALSO TRY IPA | Amber | Milk Stout

BREWER'S FOOD MATCH
Thai, Indian or seafood

AVAILABILITY
Year-round

BREWERY LOCATION
Dandenong South, VIC

BREWERY WEBSITE
www.exitbrewing.com

SAISON

LA SIRÈNE

 SAISON   6.0%   4–6°C   **WIDE-BRIMMED GLASS**

TASTING NOTES If given the choice, chances are I'd plump for La Sirène's Wild Saison – a version that's been aged with Brettanomyces to add further complexity. But La Sirène's straight Saison is itself a wonder and more readily available. Arguably the best of its kind in Australia, it looks fantastic: a glowing, cloudy orange topped with steepling foam that ticks all the boxes: floral, fruity, spicy, sweet, dry and tart. A subtly complex delight.

THE STORY While the majority of Australian brewers and their beers focus most keenly on what they can create with combinations of malt and hops, La Sirène is one of the few that has an unbridled passion for exploring the power of certain yeasts in beer.

Originating as a joint venture between two mates who'd met studying winemaking only to discover a mutual affection for the beers of Belgium, in particular fruity, spicy farmhouse styles, it was as much hobby as business. Brewing consultant Costa Nikias and microbiologist James Brown sourced a saison yeast from a family brewery in Europe, transported it to Australia and, at the second attempt, successfully cultured it up into viable form in the latter's university lab. They used it to create this fine Saison followed by a number of variants on the French/Belgian farmhouse ale style.

Now run by Costa and wife Eva, La Sirène has its own brewery in a factory in inner Melbourne that used to build tanks and has continued to explore the world of fascinating and funky beers. There have been barrel-aged fruit sours, the hugely popular (and hugely rich) Praline Belgian stout featuring hazelnuts, cacao and vanilla and, as of 2016, they were installing a coolship in a shed that they continue to fill with more and more barrels; it's a wide, flat, open 'tray' capable of holding 3,000 litres of wort that is open to the elements to be fermented by whatever is in the air of Darebin Creek.

ALSO TRY Farmhouse Red | Fleur Folie Wild Saison | Praline | Imperial Praline

BREWER'S FOOD MATCH
Enjoy with both white and red meats, full-flavoured seafood, cheese and charcuterie

AVAILABILITY
Year-round

BREWERY LOCATION
Alphington, VIC

BREWERY WEBSITE
www.lasirene.com.au

UNCOMMON CLOUD SAISON

LITTLE BANG BREWING

 SAISON   7.1%   5°C   **RED WINE TULIP GLASS**

TASTING NOTES The first trio of beers to appear from Little Bang Brewing – this hoppy saison plus a hoppy lager and a big American barley wine – showed they weren't planning to pussyfoot around. They declare the Uncommon Cloud 'whimsical' as it tends to fluctuate a little from batch to batch, but you can expect to find the saison style's typically complex fruity, spicy, sweet and dry flavours topped off with a waft of New World hops.

THE STORY At the time of writing, the hirsute duo behind Adelaide's Little Bang Brewing were well on the way to making their bang a little bigger. They started out home brewing before building a quirky 500-litre brewery in a suburban shed, entering the commercial world and doing it successfully enough to commit to brewing full time and upscaling once more.

They are Ryan Davidson and Filip Kemp, self-confessed geeks who met making computer games before the local gaming industry collapsed and they had to look elsewhere for work. Rather handily, given their blossoming love for craft beer and the process of making it themselves, the former started selling beer, the latter trained as a refrigeration mechanic.

Like many in the contemporary craft beer world, their ethos centres around creating typically off-centre beers, with

the results winning them a loyal and growing band of followers in their home state. As they grow into their larger home, expect to see that fan base, like many of their peers in SA's burgeoning brewing industry, spread beyond state lines.

ALSO TRY Icon Hoppy Lager
Galactopus Barley Wine
Beard Fiction Pale Ale

BREWER'S FOOD MATCH
Pickled herring with mustard sauce

AVAILABILITY
Year-round

BREWERY & CELLAR DOOR LOCATION
8A Union Street, Stepney, SA 5069

BREWERY WEBSITE
www.littlebang.com.au

BREAKING THE CARDINAL RULE

THE LITTLE BREWING COMPANY

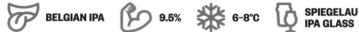 BELGIAN IPA   9.5%   6–8°C   SPIEGELAU IPA GLASS

TASTING NOTES A beer that is a hybrid of sorts of two other Little Brewing beers – its Belgian-style Mad Abbot Tripel and an IPA – combining the fruity, spicy nature of the former with the heavy hopping regime of the latter. It's a microcosm of head brewer Warwick Little's world and one that delivers grapefruit and citrus hop characters alongside spicy, clove-like phenolics from the Belgian yeast.

THE STORY The fate of Little Brewing was one I could never quite fathom. Here was a brewery that consistently made some of the best and most distinctive beers in Australia yet was lagging behind many breweries of lesser quality both in terms of sales and beer geek respect. As far as I could, in my own little way, I'd try to plug their beers whenever possible, hoping that every nudge would help.

Thus, it was with great relief that in one of my many chats with co-owner (and former winemaker, paramedic and scientist) Warwick Little in 2015 he revealed the worm was finally turning and, despite expanding, they could barely meet demand; overnight success for him and marketer-wife Kylie a mere nine years into their brewing dream...

For those unaware of the Port Macquarie brewery, they deliver on three fronts: there's the Wicked Elf range of traditional beers (pale, witbier, pilsner, etc); the Mad Abbot banner for Warwick's fine Belgian-style ales; and most recently the line that includes Breaking The Cardinal Rule. These comically titled beers are big, bold but balanced, including a few great IPAs that have perhaps done most to win over the beer crowd. Often names are inspired by Warwick, including Fastidious Bastard and Death Between The Tanks, which is how Kylie expects to find the workaholic one day.

ALSO TRY Wicked Elf Pale, Porter and Pilsner | Mad Abbot Dubbel, Tripel and Christmas Ale | Death Between The Tanks Double IPA | Fastidious Bastard IPA

BREWER'S FOOD MATCH
Duck tortelli with pomegranate and coriander

AVAILABILITY
Special release

BREWERY & CELLAR DOOR LOCATION
58 Uralla Road, Port Macquarie, NSW 2444

BREWERY WEBSITE
www.thelittlebrewingcompany.com.au

GRAND CRU

MURRAY'S

 **BELGIAN ALE**   **8.8%**   **8°C**   **STEMMED CHALICE**

TASTING NOTES Murray's must have made one of the greatest numbers of beers over its decade in business. Many have been one-offs, rebranded or short-lived. But the Grand Cru has been around since the early days and remains one of Australia's finest Belgian-inspired ales, a soft and full-bodied strong, pale golden ale featuring honeyed malts, fruity esters and a touch of spiciness.

THE STORY One of the most creative and innovative breweries in Australia – both inside and outside the bottle thanks to ever-evolving and eye-catching branding – Murray's has produced beers in pretty much every form imaginable. It started out when property developer Murray Howe decided to buy the Pub With No Beer in Taylor's Arms and not only give it beer but also its own brewery. Thus sprung up a tiny brewery that from day one began brewing bolshy beers as far from most Australian's tastes at the time as Taylor's Arms was from any significant population.

Among them were a number of Australian firsts as well as several that have gone on to become Australian cult classics, including this Grand Cru plus trailblazing double IPA Icon, no holds barred imperial stouts such as Heart of Darkness and Wild Thing, and annual barrel-aged barley wines.

The first brewer was Kiwi Graeme Mahy, who helped train up Shawn Sherlock (now at FogHorn Brewhouse, which is also listed in this book, see page 177) before heading back to his native New Zealand to brew under the 666 banner while also consulting and judging worldwide. When Shawn left in 2014, he was enticed back to a far larger brewery than he'd left and has since introduced a wealth of new beers and overseen yet more expansion at the current Port Stephens site.

ALSO TRY Angry Man Pale and Brown Fred IPA | Rudeboy Pilsner | Icon 2 IPA Wild Thing Imperial Stout Anniversary Ale

BREWER'S FOOD MATCH
Wild game, strong oily fish such as salmon, or strong cheese

AVAILABILITY
Year-round

BREWERY & CELLAR DOOR LOCATION
3443 Nelson Bay Road, Bobs Farm, NSW 2316

BREWERY WEBSITE
www.murraysbrewingco.com.au

SAISON DUVAL

NAPOLEONE BREWERY AND CIDERHOUSE

 **SAISON**   **5.7%**   **7°C**   **TULIP GLASS**

TASTING NOTES My first experience of this beer from the Yarra Valley brewery wasn't too memorable; the beer was pleasant enough, but lacked subtlety and complexity. Yet brewer Ben Waymouth has proved a quick learner on his new kit, with Napoleone's range improving fast, not least this saison, which now boasts a prominent peppery and zesty aroma, a full, softly spicy body and a tart, dry finish.

THE STORY In launching Napoleone Brewers late in 2014, the family that first started growing apples in the Yarra Valley back in the late 1940s added a third boozy bow to their string. The brewery joined Napoleone Cider and Punt Road Wines, based next door on the family's land, right in the heart of the popular tourist region.

They recruited young brewer Ben Waymouth, who'd been plying his trade at gluten-free specialists O'Brien, and gave him pretty much free rein to create what he wanted. What that meant was a mainly European and old school approach to brewing, with Ben a brewer who favours the subtle complexities of malt, Old World hops and yeast to the bolder styles of the contemporary, US-inspired craft beer world. That said, his bosses insisted he brew an American-style pale ale and the beer went on to garner Napoleone their first ever gold medal in competition.

The brewery (and cidery) is housed in a stunning building, constructed from the bones of an 1860s dairy, from which you can enjoy genuinely panoramic views across the Yarra Valley. Ben has already embarked on many collaborations with local breweries and even shared toys with the Punt Road winemakers, who have supplied the barrels in which he always has an experiment or three brewing.

ALSO TRY ESB | Breakneck Porter American Pale Ale | Rauchbier

BREWER'S FOOD MATCH
D'Affinois cheese, or double- or triple-cream brie. Anything that is delicious and will run off the plate...

AVAILABILITY
Year-round

BREWERY & CELLAR DOOR LOCATION
12 St Huberts Rd, Coldstream, VIC 3770

BREWERY WEBSITE
www.napoleone.com.au

DARK FARMHOUSE

NEW ENGLAND

 **DARK FARMHOUSE ALE**   **5.5%**   **10°C**   **WIDE TULIP GLASS**

TASTING NOTES   They have a few less than common quirks at New England brewery, including their 'Hop Cannon' for dry hopping and four open fermenters. The Dark Farmhouse makes use of the latter and is what they call a 'winter saison', thus far darker than most saisons brewed locally. It combines the chocolate and dark caramel characters of a porter with a rising tide of fruity esters in what's a hearty, full-bodied beer.

THE STORY   New England opened in 2013 with a mission to bring locally brewed beer back to the agricultural region around its hometown of Uralla, located on the Northern Tablelands on the road connecting Armidale and Tamworth. Built inside a former woolshed and with a flying ram forming its logo, there's little doubt that its allegiances lie within its rural NSW community – even if word has spread and you'll find its beers in the more discerning beer bars and bottleshops of the wider East Coast.

Operating on gear bought from Bridge Road in Beechworth when the Victorians expanded, and with a brewer who spent time at sour- and wild-beer specialists Jolly Pumpkin in the States, they're a little more adventurous than some Aussie brewing outposts. They do a fine line in hopped-up ales, produce genuine English-style real ales and are happy to experiment with unusual ingredients too; even their very quaffable golden ale comes packing a fruity Belgian yeast.

There's a tight policy on freshness too: any beer not sold in three months is dumped, other than those that are suitable for sticking around a bit longer. And the best place to get them as fresh as possible is by heading to the cellar door itself. There you'll find a broad range of regulars and seasonals and locally made cheese and jerky to accompany it.

ALSO TRY   New Englander Golden Ale New Englander Hop Cannon IPA New Englander Brown Ale New Englander Pale Ale

BREWER'S FOOD MATCH
Enchiladas in a spicy adobo sauce

AVAILABILITY
Seasonal: winter

BREWERY & CELLAR DOOR LOCATION
19 Bridge Street, Uralla, NSW 2358

BREWERY WEBSITE
www.newenglandbrewing.com.au

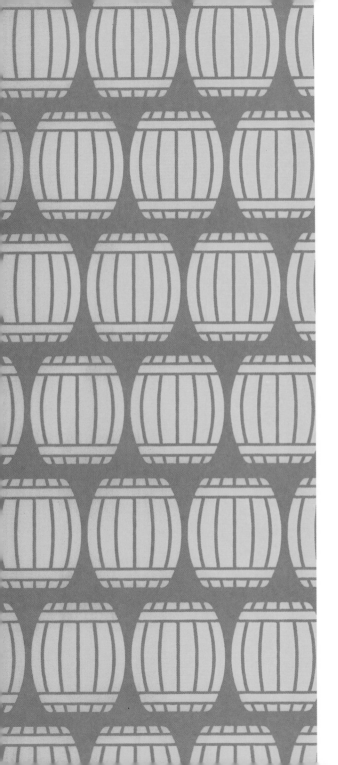

BOATROCKER BREWERY

It's been one of the many great pleasures of my time immersed in the Australian craft beer scene to have enjoyed the Boatrocker journey pretty much from day one. I recall trying the brewery's very first beer, Alpha Queen, while sprawled on cushions in the front window of Grumpy's Green in Fitzroy; enjoying its bold combination of English malts and New World hops that together created a beer with more character than most American-style pale ales of the period.

Then, after noticing that the beer was contract-brewed at a time when the practice was largely looked down upon – the result, in part, of some unscrupulous operators with no care for quality or ingredients, paying for beer that they would try to sell with little more than a marketing concept – it was refreshing to see that Boatrocker's founders, Matt and Andrea Houghton, were totally upfront about their setup while others in the same situation tried to obfuscate.

I later brought Matt in to be part of the tiny team that launched Good Beer Week in 2011 (for the rather prosaic reason that I knew he'd built his own website and we needed one on the cheap – i.e. free – for the festival) and have since enjoyed bouncing ideas around with him (or, perhaps more accurately, bemoaning elements of the industry that we feel could be better and trying to find solutions). Boatrocker in nature as much as name, Matt's proved to be an outspoken, often spikily so, addition to Australia's beer industry, with his opinions intended to shake things up as much as some of his more experimental beers.

For the first few years of the brewing company's life, there would have been little to prepare those who didn't know Matt for what was to come. As he and Andrea built their brand and saved up for their own brewery, the beers were well made examples of relatively common or garden styles: in addition to the Alpha Queen came gold medal-winning German pilsner Hoppbier, a fruity summer ale called SMASH, and Hop Bomb IPA. But once their brewery – picked up from a venture that never got off the ground in Tasmania – was in place in Melbourne's southeastern suburb of Braeside, the true colours began to show.

Matt had long been an obsessive fan of beers from Belgium, once trying to culture up yeast from an imported bottle and making multiple tours of the country, writing about one of them for my Crafty Pint website. Thus, when he had his own toys to play with, it was to Belgium that he looked.

The very first brew that went through the system was a statement of intent. The hoppy wort went straight into wine barrels he'd bought from Yering Station and there the liquid sat for two and a half years, naturally souring and taking on all manner of funky, oaky characters. It was the start of what he hopes will become Australia's largest sour beer program. Some of the unblended, uncarbonated beer was bottled and released late in 2015 as Brambic, short for Braeside lambic, in recognition that this was Boatrocker's tribute to the idiosyncratic beers from the Lembeek region of Belgium.

The beer was one of a number of special releases to leave the brewery at that time as it was then that Matt opened the giant, homemade barn doors of an Australian first: Boatrocker's dedicated Barrel Room and bar. Across the road from the brewery, a second warehouse has been lined with racks of barrels and puncheons. Some have come from wineries, others from local distilleries and a number from American bourbon makers; the aim is to have more than 300 filled with around 70,000 litres of beer that will be released either as they are or blended between barrels and with fresh beers. In the middle is a bar decorated with pink flamingoes serviced by 15 taps protruding from the outer wall of a cool room.

While Matt's Belgian obsession has been sated in numerous ways – saisons straight and soured; barrel-aged strong ales; the aforementioned lambic-style beers and so on – the experimentation at Boatrocker hasn't been limited to that part of the world. Indeed, the beer the brewery has become best known for in beer geek circles is Ramjet, a luscious whisky barrel-aged imperial stout that is featured elsewhere in this book (see page 222).

Boatrocker has also released a series of German-inspired Berliner Weisse-style sours, often showcasing different fruits, plus strong ales and barrel-aged barley wines. At the same time, the core range remains in place to do the unit-shifting with SMASH now part of second 'sub brand' Big Love and called Suburban Pale.

The introduction of the Big Love brand followed the other significant moment for Boatrocker in 2015. A mutual friend brought together Matt and the Made By HAND team formed by four of the men who had started Little Creatures. They initially met late in 2014, when Matt took along bottles of all of his beers for them to sample. A few months later, Howard Cearns, Adrian Fini, Nic Trimboli and David Martin took a 33 per cent share in Boatrocker, enabling, among other things, the development of the Barrel Room project to accelerate.

The foursome's track record suggests they tend to back winners and Boatrocker's story to date suggests Matt and Andrea's little creature will prove to be yet another.

WHEAT
BEERS

WHEAT BEERS

Wheat, both in malted and unmalted form, is used in a wide variety of beers. It can be used in beers such as golden ales to add body or improve head retention.

When talking about wheat beers as a category, however, it is generally understood to mean styles also referred to as 'white' beers that are characterised by the aromas and flavours derived from their yeasts. The two main families originate in Germany and Belgium.

In Germany, these weissbiers come in a number of forms, with the most common being the cloudy Hefeweizen (literally translated as 'yeast wheat') the bright, filtered Kristalweizen, the dark Dunkelweizen ('dark wheat') and stronger, maltier variants called Weizenbock (literally 'wheat strong').

The unique yeast strains found in these beers, most famously those belonging to the world's oldest existing brewery, Weihenstephan, create distinctive fruity and spicy characters. These are usually described as banana, clove and even bubblegum. The beers also feature a high proportion of wheat malt in the grain bill, normally 50 per cent. Hop influence is barely noticeable, with these beers low in bitterness, too.

Belgian witbiers, which means simply 'white beers', feature yeast strains that also create fruity, spicy and herbal aromas and flavours, but leaning more towards citrus in terms of fruit and peppery spices. They traditionally feature the use of adjuncts within the brewing process too, commonly fruit and spice. Most common are ground coriander and citrus peel, although it is not unusual to find the likes of cardamom, star anise, pepper, cinnamon and others used in witbiers. Again, there is usually up to 50 per cent wheat within the grain bill and hop presence is mild.

In the case of both German and Belgian styles, expect sweet malt flavours alongside those fruity, spicy characteristics and also a refreshingly dry and tart finish.

With their light, fruity and refreshing nature, in many countries they are regarded as great warm weather beers. Certainly, that is the case in Australia with brewers often releasing witbiers and Hefeweizen as spring or summer seasonals. There are a number of good examples brewed here, and at one stage it appeared that almost every new microbrewery, especially in WA, would include one or the other as part of their core range.

You can also find a handful of beers categorised as American wheat beers. These use more neutral yeast strains – in other words, yeasts that give off little in the way of fruity or spicy characters as by-products during fermentation –

but still use high proportions of wheat, usually in combination with copious amounts of New World hops. The Wayfarer USA included overleaf is one such example, but there are several beers in the Session Beers chapter (see page 48) that also contain significant percentages of wheat yet are tagged golden or summer ales.

There are also New World twists on other traditional wheat beer styles, such as highly hopped, higher alcohol witbiers or Weizenbock. For example, in the ongoing hunt to discover new territories, the past few years have seen a number of releases, usually to mark special occasions or the result of collaborations between different breweries, tagged as Hopfenweizenbock ('hops wheat strong'); the head brewer of Weihenstephan even created one especially for the Australian market to coincide with his visit to the country in 2014, using new Australian hop varieties to add a tropical nuance to one of his brewery's classic beers.

A DOZEN MORE TO TRY

BURLEIGH BREWING	**MOO BREW**
Hef	Hefeweizen
GOODIESON BREWERY	**WHITE RABBIT**
Wheat Beer	White Ale
THE LITTLE BREWING COMPANY	**REDOAK**
Wicked Elf Witbier	Weizen Doppelbock
FERAL BREWING	**LA SIRÈNE**
White	Florette
RED HILL BREWERY	**3 RAVENS BREWERY**
Weizenbock	White
PRICKLY MOSES	**MATILDA BAY**
ChainSAW	Redback Original

DOCTOR'S ORDERS BREWING

 WITBIER   7.5%   6°C   **SPIEGELAU STEMMED PILSNER GLASS**

TASTING NOTES As Doctor's Orders beers goes, the Zephyr is at the saner end of the spectrum. No squid ink, no salt, no barrel action, no double-figure alcohol content. For all that, it's possibly his finest: a beefed-up take on Belgian witbiers (typically very pale and cloudy, softly spicy, citrusy ales) that uses coriander, and lemon myrtle instead of citrus peel and packs plenty of citrusy, softly spicy goodness into its creamy body.

THE STORY The most commonly used term for brewery-less brewers who use others' equipment is a 'gypsy' brewer. And the most commonly used term for two brewers working together is a collaboration. However, Darren Robinson of Doctor's Orders prefers to use 'cuckoo' for the former (as he's taking over someone's nest to lay his beery eggs), and when he collaborates at Adelaide's Wheaty brewpub (which he does often), they use the phrase 'spooning', which originates from New Zealand's Yeastie Boys.

All of which is a rather longwinded way of saying that Darren is a spooning cuckoo, a term that seems suitably off-the-wall for one of Australia's more idiosyncratic brewers. A fanatical home brewer who has taken many of his ideas into the public realm, often as Australian firsts of a particular beer style.

He's brewed a German-style sour with squid ink, created a beer designed to be the mixer with gin and placed many a beer within oak. He's also collaborated with brewers big and small here and overseas and, as of 2014, started packaging his beers in eye-catching bottles so that more people could sample a little of what the doctor ordered.

ALSO TRY Prescription 12 | Plasma Iron Lung

BREWER'S FOOD MATCH
Snapper, cod, oysters, scallops, mussels, pasta, tacos

AVAILABILITY
Seasonal: summer

BREWERY & CELLAR DOOR LOCATION
'Gypsy' brewers

BREWERY WEBSITE
www.doctorsordersbrewing.com

WAYFARER USA

GREEN BEACON

 **AMERICAN**   **4.9%**   **6-8°C**   **SPIEGELAU AMERICAN WHEAT BEER GLASS**

TASTING NOTES There seems to have been more noise generated in Green Beacon's hometown of Brisbane about some of their hoppier beers. But, from the first mouthful from my first can of this American wheat beer I was sold: light on the palate, clean, delicately hopped and refreshing; it came across as the sort of beer Brisvegans should be packing first in their summer picnic baskets.

THE STORY Green Beacon was one of the first breweries to open in Brisbane at the start of the city's recent craft beer explosion. Modelled on the format that's been so successful for the likes of Mountain Goat: industrial warehouse in which you can enjoy beers in the company of the stainless steel in which they were made, it's since been joined by more as the Queensland capital has developed into a thriving hub of quality beer unthinkable a few years ago.

As with many young breweries, the quality of the beers improved noticeably in the first couple of years after opening. Over time, the lineup has evolved – with the brewers not afraid to change the beer attached to one of their nautically themed names – although the heart of their range is now locked down. That's not least because four of them are available in cans after Green Beacon

became the first Queensland micro to install a canning line.

That said, the fact their beers are packaged hasn't made them much easier to find outside their hometown. The change in the beer scene Green Beacon helped fire has been so dramatic pretty much everything that leaves their warehouse is snapped up locally – another reason to head north and explore one of the most colourful beer scenes in the country.

ALSO TRY 3 Bolt Pale Ale | Penny Porter Cross Knot Kolsch | Windjammer IPA Grappler New World Pilsner

BREWER'S FOOD MATCH
Barbecued octopus, chorizo, rocket, caramelised red onion and a zesty citrus dressing

AVAILABILITY
Year-round

BREWERY & CELLAR DOOR LOCATION
26 Helen Street, Teneriffe, QLD 4005

BREWERY WEBSITE
www.greenbeacon.com.au

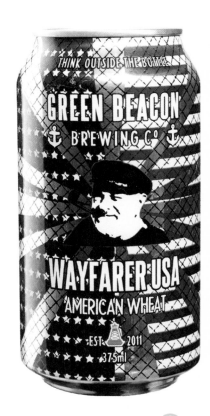

WITBIER

HIMMEL HÜND

 WITBIER   **4.5%**   **2–4°C**    **PILSNER/ POKAL GLASS**

TASTING NOTES In a beer landscape that, at the craftier end at least, is rather fond of hoppy beers, when a brewer launches with something different it tends to catch the eye. Thus it was with Annabel Meagher announcing Himmel Hünd to the world with a beer brewed in tribute to the European ales that had kick-started her love affair with good beer. A lovely, full-flavoured and faithfully citrusy and spicy take on the Belgian witbier style.

THE STORY There's a fondness within the Australian beer world for naming breweries after animals, particularly dogs. Yet, while we have Moon Dog, Black Dog, HopDog and Spotty Dog, there is only one Hünd: the brewing company launched in 2014 by Annabel Meagher and her partner Henry.

   Having been turned on to beer while studying and working in Bavaria, Annabel had gone from home-brewing student to work experience at Matilda Bay in Port Melbourne before it was shut down by CUB/SABMiller. Soon afterwards, she and Henry launched their 'gypsy' brewing company, first with the Witbier then a traditional Vienna Lager brewed at various locations around Victoria.

   As for the dog theme, it turns out Himmel Hünd means 'Sky Dog' in German (German language was one of many degrees Annabel collected before choosing the life of a brewer) and her Australian cattle dog is called Skey. He appears in cartoon form on the Witbier's label, earning his place there by helping Himmel Hünd snag a gold for packaging at the Australian International Beer Awards just months after launching.

ALSO TRY Vienna Lager

BREWER'S FOOD MATCH
Spicy Mexican dishes

AVAILABILITY
Year-round

BREWERY LOCATION
Moolap, VIC

BREWERY WEBSITE
www.himmelhund.com

HEFEWEIZEN

LITTLE RIVERS

 HEFEWEIZEN　 4.8%　 3–4°C　 **BAVARIAN WEIZEN GLASS**

TASTING NOTES Little Rivers Hefeweizen seems to have carved something of a niche in Tasmania. On my last visit, it was pouring at several venues and, when checking out a bottleshop midweek, a customer came in and requested it without even scouring the shelves. It's at the fruitier, richer end of the hefe scale – lots of candied banana, sweet lemon and sherbet alongside softer spices – yet finishes clean and relatively dry.

THE STORY Such was the relative prevalence of Little Rivers's beers on a recent trip to Tasmania, it came as some surprise to arrive at the brewery and discover just how tiny the operation was. At the end of a beautiful, winding drive through the forests of the state's northeast I found head brewer Chris Carins and partner Jess in their unassuming brewery venue a block back from Scottsdale's main road. Through the back was the brewery upon which he'd launched the business: a mere 250-litre kit through which he had somehow brewed well in excess of 30,000 litres in the previous 12 months – with every last drop then packaged and delivered around the state by the tiny family team that makes up Little Rivers.

Since then, they've responded to growing demand by installing a 2,000-litre brewery in their shed. It's one of the largest setups in Tasmania now and, putting things in context, produces one litre of beer per person living in Scottsdale every time Chris brews, meaning it's just as well the rest of the state is taking them to heart.

ALSO TRY European Dark Lager | Kolsch Pale Ale

BREWER'S FOOD MATCH
Goes great with Bavarian cured meats, sausages and hams

AVAILABILITY
Year-round

BREWERY & CELLAR DOOR LOCATION
22 Victoria Street, Scottsdale, TAS 7260

BREWERY WEBSITE
www.lrbrewing.com.au

SPECIALTY BEERS

SPECIALTY BEERS

When opening this chapter in *150 Great Australian Beers*, I wrote: "If there is a defining rule in the brave new world of craft brewing it is that there are no rules. Every beer style created and recorded since beer's very earliest days thousands of years ago is there to be plundered and reinterpreted. Traditional beers are there to be reinvented and reinvigorated. Style categories are there to be thrown into a giant melting pot and turned into something new. And there is no limit to the ingredients you can use, the processes through which beer can pass before being consumed, or the vessels in which it can be fermented, conditioned, packaged or served."

If that was true in 2014, it's even more the case now. Sure, the levels of experimentation occasionally swerve into daft territory, particularly when brewers try to catch punters' attention at the annual GABS festival and media attention tends to focus on the wacky ingredients, thus risking making the craft beer industry look childish to outsiders. Yet, even there, some of the wilder experiments become permanent releases or inspire brewers to try things they might never have considered without such a platform.

The situation now is really a case of looking back and forwards – maybe even sideways – simultaneously. Today's craft brewers are taking us back to how the beer world used to be before it became little more than a homogenous commodity in the 20th century, but many are also taking drinkers to places they've never been before.

Grain and grape are being combined in beers that feature unfermented wine wort, sometimes wine itself. Collaborations between brewers, once a novelty, are ten a penny, often leading to unique results; what's more, brewers aren't content to just work with other brewers: musicians, artists, farmers, novelists, beard balm manufacturers – anyone is fair game as long as they have an idea and enthusiasm. There isn't a wooden barrel in existence – new French or American oak, wine, whisky, Cognac, rum, you name it – that a brewer somewhere won't have used to give their beer added complexity.

Indeed, for almost half of the beers that you'll find in the coming pages the brewers have used barrels at some stage before packaging and releasing them to the public. For centuries, all beers would be packaged and transported in, and served from, wooden barrels. Today, in almost every case, the journey from milled grain to finished beer takes place exclusively within steel vessels.

However, when contemporary brewers use wooden casks and barrels it is to achieve one or more of four outcomes. They may wish to add some oaky characteristics to their beer, such as in Feral Brewing's fantastic Barrel Fermented Hog (also referred to as BFH), a semi-regularly brewed version of their all conquering Hop Hog that is fermented for a few days in fresh oak barrels.

In other cases, the goal is to pick up flavours or aromas from the previous inhabitant of the barrel, whether that is a wine, a spirit or even just the character of new, untainted oak. Increasingly, and sometimes in combination with that goal, the intention is to allow wild bacteria either already present in the barrel or added by the brewer to 'infect' the beer, usually to give it some of the sour or barnyard characteristics described in the introduction to the Belgian beers chapter. On occasion, other ingredients are added: fruit, spirit-soaked chillies, chocolate or other spices.

The final use for barrels is to allow slow and gentle oxidation of beer. Normally, brewers or vendors of beer wish to avoid oxidation at all costs as, particularly in lighter, hop forward beers, it can create unwanted flavours and aromas. But in stronger beers, particularly strong dark Belgian ales, imperial stouts and porters or barley wines, it can lead to desirable changes in the base beer. Oxidation can soften the roasty, harsher edges in big stouts and add caramel or vanilla notes. Likewise, in some beers it can lend them a fortified, sherry-like character.

Perhaps the most exciting niche within the local beer industry, however, is where brewers are experimenting with spontaneous fermentation. This sees brewers leave their wort open to the elements so that the yeasts and other microflora in their native habitat go to work fermenting the beer instead of pitching bought or house yeasts into them. This technique isn't without its risks and often brewers will blend several vintages or types of such beers to achieve a palatable result. What it promises is the potential to create beers that are truly of their place, in that the particular yeasts local to the brewery contribute to the flavours and aromas. Two Metre Tall in Tasmania and Melbourne's La Sirène, in particular, are exploring this in earnest, the former a genuine farmhouse brewery, the latter creating what might be tagged 'urban farmhouse' ales.

Either way, whether with or without barrels, by innovating with beer's traditional four ingredients or throwing everything including the kitchen sink and your surrounds into a brew, you will find beers out there limited by nothing more than a brewer's imagination. Heck, not one but two of the beers in this chapter feature seawater.

Not all experiments work, but when they do they can be fantastic experiences that push the envelope for beer ever further.

--- A DOZEN MORE TO TRY ---

FERAL BREWING
Watermelon Warhead and BFH

STONE & WOOD BREWING
Stone Beer

EAGLE BAY BREWING AND MANE LIQUOR
Black & Tannin

HOPDOG BEERWORKS
Alluvial Peach

LA SIRÈNE
Spontaneously Fermented Series

MOO BREW
Harvest Ales

MOON DOG BREWERY
Jumping The Shark

MURRAY'S CRAFT BREWERY
Anniversary Ales

HOLGATE BREWHOUSE
Beelzebub's Jewels

SEVEN SHEDS
Smokin' Bagpipes

MERCHANT BREWING
Earl Pear

BAROSSA VALLEY BREWING
3Some

DARK

3 RAVENS

 SMOKE BEER   **5.0%**   **8–10°C**   **STANGE GLASS**

TASTING NOTES One of few smoked beers made with regularity in Australia, 3 Ravens Dark is inspired by the unique rauch biers of Bamberg, Germany. Brewed with smoked malts from Germany, the result is a dark amber beer that has distinct sweet smoky and smoked meat characters. It might sound odd if you've never had a smoked beer, but it works. They're versatile food beers, too.

THE STORY 3 Ravens was started well over a decade ago by a group of engineering mates in a warehouse in Thornbury. Yet the European-inspired, somewhat gothic brewery almost didn't make it to its tenth birthday. The brewery and site were put up for sale and it looked like one Melbourne's oldest and most idiosyncratic breweries could be lost. Instead, WA's Mash Brewing – looking for an eastern outpost – stepped in, bought the whole lot and gave it new life.

It's since expanded significantly, brewing Mash beers for the East Coast, and winning a series of top trophies for beers as diverse as this Dark, its English Ale and the Berliner Weisse, released under the Mash banner. The expansion hasn't just been on the brewing front either, with the once private 'Pleasure Palace' bar open every Friday – and occasionally for special events – thus becoming a welcome addition to Thornbury's growing number of good beer venues.

ALSO TRY English | White | Black | 55 Colourful 'Little Raven' one-offs

BREWER'S FOOD MATCH
Steak tartare, Brillat-Savarin triple-cream brie, chargrilled meats and vegetables

AVAILABILITY
Year-round

BREWERY & CELLAR DOOR LOCATION
1 Theobald Street, Thornbury, VIC 3071

BREWERY WEBSITE
www.3ravens.com.au

BIG 'N' BEARDY

7 CENT BREWERY

 IMPERIAL STOUT **9.8%**  **12°C** **SNIFTER GLASS**

TASTING NOTES As complex as you'd imagine for a Russian imperial stout that spent almost a year inside a whisky barrel that formerly housed a 14 per cent Belgian ale, created as a collaboration between a Norwegian and Aussie brewer. The roast, coffee and dark chocolate you'd expect of the base beer are joined by flashes of whisky, stewed fruits, oaky vanilla and leathery char.

THE STORY Three home-brewing mates who met while studying engineering at uni had a big night brewing and drinking in the shed at the back of one of their parents' homes. It ended with them failing to come up with a name for their brewery and instead, setting fire to an old sofa. The following morning, they found seven cents among the wreckage.

Slowly building their brewery (in that same shed) while retaining other jobs, they do have a core beer range, but they have been catching the eye more with their frequently ridiculous and outrageously long-in-the-making specials. Big 'n' Beardy is one standout, but others, such as the sour cherry porter Glass Case of Emotion, which was 18 months in development, are equally enticing for the adventurous palate.

ALSO TRY Glass Case of Emotion (if it returns)

BREWER'S FOOD MATCH
Roquefort cheese or vanilla ice cream (in the beer if you're feeling brave!)

AVAILABILITY
Seasonal

BREWERY LOCATION
Gisborne South, VIC

BREWERY WEBSITE
www.7cent.com.au

SEX, DRUGS AND ROCKY ROAD

BACCHUS BREWING CO.

 SPECIALTY 8.5% 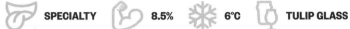 6°C TULIP GLASS

TASTING NOTES The best known of many Bacchus beers designed to taste like something not beer was debuted at the 2013 GABS Festival – the place to find more odd beers under one roof than any other – and took second in the People's Choice vote. Peanuts, sour cherries, chocolate, vanilla and rose water are used to recreate rocky road in liquid form, resulting in something akin to a perfumed, sweet English strong ale.

THE STORY Queensland's Bacchus is a genuine outlier in the world of Australian brewing. The brainchild of home-brewing former scrap-metal trader Ross Kenrick, its team of brewers is responsible for well over 100 different brews each year. Many are just single keg releases too, created on the row of 50-litre mini-brewhouses that line one wall of the Capalaba warehouse unit that is also home to a brewery bar.

Many are genuine flights of fancy, going well beyond even Sex, Drugs And Rocky Road for their inspiration or desired end goal; Ross has had his brewers throw chickens and shellfish into brews in the past. Such small-batch brewing makes it a low risk approach – if a concept doesn't work out, it's at least likely to be interesting and, at worst, it's only 50 litres of experiment that requires disposing.

That said, what's perhaps most remarkable is how often the ideas in Ross' head work out – no matter how ridiculous or far-fetched they seem; one year, Bacchus was shortlisted for Champion Small Australian Brewery. The approach also allows for all areas to be explored: from high octane, barrel-aged beers to all manner of sours and everything in between. Drop in at pretty much any time and you'll be able to sample from multiple banks of taps while watching the brewers at work.

ALSO TRY White Chocolate & Raspberry Pilsner | Mosaic IPA | Cunning Ninja's Imperial IPA | Queensland Ale | Big Red (Cock Ale)

BREWER'S FOOD MATCH
Enjoy after dinner

AVAILABILITY
Year-round

BREWERY & CELLAR DOOR LOCATION
2 Christine Place, Capalaba, QLD 4157

BREWERY WEBSITE
www.bacchusbrewing.com.au

THE DUKE OF YORK

BEATEN TRACK

 **BARLEY WINE** **11.3%** **4°C** **BRANDY BALLOON**

TASTING NOTES His summer ale might be the biggest seller, but Nick Galton-Fenzi's The Duke of York is the house specialty, named after the pub destroyed in the Boulder earthquake of 2010. It's a huge coming together of eight hops, six of which are American, measures 11.3 per cent ABV and is aged before release to mellow out. And mellow it does, its red body smooth and full, with a rich, fortified malt character dominating and any boozy heat well hidden.

THE STORY There was once a number of breweries in the WA Goldfields city of Kalgoorlie-Boulder. But by the time a bunch of home brewers who called the city home embarked on the long, slow process that led to the opening of Beaten Track Brewery in 2010, there had been nothing since the early 80s.

Now, under the guidance of one of those home brewers, Nick Galton-Fenzi, the city may still only have one brewery but it's one that pumps out a phenomenal number of beers throughout the year, most named after WA roads and highways or other iconic spots. There's a sizeable core range that stays on the safer side but encompasses styles from here, Europe, the UK and the States, then an ever-changing line-up of specials that includes this barley wine but also nitro beers, sours, hop bombs and more.

At the time of writing, they were limited to a license that only allows sampling and take-home sales, although the $20 sampler gets you tastes of six beers. Otherwise, you can find the beers around Perth where the splendid Mane Liquor bottleshop handles their distribution.

ALSO TRY Gunbarrel Black IPA Gibb River Rye | Youngs Scotch Ale Sandstone Summer Ale

BREWER'S FOOD MATCH
After-dinner fruit and soft cheese platter

AVAILABILITY
Seasonal: autumn

BREWERY & CELLAR DOOR LOCATION
25A Dwyer Street, Boulder, WA 6432

BREWERY WEBSITE
www.beatentrackbrewery.com.au

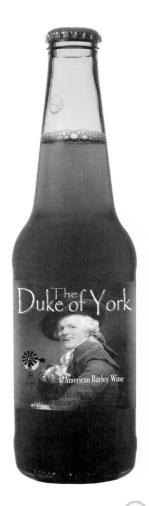

RAMJET

BOATROCKER BREWERY

 IMPERIAL STOUT   **11.4%**    **6–8°C**   **LARGE SNIFTER GLASS**

TASTING NOTES A beer that tends to get more beer geeks drooling more readily than pretty much any other, this annual release from Boatrocker is luscious decadence writ large. A rich, creamy imperial stout that's aged in Starward Whisky barrels, where it takes on vanilla and spicy whisky characteristics, Ramjet's popularity led to the creation of a brother beer: Roger Ramjet, which is aged in bourbon barrels.

THE STORY Only time will tell, but few in the know would bet against Boatrocker becoming an iconic Australian brewery. It started out as a contract brewer, with full flavoured American-style pale ale Alpha Queen being the first release, followed by gold medal-winning pilsner Hoppbier. But it's since Matt Houghton, who founded the business with wife Andrea, moved into his own place in 2013 that things have got really interesting.

Along with bold beers like Ramjet, he's been able to indulge his fascination with Belgian beer culture, creating all manner of barrel-aged beauties, some naturally soured, some inoculated, as well as opening Australia's first dedicated Barrel Room bar across the road from the brewery. There, 300 or more barrels will be filled with various beers, some to be blended over time. His endeavours caught the eye of the guys behind Little

Creatures, with Made by HAND taking a third share in Boatrocker in 2015, giving one more reason why success looks so likely for this genuine innovator.

For their full story, see page 204.

ALSO TRY Big Love Suburban Pale Hoppbier Pilsner | Mitte Berliner Weisse Brambic (Braeside lambic) Banshee Barley Wine

---

BREWER'S FOOD MATCH
Blue cheese

AVAILABILITY
Annual release

BREWERY LOCATION
51 Macbeth Stret, Braeside, VIC 3195

CELLAR DOOR LOCATION
34 Macbeth Street, Braeside, VIC 3195

BREWERY WEBSITE
www.boatrocker.com.au

DARK HARVEST

BRIDGE ROAD BREWERS

 HARVEST ALE   6.6%   6°C   IPA GLASS

TASTING NOTES Ben Kraus releases so many beers and embarks on so many innovative ventures that choosing one beer to include has been trickier than most. But the Dark Harvest isn't just a great beer – a wonderful choc-orange take on the black IPA style – it also encapsulates so much of what he does. Originally a collaboration with Danish legend Mikkeller, it uses freshly harvested wet hops from a nearby farm and was originally brewed overnight due to Mikkel's schedule – the sort of quirk that Ben seems to thrive upon.

THE STORY The young Ben went to Europe to learn winemaking and returned a brewer, with partner Maria leaving Austria to start life and a family with him in his hometown of Beechworth. They built the original Bridge Road Brewers on his parents' land on Bridge Road before moving soon afterwards to the old coach house and stables, where they have steadily expanded and created a popular, family-friendly venue based around his evolving range of beers and great pizzas and pretzels.

Probably the foremost brewing advocate of new Australian hops, which he showcases in a single hop IPA series as well as educational 'Hops 101' packs, Ben is also a pioneer in the world of collaborations. He's worked with brewers –

in Beechworth and overseas – with the most extravagant venture seeing him and ex-Nøgne Ø legend Kjetil sending beers in barrels across the planet by sea.

Bridge Road is probably best known for its Beechworth Pale Ale and Australia's longest continuously brewed Saison, but the brewery has a roster as long as it is colourful. What's becoming an ever-bolder anniversary release, the black Belgian IPA B2 Bomber is much sought after, while recent years have seen Ben explore the worlds of bacteria and unusual yeasts.

ALSO TRY Beechworth Pale Ale Chevalier Saison | Bling Bling Double IPA Harvest Ale | B2 Bomber | Single Hop IPAs Collaborative sour beer ventures

BREWER'S FOOD MATCH
Pair with moderately rich dishes
of meat or game

AVAILABILITY
Seasonal

BREWERY LOCATION
50 Ford Street Beechworth,
VIC 3747

BREWERY WEBSITE
www.bridgeroadbrewers.com.au

WEE HEAVY

CAPTAIN BLIGH'S

 WEE HEAVY   **8.8%**   **8°C**   **NONIC GLASS**

TASTING NOTES This big Scotch ale is a veritable meal in a glass, originally brewed with Tasmanian whisky legend Bill Lark, who gave Bligh's barrels in which to age the beer. The 'Devil's Cut' – the whisky left in the barrel – took the beer to around 9 per cent ABV and added further spicy, fruity complexity and lushness to what was already rich and malty to start with.

THE STORY Psychiatric nurse Steve Brooks and novelist wife Karen initially headed to Tasmania to care for a sick friend. Once there, they had ample opportunity to take stock and Steve decided that rather than return to nursing he would pursue his love of beer and brewing, one that had been with him since the 1980s when he worked at Bendigo's Rifle Brigade Pub Brewery.

He took over Captain Bligh's Tasmanian Cider, added beer to the roster, then knocked the cider on the head and introduced beer jams as a sideline instead. His brewery is based in a building with a long brewing history: known as the Tasmanian Brewery Building, it started as Punshon's Brewery in the 1830s, becoming the James Tasmanian Pale Ale Brewery, then The Adams Brewery and finally the Co-Operative Brewery before ceasing brewing for decades.

Bligh's schtick is brewing 'Colonial Ales', which means beers brewed to Tasmania's 19th century colonial laws and with local ingredients. Most are British in inspiration and come with an historic bent, upon which Steve, as much natural raconteur as brewer, is more than happy to expound if you catch him working at the brewery.

ALSO TRY Anneke Red Ale
HIPA (Hobart India Pale Ale)
Six Guinea Pale Ale

☆

BREWER'S FOOD MATCH
Irish stew

AVAILABILITY
Seasonal: winter

BREWERY & CELLAR DOOR LOCATION
64 Warwick Street, Hobart, TAS 7000

BREWERY WEBSITE
www.captainblighs.com.au

BARREL-AGED SOUR SAISON

FLAT ROCK BREW CAFÉ

 SOUR SAISON **7.6%** **5–8°C** **TULIP GLASS**

TASTING NOTES Barely a week passes without a new beer hitting Flat Rock's taps. Some never return but one special they keep creating is this unique sour saison. The base beer spends six months in Chardonnay barrels before being served to drinkers. The result is a beer with an amazing deep golden colour and incredible clarity. Creamily smooth, mixing a touch of sweet with a spot of sour, it presents rather like a dessert wine.

THE STORY If the term brewpub could be used as an adjective as well as a noun, it would be fair to describe the Flat Rock Brew Café in the Sydney suburb of Naremburn as a brewpubby brewpub. The cosy little joint sits in an unlikely spot next to a busy junction, but don't let its size or location put you off: it's got a big heart and produces some of the most interesting and exciting beers in Australia – just in very small amounts.

The brewery where the magic takes place (or at least starts) is found underneath the venue part of the Brew Café and is one for which the term 'nano' – smaller than 'micro' but bigger than 'pico' in beer geek terminology – could be applied. Because of its small size and Flat Rock's owners' and brewers' desire to search relentlessly for new and innovative beers, it turns out dozens of different

brews each year, with only a few of them anything approaching 'regular' status on the lineup of taps and hand pumps upstairs.

Many of the beers are only part way to being finished when they leave their fermenters, too. There's a collection of barrels of various origins filled with beer and sometimes bacteria or fruit plus casks that allow the venue to offer genuine English-style real ale. Add in great food from the kitchen upstairs and quirky events, and you've got the dictionary definition of brewpub. And brewpubby, of course.

ALSO TRY English Bitter | Red Rye IPA Devil's Pond Imperial Stout

---

BREWER'S FOOD MATCH
Roasted wild poultry, guinea fowl or partridge

AVAILABILITY
Seasonal

BREWERY & CELLAR DOOR LOCATION
290 Willoughby Road, Naremburn, NSW 2065

BREWERY WEBSITE
www.flatrockbrewcafe.com.au

SUPERBEAST

HOPDOG BEERWORKS

 **BARLEY WINE**   **10.5%**   **6–8°C**   **POCO GRANDE**

TASTING NOTES HopDog's annual birthday beer changes each year. But each shares characteristics in common: they're always massive, always chockfull of hops and usually overloaded with some ingredient, such as the year brewer Tim Thomas went nuts with smoked malts. The most recent (at time of writing) was an imperial black IPA inspired by the sort of metal Tim likes to brew to, yet managed a depth and balance that belied its insanity.

THE STORY Following a long and well-travelled journey through a number of Australian breweries, Tim Thomas decided to head out on his own with his wife, establishing HopDog BeerWorks in an industrial unit in Nowra, two hours south of Sydney. Initially brewing on what was little more than a home-brew kit, he nevertheless quickly caught the eyes of the nerdier types of the beer world for his frequently oddball creations.

Quality and consistency didn't always match the heights of his ambition but, over time, as demand has increased and the brewery has expanded so has the standard of beers. That doesn't mean there's been any reining in of the brewer's imagination – quite the opposite, in fact.

All manner of barrels have been filled with beer, sometimes with fruit, spices or other ingredients added, while bugs and bacteria have been allowed to go to work on many releases too. It's a sign of how broad the HopDog range is that, when deciding which beer to feature in this book, brews as varied as his Horns Up rye IPA, sour and fruity, barrel-aged Alluvial Peach, a traditional porter and this evolving annual beast were all considered.

ALSO TRY Horns Up | Alluvial Peach 6TenK Porter | Redhopulous

BREWER'S FOOD MATCH
Cheese, especially Maffra cheddar with an awesome quince paste

AVAILABILITY
Seasonal

BREWERY & CELLAR DOOR LOCATION
2/175 Princes Highway, South Nowra, NSW 2541

BREWERY WEBSITE
www.hopdog.com.au

GINGER BEER

MATSO'S

 **GINGER BEER**   **3.5%**   ❄ **ICE COLD AND POURED OVER ICE**   **TALL GLASS**

TASTING NOTES By Matso's standards this is fairly tame given the Broome brewer also releases beers featuring chillies, mangoes and desert limes. They also release more 'standard' beers, but to feature one of those would seem to miss the point. And, anyway, in the world of ginger beers this one – despite being only 3.5 per cent ABV – is a fiery beast, boasting enough spritz and ginger to make your eyes water.

THE STORY It's often said there's nowhere in Australia quite like Broome. And it's fair to say there's nothing in the Aussie beer world quite like Matso's, the brewery that sold its first beer in the town in the late 90s. Situated in the striking, heritage-listed former Union Bank building, it's as much tourist attraction as brewpub, making a feature of its tropical location in many of its releases.

As well as this Ginger Beer, you'll find a Lychee Beer, a Chilli Beer and a Mango Beer. Having long outgrown their onsite brewery, the vast majority of Matso's beers are brewed under contract far from the tropical bay the business calls home, yet they command a loyal following, albeit one with little crossover into the country's hardcore beer geek world.

While many serious beer drinkers will dismiss the Matso's schtick as gimmicky, it's worth noting the brewery's longevity. It's survived as long as Mountain Goat (now part of Asahi) and, in 2015, marked its 18th birthday by brewing an anniversary version of the Ginger Beer: no less than an American-style barley wine infused with ginger, natural spices then aged on oak staves soaked in dark rum.

ALSO TRY Mango Beer
Bishop's Best Dark Lager | Session Ale

BREWER'S FOOD MATCH
Pork belly with pickled papaya, red onion, mint, coriander, cashews and Thai dressing

AVAILABILITY
Year-round

BREWERY LOCATION
60 Hamersley Street, Broome, WA 6725

BREWERY WEBSITE
www.matsos.com.au

BLACK LUNG

MOON DOG

 IMPERIAL STOUT   **8.8%**   **8–10°C**   **TULIP GLASS**

TASTING NOTES The Black Lung changes each year – not the base beer but the type of oak in which the smoky stout is aged. One thing that never changes is the anticipation that awaits its release, which is always met by the quality of the beer. There's always dark chocolate, smokiness, oak, roast bitterness and usually some fortified, fruity booze. And I always thoroughly enjoy it.

THE STORY With their biggest selling Love Tap lager having gradually receded from its initial 7.1 per cent ABV to 5.0 and other 'normal' beers joining the regular lineup, one might suspect that Moon Dog, the Melbourne brewery that kick-started the third wave of eccentric, no-limits brewing in Australia, is growing up.

Yet the brewery launched by two brothers and their mate retains its madcap charm and outrageous silliness. After all, no brewery that makes two beers designed to be mixed as one, like a cocktail – then rigs up two taps at its brewery bar with a cocktail shaker to do just that – or recreates champagne in beer form (really well) or brews a beer with 5,800 Redskin lollies, can ever be said to be suffering from an overdose of maturity. Its backstreet industrial brewery and bar – midway between a brothel and CUB's headquarters – is also a must visit.

ALSO TRY Henry Ford's Girthsome Fjord Jumping The Shark (annual variations) Perverse Sexual Amalgam Jukebox Hero

---

☆

BREWER'S FOOD MATCH
Smoked brisket

AVAILABILITY
Seasonal

BREWERY & CELLAR DOOR LOCATION
17 Duke Street, Abbotsford, VIC 3067

BREWERY WEBSITE
www.moondogbrewing.com.au

FRESHIE SALT & PEPPER GOSE

NOMAD BREWING

 GOSE 4.5% 6-8°C TEKU GLASS

TASTING NOTES Quite how we ended up with two beers featuring seawater in this book... If anything it's a sign of how far the beer world has come in the past decade – and how innovative brewers are becoming. Far less crazy than Two Metre Tall's Salty Sea Stout (page 234), this take on the German Gose style nevertheless saw its brewers wade into the waters off Sydney's Northern Beaches before creating a light, refreshing, lightly sour and acidic, spicy, citric ale.

THE STORY In the space of a few months, Australia gained two breweries that were joint ventures between locals and international brewers who had initially visited to launch their own beers only to become enamoured by what they found here. Nomad was the first to open, the lovechild of Italian brewer Leo di Vicenzo of Birra del Borgo and his Australian importers at Experienceit Beverages.

The nomad in question was head brewer Brooks Caretta, a young brewer who had previously run operations for Leo in Italy and New York City. From the off, working closely with Leo on his regular visits to the brewery, he set about creating beers with subtle local twists. Using seawater in the Freshie may seem a little extreme, but other beers in the lineup have used coffee, desert limes, muscat

raisins, bush tomatoes, riberries and finger limes, often to good effect.

The joint venture has conducted further joint ventures too, often with other international brewers on Experienceit's roster, including international behemoths such as Victory Beer from Pennsylvania, Stone Brewing from San Diego and Tampa's Cigar City.

ALSO TRY Long Trip Saison | Jet Lag IPA Berry Cubana

BREWER'S FOOD MATCH
Salt and pepper squid, rock oysters, beer-battered fish and chips (with Freshie as the beer, naturally!)

AVAILABILITY
Year-round

BREWERY & CELLAR DOOR LOCATION
5 Sydenham Road, Brookvale, NSW 2100

BREWERY WEBSITE
www.nomadbrewingco.com.au

GLUTEN FREE BELGIAN ALE

O'BRIEN

 GF BELGIAN ALE 6.0% 8°C CHALICE

TASTING NOTES The first beer to win a trophy for Best Gluten Free Beer at the Australian International Beer Awards is this Belgian-style ale, a seasonal release from Ballarat's O'Brien's. A golden ale brewed with sorghum and millet with pleasant sweet, fruity and spicy characters derived, mostly, from the choice of yeast along with additions of Belgian candi sugar and coriander seeds.

THE STORY When they took home the above trophy from the 2013 Australian International Beer Awards, it was the culmination of a long road for John O'Brien. He first started out on his mission to create a decent tasting gluten-free beer back in 1998 when he was diagnosed with coeliac disease.

It took until 2005 for the first O'Brien beer to be released and a further eight years before his Belgian Ale won the trophy, but along with brewing colleague and fellow coeliac sufferer Andrew Lavery, he is now responsible for a series of impressive gluten-free beers.

As awareness of the disease has grown, more GF beers have come onto the market, while a small number of brewers have played with the use of enzymes to reduce the gluten within beers brewed

with barley, in order to make them 'gluten reduced'. O'Brien led the way, however, with several of their core beers found in the fridges of major retailers nationwide and some, including specials such as their India Pale Ale – standing up well, whether you take into account the use of sorghum and millet or not.

ALSO TRY Black Lager | India Pale Ale Brown Ale

BREWER'S FOOD MATCH
Thai-inspired baked salmon with sweet potato mash and a mango salsa, or for more relaxed times, soft blue cheese and fig paste on rice crackers

AVAILABILITY
Seasonal: autumn

BREWERY & CELLAR DOOR LOCATION
36 Gregory Street West, Wendouree, VIC 3355

BREWERY WEBSITE
www.rebellionbrewing.com.au

SPECIAL RESERVE

REDOAK

 **BARLEY WINE** **12.5%** **8°C** **BALLOON GLASS**

TASTING NOTES A beer that you can only try at Redoak's Sydney venue and that will set you back a cool $70 for a bottle is worth the effort. A barley wine that undergoes three separate fermentations and spends time ageing on oak is as much fortified Pedro Ximenez as beer. Luxuriant and velvety, this gently warming treat runs the full gamut from vanilla, oak and chocolate through dates and raisins to its liqueur-like finish.

THE STORY Redoak, run by brother and sister pair David and Janet Hollyoak, is the Australian beer world's greatest enigma. Ever since he says he was hoodwinked into allowing 'spies' from one of the major breweries posing as home brewers onto a brewery tour, David has refused to open the doors of his Camden brewery to anybody. It means that the secrets of the country's most successful brewery in terms of global award success – this Special Reserve has won copious major titles, as have many of its stablemates – remain just that: closely guarded secrets.

Whether the enigma will ever be unravelled – David says he will open the doors to the brewery once there are no more contracted taps in Australia – remains to be seen. But so many of the beers created by this passionate advocate for small, independent Australian brewers, who has been brewing since the age of 14, are truly delicious that it's easy to forgive the shroud of mystery.

ALSO TRY Bitter | Chateau Sour Baltic Porter | Wee Heavy | Organic Pale Ale Weizen Dopplebock

BREWER'S FOOD MATCH
A bold vintage cheddar with muscatels, walnuts, dried fruit and lavosh

AVAILABILITY
Year-round

BREWERY & CELLAR DOOR LOCATION
201 Clarence Street, Sydney, NSW 2000

BREWERY WEBSITE
www.redoak.com.au

RED SKY

SHENANIGANS BREWING

 RED IPA **6.5%** **7–8°C** **IPA GLASS OR GOBLET**

TASTING NOTES Using herbs and spices well in beer can be a tricky business, particularly outside the styles that typically feature them, such as Belgian witbiers. But Sydney's Shenanigans combined the flavours and aromas (and colouring) of jasmine and hibiscus with the hop and malt characters of this red IPA with such aplomb you almost want to put on Stevie Wonder's *Ebony and Ivory* while drinking it.

THE STORY Home-brewing buddies Sam Haldane and Dan Beers (yes, really) launched their brewing company, Shenanigans, in early 2014 and have swiftly built a reputation as one of the finest among the many breweries that call Sydney's inner west home. They don't have a home of their own yet, initially brewing at Marrickville's Batch Brewing, but now popping up at various NSW breweries – but that hasn't stopped them making good beers consistently well.

Their flagship is the Winston pale ale, a fine take on a popular style, but they are often more extravagant in their goals. As well as this seriously fantastic red IPA, they've released beers featuring chillies, rum-soaked oak and coffee in their brews, with their limited releases often going by the wholly appropriate name 'Stunt Beers'.

ALSO TRY Winston | Stunt Beers

BREWER'S FOOD MATCH
Berry-flavoured sorbet or dessert, or anything with chilli

AVAILABILITY
Seasonal: spring

BREWERY LOCATION
Contract-brewed

BREWERY WEBSITE
www.shenanigansbrewing.com.au

TWO BIRDS BREWING

 SPECIALTY **5.2%** **4-6°C** **TULIP GLASS**

TASTING NOTES This beer was conceived as something of a joke for a festival while eating tacos in the US, and retains a love–hate reputation among beer lovers. It's a pain to brew (due to the preparation of countless limes), but Two Birds' Taco is a fun, quirky, enjoyable (unless you're in the hate camp) take on tacos that collects medals wherever it goes. A crisp, fruity pale ale that combines corn, coriander and lime with citrusy American hops with success.

THE STORY Brewers Jayne Lewis and Danielle Allen (old friends from Perth, now decamped to Melbourne and Sydney respectively) decided while on holiday in the US in 2010 to start Australia's first female-owned brewing company. Initially establishing themselves with colourfully packaged beers brewed under license – Golden and Sunset ales being the first pair – they have since opened the splendid Two Birds Nest in Spotswood, which houses their expanding brewery upon which they brew their draught beer as well as a great venue.

They've grown fast, while at the same time raising the profile for women in the local brewing industry. They've done this in part by winning countless trophies – Champion Large Brewery at the Craft Beer Awards two years running plus consecutive Champion Beer at the UK's Wetherspoon's Real Ale Festival among them – but also via the Pink Boots Society. In 2015, they even combined the two when the Neneh Cherry Saison they brewed with the Pink Boots Society was named Champion French/Belgian Ale.

ALSO TRY Golden Ale | Sunset Ale Bantam IPA

BREWER'S FOOD MATCH
Tacos, of course! It also pairs well with Vietnamese food – think lemongrass and beef rice vermicelli salad with lots of fish sauce.

AVAILABILITY
Year-round

BREWERY & CELLAR DOOR LOCATION
136 Hall Street, Spotswood, VIC 3015

BREWERY WEBSITE
www.twobirdsbrewing.com.au

SALTY SEA STOUT

TWO METRE TALL

 SOUR STOUT   **5.1%**   **8-12°C**   **RED WINE GLASS**

TASTING NOTES A beer that, in its own way, perhaps tells you everything you need to know about Tasmania's unique Two Metre Tall, not least in that it will probably divide opinion like no other beer. Brewed with Bruny Island seawater, seaweed, oysters and mussels as well as Two Metre Tall's ineffable touch, it's salty, sweet, acidic, tangy, fruity, unique and – to some – the greatest beer ever made.

THE STORY A story of redemption unlike any other in Australia, Two Metre Tall is found on a huge tract of farmland in the Derwent Valley. Set up by Ashley and Jane Huntington after they returned from winemaking in France, the initial intention was to plant vines on a slope that Ashley reckoned was the most ideal for pinot in the state, but he ended up trying his hand at beer and cider instead.

His earliest days as a brewer didn't go as expected. Ashley tried to introduce some of the techniques he'd applied to pinot noir to brewing and ended up with such unpleasant results he was left, in his words, 'disturbed'. However, rather than seek the safety of textbooks and brewing as the vast majority of brewers do, he decided to explore elements of the unpleasantness that intrigued him.

He encouraged wild yeasts and bacteria from his farm to take up home in his beers and ciders, but the results failed to impress many customers; indeed, some in the industry turned against him. Yet today, as he approaches a mastery of his farmhouse ales, and the beer world embraces spontaneous fermented beers and ciders, he is increasingly recognised as something of a visionary, one who is closing in on his dream of creating a 100 per cent estate ale – a beer that's brewed with grain and hops he's grown and fermented with the yeasts in the air.

For their full story, see page 236.

ALSO TRY Cleansing Ale (the older the better) | Derwent Aromatic Spelt Ale Huon Dark Ale | Original Soured Ale Raspberry Wild Cider | Sour Cherry Ale

---

BREWER'S FOOD MATCH
Hearty fare! For a novel take on 'beef and reef', serve this with a hearty beef stew and fresh crusty bread.

AVAILABILITY
Will be brewed again if conditions in the Tasmanian oyster industry are right

BREWERY & CELLAR DOOR LOCATION
2862 Lyell Highway, Hayes, TAS 7140

BREWERY WEBSITE
www.2mt.com.au

BARLEY WINE

VAN DIEMAN BREWING

 **BARLEY WINE**   **14%**   **12–18°C**   **SNIFTER GLASS**

TASTING NOTES A late change to the Van Dieman entry, which was originally going to be Will Tatchell's annual Hedgerow release: a barrel-aged sour featuring ingredients sourced from the family farm in Evandale. Then this huge barley wine aged in Muscat barrels arrived and took the guernsey. The 12 months in oak was well spent as the end beer is a true after dinner sipper, throwing up characteristics encompassing Christmas spices, Negronis, champagne, oak, acidity, bitters and more.

THE STORY Having learnt his brewing trade at traditional breweries in the UK, Will Tatchell returned to his parents' farm in Evandale, just south of Launceston, and set about building a brewery upon which he could brew traditional, mainly British-inspired ales. The Van Dieman beers take their names from closer to home, however: Jacob's Ladder mountain drive and Ragged Jack peak.

The scope of Will's brewing has broadened (as has the size of his family) over the years. The beer that was originally to feature here, the Hedgerow sour, was among the more adventurous of his projects – at least until he embarked upon a mission to turn his family's farm into a brewery.

In a similar manner to fellow Tasmanians Two Metre Tall, he plans to develop an 'estate ale' brewed with ingredients harvested from the farm: homegrown barley and hops, local water and a yeast strain isolated from those present in the natural environment.

ALSO TRY Jacob's Ladder Amber Ragged Jack Pale | Giblin Imperial Stout Enigma Harvest IPA

BREWER'S FOOD MATCH
Sticky date pudding or as an alternative to dessert wine

AVAILABILITY
Limited release

BREWERY LOCATION
537 White Hills Road, White Hills, TAS 7258

CELLAR DOOR LOCATION
Josef Chromy Wines, 370 Relbia Road, Relbia, TAS 7258

BREWERY WEBSITE
www.vandiemanbrewing.com.au

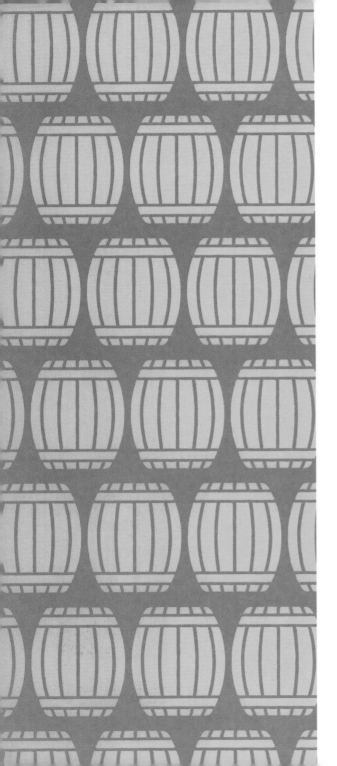

TWO METRE TALL

Unique. It's a word bandied about freely. But it's safe to say that, however you look at Tasmania's Two Metre Tall, it is unique.

Its brewery setup: uniquely constructed (and deconstructed) by brewer Ashley Huntington over the years to suit his particular needs. Its beers: unlike anything else in Australia, if not the world, and becoming intentionally more so over time. Its story: unique, littered with extreme lows and, latterly, highs that, were the story transplanted to the script of one of those Hollywood sports movies, it would be dismissed as too far-fetched.

And as for its co-founder and brewer, well, I don't think there's room in the world for too many Ashley Huntingtons. Outrageously impassioned, fiercely driven and bloody-minded, wantonly creative, wildly charismatic and unbound by parameters, he is, above all else, what makes Two Metre Tall unique (as well as being two metres tall).

Telling the story of what Ashley and wife Jane have been up to on their sprawling farm, Charlemont, in the Derwent Valley could fill an entire book. They returned to Tasmania after making wine in the Languedoc region of France, where Ashley garnered attention for the quality of his wine, his use of innovative techniques and his eye-popping charisma. Their intention was to plant vines – Ashley reckoned one slope in particular on their 600-hectare farm was the finest in all Tasmania for pinot grapes.

Yet, instead, he turned to brewing. But not brewing as most people would understand it. From the start, there was the goal of creating a 100 per cent estate ale: featuring hops grown on the farm, local water, barley grown and malted onsite and fermented by yeasts and other microflora native to the farm. It's a goal they're most of the way towards achieving by 2016, with only the onsite malting missing.

The intervening years, however, have been a wild ride, one coloured by experimentation (deliberate and otherwise), disaster, innovation, rejection, enlightenment, abuse and, ultimately, vindication.

The cause of much of the rejection and abuse can be traced to the early years. In trying to apply a particular wine-making technique to his malt, some early results were, in his words: "remarkably unpleasant". Yet, rather than retreat to brewing manuals, he was fascinated by elements of this unpleasantness, particularly an acidity he wished to explore further.

Thus he continued to follow his own path, celebrating variations in his batches and allowing wild yeasts and bacteria into his beers – even adding expansion chambers to his tanks to make them more atmospheric.

While there were some as fascinated with his beers and techniques as he was, there were far more who picked them up, were met with unexpected sour, acidic or funky characters and took umbrage. Entire pallets were returned to the farm by disgruntled customers and criticism swirled, occasionally and most aggressively from fellow brewers who saw his approach as potentially damaging to the cause of the fledgling microbrewing industry.

Two Metre Tall's bottles come with the most intricately detailed labels (several on each bottle in fact) spelling out the ethos of the brewery, what's gone into them, when the liquid was brewed and when bottled. Yet, for all that, it's easy to wonder whether a note on, say, the Cleansing Ale, explaining that the beer would gradually become sour and acidic over time might, in those early days, have saved some confusion and, thus, heartache. On the other hand, within a beer market still coming to terms with fruitily hopped beers, it's doubtful anything would have prepared many for Ashley's fluctuating and fanciful beers and ciders, especially when he was still learning along the way.

In 2012, while they were selling enough beer to survive, the rejection and criticisms were taking their toll. Then Ashley was awarded a Churchill Fellowship that saw him travel to Europe and the States. There, he visited iconic breweries, old and new, that were making sour and spontaneously fermented beers that were cherished and much sought after.

It was his 'Eureka!' moment; emboldened, he returned to Tasmania with renewed vigour and has never looked back. As the popularity of sour and farmhouse-style beers has risen in Australia, many drinkers have approached Two Metre Tall from a different perspective and his appearances at events now sell out. The breadth of beers and ciders – sometimes both combined, often featuring locally sourced organic fruits – has grown; he's even brewed a quirky stout featuring sea water, oysters and mussels that's featured in this book (see page 234).

In 2015, America's prestigious Shelton Brothers started the process of importing his beers to the US – a market notoriously tough to break. Then, when four-time world's best restaurant Noma embarked upon an 11 week residency in Sydney in 2016, its sommelier chose to pair the opening dish in its degustation with something other than wine.

They commissioned instead Snakebite, a barrel-aged cider and sour beer blend from Two Metre Tall. And if the head sommelier from perhaps the world's best restaurant likes what you're creating, chances are you're on the right track.

HOW THE BEERS WERE CHOSEN

There are downsides to the seemingly inexorable beer renaissance. For brewers, these could include facing ingredient shortages or a stiffer challenge to find and then retain stockists. For vendors and drinkers, it might be hard to keep up with all the new arrivals, with both locally brewed and imported beers landing in ever greater numbers.

For me, in compiling this book, the major downside was working out which beers and breweries would make the pages, given there was a limited number of those to fill. In less than two years since the final version of *150 Great Australian Beers* went to print, the number of Australian brewing companies has risen sharply to historically high levels well in excess of 300 – between typing this sentence and the finished book landing on shelves, I'd guess that another dozen at least will have opened or sold their first beer.

Adding to the challenge this time around was the decision to include beers even if they weren't available in packaged form. The vast majority to make the pages are available in cans or bottles, but there are a few beers that come in draught form only, often from breweries who don't package at all.

The previous book lined up 150 of the best and most interesting beers available in Australia at the time, which meant there were multiple entries for many breweries. This time around, in an attempt to capture as much of the flavour of the current Australian beer world as possible, I decided to only feature one beer from each brewer. Thus, there are 150 different brewing companies featured rather than the 80-odd last time around (itself another challenge for which the phrase 'herding cats' could have been invented), with each entry also suggesting some other beers from their respective ranges to check out.

For each of these brewing companies, the beer chosen might be their most popular, their best (well, in my opinion, at least), or their most interesting. Taking this approach means that, because there are breweries with two, three, four or more beers in their lineup that could be regarded as among the best for their style in the country, there will be chapters in which a beer is 'missing'; for example, you may think Bridge Road's Beechworth Pale Ale should be in the Pale Ales chapter, but the brewery's main entry is Dark Harvest in the Specialty chapter, because it is a beer that I believe encapsulates more of what the Beechworth brewer is about. So, alongside each style-based chapter introduction, I've included another dozen great beers that would be worthy of a spot in the chapter.

Elsewhere, the key aim was to present as broad and diverse a snapshot of the contemporary beer industry as possible, to ensure that all the key players were featured along with a colourful selection of those who are so small, young or remote that you may not have heard of them – or come across their beers, at least. With 150 slots and more than 300 candidates to choose from, that still means plenty of names aren't featured, some of which might be your personal favourites. And addressing this is perhaps best achieved by looking at the main reasons for their exclusion.

Some chose not to be included. There were a few breweries who never responded to requests for information or samples in the months leading up to the deadline. And there were others who don't package their beer who said it was impractical to package samples for consideration. On this note, it's worth offering particular thanks to Shawn Sherlock (FogHorn Brewhouse), Vince de Soyres (Flat Rock Brew Café), Chris Sewell (then head brewer at Illawarra Brewing Company), Craig Eulenstein (then head brewer at The Monk), Lachlan MacBean (Grainfed) and Eddie Oldfield (Black Hops Brewing), all of whom were willing to go the extra mile to get samples of otherwise draught-only beer to me by various means.

Then there are some I've not yet visited in person or whose beers I hadn't located on tap or in bottle, including the very many who opened in the months prior to this book going to print. Furthermore, there are brands that are little more than a business owner picking a style from a contract brewer so they can offer their own branded beer at a winery or in a local region without any real interest in the beer itself. Plus there are some that for other reasons, such as extremely limited reach or poor quality beer, don't warrant consideration. A couple featured in the last book missed out through a desire to get as many new faces in as possible; hopefully, their presence in the last book is recompense enough for being cut this time.

As for the country's major breweries, aside from Boag's Premium, there's nothing one might call 'mainstream' in the lineup. You might ask why would anyone call a book *The Great Australian Beer Guide* and not have the country's biggest selling brands in there?

While almost my entire working life is spent writing about the country's craft beer industry – thus most commonly smaller, independent breweries – this book is not exclusive. There are several beers in here from Kirin/Lion, one from SABMiller/CUB and one owned by Asahi, but they're chosen for being beers that I think stand up in terms of flavour and aromas and/or have a good story to them. It's worth noting that the

iconic Cascade Brewery in Hobart was due to feature via its First Harvest beer, but we were informed by CUB right on the deadline that the beer was not being brewed in 2016 after all, leading to some rather painful last-minute rewriting and reshuffling of the book.

As for other mainstream brands, there's no doubting the big-name lagers are technically well-executed beers, but if you've spent any amount of time drinking more characterful beers from smaller producers, while you may have occasionally had to ride the rollercoaster in terms of coming across some technically less than well executed beers, returning to an industrial lager is a little like giving up coffee from your local roaster and pouring yourself a cup of Nescafé with two sugars. It's still hot, wet and contains caffeine but it's a lowest common denominator form of that product.

Similarly, a beer's huge popularity isn't enough to warrant inclusion. The likes of VB and XXXX Gold may duke it out to be Australia's most consumed brand, but basing the selection on volume of sales would be the beer equivalent of the World Music Awards, the glitzy ceremony occasionally hosted by the royal family of Monaco that awards gongs to artists purely on the number of records they've sold. Sales, in any field, need not be synonymous with quality, and selection here places more value on qualities such as flavour, aroma, innovation, creativity and so on.

The other big player in the local market with international links, the Australian Beer Co (a joint venture between Yellow Tail wine producer Casella and Coca-Cola Amatil) that is behind the Yenda beer range, doesn't feature. To my mind, it has yet to produce a year-round beer impressive enough, especially given advantages that include an operation into which CCA poured $46 million when the joint venture was announced, to outweigh the negatives of a marketing campaign that looks to portray the brand as a homely little operation from rural New South Wales when in reality it is a joint venture between two vastly resourced global players.

So, while the above means this book is no encyclopedia, it is an attempt to encapsulate the very many wonderful things happening in the Australian beer world today at a time when the ground is shifting like never before. It should act as a reference point of a moment in time and also, I hope, as a springboard from which readers will launch into fresh, flavoursome and enjoyable adventures in beer.

INDEX

alcohol   11, 20, 22, 27
ales
    'gateway'   50
    'golden'   50
    'summer'   50
amber ales *see* reds & amber ales
barley   20
barrels   23
beer
    in Australia   10–18
    enjoying   25
    festivals   15–16
    and food   26–7
    glasses   24–5
    gluten-free   21
    how selected   238
    'indie beer'   17
    ingredients   20–3
    mid-strength   50
    mixed fermentation   23
    serving   24–5
    storing   25
    temperature   24, 25
breweries
    Akasha Brewing Company (NSW)   136
    Australian Beer Co.   18, 239
    Australian Brewery (NSW)   192
    Bad Shepherd Brewing (VIC)   156
    Bacchus Brewing Co. (QLD)   220
    Balmain Brewing Company (NSW)   33
    Bandicoot Brewing (VIC)   193
    Barossa Valley Brewing (SA)   70
    Barrow Boys Brewing Co. (VIC)   34
    Batch Brewing Co. (NSW)   90
    Beard and Brau (QLD)   194
    BentSpoke Brewing Co (ACT)   91, 186
    Bacchus Brewing Co. (QLD)   220
    Beaten Track (WA)   221
    Big Shed Brewing Concern (SA)   15, 157
    Black Dog Brewery (VIC)   174
    Black Duck Brewery (NSW)   137
    Black Hops (QLD)   195, 239
    Blackman's Brewery (VIC)   35
    Boatrocker Brewery (VIC)   14, 191, 204, 222
    Bootleg Brewery (WA)   12, 119
    Boston Brewing (WA)   71
    Brew Corp (WA)   113

Brewboys (SA)   120
BrewCult (VIC)   52
Brewtel Brewers (QLD)   85
Bridge Road Brewers (VIC)   13, 22, 223, 238
Bright Brewery (VIC)   72, 89
Brisbane Brewing Co (QLD)   73, 84
Brookes Beer (VIC)   138, 158
Burleigh Brewing Company   74, 85
Captain Bligh's (TAS)   224
Cascade (TAS)   239
Castlemaine Brewing (VIC)   138
Catchment (QLD)   85
Cavalier Brewing (VIC)   159
Cheeky Monkey (WA)   122
Clare Valley Brewing Company   47, 175
Colonial Brewing (WA)   53
Coopers   18, 176
Cowaramup Brewing Company   123
Croft Brewing (QLD)   196
Dainton Family Brewery (VIC)   139
Doctor's Orders Brewing (NSW)   210
Eagle Bay Brewing (WA)   124
Edge Brewing Project (VIC)   36
Ekim Brewing (NSW)   102
Emerson's (NZ)   18
Endeavour Vintage Beer Co   75
Exit Brewing (VIC)   15, 197
Feral Brewing Company (WA)   13, 18, 71, 92, 103, 112, 217
Fixation Brewing Company (NSW)   93
Flat Rock Brew Café (NSW)   225, 239
FogHorn Brewhouse (NSW)   177, 201
Fortitude Brewing Company (QLD)   54, 148
Four Hearts Brewing (QLD)   55, 85
4 Pines (NSW)   18, 118
Fox Hat (SA)   178
Gage Roads (WA)   18, 56
Grainfed (NSW)   140, 239
Grand Ridge (VIC)   12, 125
Green Beacon (QLD)   185, 211
Grifter Brewing Co., The (NSW)   15, 94
Hahn Brewery (NSW)   12
Hargreaves Hill (VIC)   126
Hawkers Beer (VIC)   13, 47, 63, 95
Hawthorn Brewing (NSW)   96
Himmel Hünd (VIC)   212
Hix Beer (VIC)   160
Hobart Brewing Company (TAS)   161

Holgate Brewhouse (VIC)   12, 162
Hop Nation (VIC)   141
HopDog BeerWorks (NSW)   226
Hunter Beer Co. (NSW)   37
Illawarra Brewing Company (NSW)   97, 239
James Boag's (TAS)   38
James Squire (NSW)   15, 18, 163
Kaiju! Beer (VIC)   98
Kick|Snare (TAS)   99
Killer Sprocket (VIC)   142
Knappstein (SA)   18, 39
Kooinda (VIC)   100
La Sirène (VIC)   14, 198
Last Drop Brewery (WA)   14, 40
Last Rites Brewing Company (TAS)   101
Little Bang Brewing (SA)   199
Little Brewing Company, The (NSW)   200
Little Creatures (WA & VIC)   12, 15, 18, 47, 50, 68, 76, 113, 163
Little Rivers (TAS)   213
Lobethal Bierhaus (SA)   127
Lord Nelson Brewery (NSW)   121
Macarthur Grange (NSW)   60
Malt Shovel Brewery (VIC)   12
Mash Brewing (WA)   41, 61, 65, 103, 117
Matilda Bay (TAS)   12, 18, 77, 102, 103
Matso's (WA)   227
Mildura Brewery (VIC)   41
Mismatch (SA)   15, 47143
Modus Operandi (NSW)   144
Monk Craft Brewery Kitchen (WA)   128, 239
Moo Brew (TAS)   21, 63, 161, 179
Moon Dog (VIC)   228
Mornington Peninsula Brewery (VIC)   164
Morrison Brewery (TAS)   101, 145
Mountain Goat (VIC)   12, 16, 17, 93, 125, 146
Murray's (NSW)   201
Nail Brewing (WA)   12, 147
Napoleone Brewery and Ciderhouse (VIC)   202
New England Brewing Co (NSW)   203
Newstead Brewing Co (QLD)   85, 104
Noisy Minor (QLD)   54, 148
Nomad Brewing (NSW)   229
O'Brien (VIC)   230
One Mile Brewery (NT)   16
Pact Beer (ACT)   16, 78

Pirate Life Brewing (SA)   13, 46, 105
Prancing Pony Brewery (SA)   47, 149
Prickly Moses (VIC)   57, 78
Public Brewery (VIC) 58
Quiet Deeds (VIC)   165
Red Duck (VIC)   106, 117
Red Hill Brewery (VIC)   180
Redoak (NSW)   231
Rehn Bier (SA)   181
Riders Brew Co (VIC)   79
Riverside Brewing Company (NSW)   107, 136
Robe Town Brewery (SA)   166
Rocks Brewing (NSW)   167
7 Cent Brewery (VIC)   219
Seven Sheds (TAS)   17, 129, 155
Shark Island (NSW)   59
Shenanigans Brewing (NSW)   232
Six String Brewing Co. (NSW)   150
Smiling Samoyed (SA)   108
Southern Bay Brew Co. (VIC)   109
Southwark (SA)   182
Stockade Brew Co (NSW)   60
Stone & Wood (NSW)   13, 18, 47, 60, 61, 64, 81, 93
Sydney Brewery (NSW)   42
Temple Brewing Company (VIC)   43, 69
Thirsty Crow (NSW)   183
3 Ravens (VIC)   218
Thunder Road (VIC)   62
Tooborac Brewery (VIC)   63, 80
Two Birds Brewing (VIC)   233
2 Brothers Brewery (VIC)   32
Two Metre Tall (TAS)   14, 234, 236
Vale Brewing (SA)   44, 178
Van Dieman Brewing (TAS)   235
Venom (VIC)   63
Wolf of the Willows (VIC)   81
Watts River Brewing (VIC)   110
Wayward (NSW)   151
Wheaty Brewing Corps (SA)   111
White Rabbit (VIC)   168
Wig & Pen (ACT)   184
Wolf of the Willows   81
Woolshed Brewery (SA)   169
Young Henrys (NSW)   15, 130
Yulli's Brews (NSW)   82
Yak Ales   18

brewing
    Australian, history of   10–11
    contemporary   14–16
    industrialisation of   11
    ingredients   19, 20–3
    process   19–23
Brewsvegas festival   16
British & Irish ales   12, 117
    Bruce   127
    Cowaramup Special Pale   123
    Eagle Bay ESB   124
    4 Pines ESB   118
    Hargreaves Hill ESB   126
    Kentish Ale   129
    Moonshine   125
    Old Admiral   121
    Old Reliable Pale Ale   122
    Raging Bull   119
    Seeing Double   120
    Special Pale   123
    Vintage   128
    Young Henrys Real Ale   130
browns, darks & porters   11, 155
    Brookes Brown Ale   158
    Butcher Porter   167
    Cavalier Brown Ale   159
    Frankenbrown   157
    Hazelnut Brown   156
    Hix Brown Ale   160
    Iron Pot Rye Porter   161
    Jack of Spades Porter   163
    Judas The Dark   169
    Mornington Brown Ale   164
    Quiet Deeds Vanilla Porter   165
    Solstice Baltic Porter   166
    Temptress   162
    White Rabbit Dark Ale   155, 168
craft beer   10, 13, 17, 18, 47
    Australia's first   11–12, 16, 28
dark ales see browns, darks & porters
dubbels   191
dunkelweizens   209
enjoying beer   24–5
Flanders see French & Belgian ales
food matching   26–7

French & Belgian ales   25, 135, 190–1
    Belgian Bombshell   193
    Beach House Saison   195
    Bon Chiens   194
    Breaking The Cardinal Rule   200
    Dark Farmhouse   203
    Exit Saison   197
    La Sirène Saison   198
    Murray's Grand Cru   201
    Saison D'Hérétique   192
    Saison Duval   202
    Saison Grenade   196
    Uncommon Cloud Saison   199
glasses   24
gluten-free   21
Good Beer Week   16, 205
gueuzes   190, 191
gypsy brewer   210
hefeweizens   22, 179, 180, 209, 213
hopfenweizenbocks   209
hops   21–2, 65, 68–9, 117, 223
imperial stouts see stouts & imperial stouts
ingredients   15, 21–3, 68–9, 117, 181
India Pale Ales   93
    Australian IPA   96
    Bengal IPA   106
    Big Sur   94
    Black IPA   100
    Copy Cat AIPA   103
    Cthulhu Black   IPA   98
    Dead Man's Revenge   101
    Fixation IPA   93
    Hawkers IPA   95
    Hel   102
    Hop Hog   92, 113
    Hop Bazooka   109
    Mo & Co IPA   97
    Non Corps Promise   111
    Pirate Life IIPA   105
    777 Imperial IPA   107
    Smiling Samoyed IPA   108
    Sprocket   91
    Stompbox   99
    Two to the Valley IPA   104
    West Coast IPA   90
    Watts River IPA   110

kristalweizens 209

lagers 10, 11, 30-1
    American Amber Lager 44
    Blackman's Unfiltered Lager 35
    Bock 33
    Cool Hops 36
    Hunter Bock 37
    James Boag's Premium Lager 38
    Knappstein Reserve Lager 39
    Kung Foo Rice Lager 32
    Last Drop Pilsner 40
    Lovedale Lager 42
    Powerstance Pilsner 43
    Stefano's Pilsner 41
    Stormy Lager 34

lambics 23, 97, 190, 191, 205, 222

malt 20-1

mash 19, 23

microbrewery 192

oud bruins see French and Belgian ales

pale ales 10, 23, 68-9
    Alpha Pale Ale 77
    Alpha Queen 14
    Blowhard Pale Ale 72
    BPA 73
    Growers Pale 75
    Gunslinger American Pale Ale 80
    Hawkers 47
    Hop Heaven 70
    Little Creatures Pale Ale 12, 68, 76, 113
    Mt Tennent Pale Ale 78
    Norman Australian Ale 82
    Riders XPA 79
    Rye Pale Ale 71
    28 Pale 74
    XPA 81
    see also India Pale Ales

Pirate Life 47

porters see browns, darks & porters

quadrupels 190

reds & amber ales 135
    Admiral Ackbar 148
    Archie's Red Ale 143
    Castlemaine Red 138
    Charmer 151
    Fancy Pants 146

Fire Within 136
    Former Tenant Red IPA 144
    Heron's Craic 137
    Irish Red 145
    Killer Sprocket Amber Ale 142
    Nail Brewing Red Ale 147
    Prancing Pony India Red Ale 149
    Red Eye Rye 139
    Six String Dark Red IPA 150
    The Buzz 141
    3 Sons 140

saisons 22, 190, 191, 197, 202, 205

session beers 50-51
    Brunswick Bitter 62
    Colonial Draught (formerly Kölsch) 53
    Featherweight Ale 58
    Golden Ale (Fortitude) 54
    Golden Ale (Venom) 63
    Greenhills 59
    Ipswich Challenger 55
    Pacific Ale 61
    Reset Robot 52
    Single Fin 56
    Spotted Ale 57
    The Sesh 60

specialty beers 15, 216-17
    Barley Wine 235
    Barrel Aged Sour Saison 225
    Big 'n Beardy 219
    Black Lung 228
    Dark Harvest 223
    Freshie Salt & Pepper Gose 229
    Ginger Beer 227
    O'Brien Gluten Free Belgian Ale 230
    Ramjet 222
    Red Sky 232
    Redoak Special Reserve 231
    Salty Sea Stout 234
    Sex, Drugs & Rocky Road 220
    Superbeast 226
    Taco Beer 233
    The Duke of York 221
    3 Ravens Dark 218
    Van Dieman Barley Wine 235
    Wee Heavy 224

squid ink 210

Stone & Wood   64

storing beer   25

stouts & imperial stouts   11, 172–3

    Coopers Best Extra Stout   176

    Dead Dog Stout   174

    King Kong Stout   175

    Moo Brew Stout   179

    Phat Mongrel   178

    Red Hill Imperial Stout   180

    Rehn Bier Extra Stout   181

    Sligo Extra Stout   177

    Southwark Old Stout   182

    Thirsty Crow Vanilla Milk Stout   183

    Velvet Cream   184

temperature   24, 25

tripels   190

Two Metre Tall   236

water   23

weizenbocks

wheat beers   190, 209

    Hefeweizen   213

    Wayfarer USA   211

    Witbier   212

    Zephyr   210

witbiers   22, 23, 26, 31, 135, 190, 209

wort   17, 19, 21, 23, 31, 190, 216, 217

yeast   22–3, 191

Acknowledgements

One thing that has become abundantly apparent in six or so years of writing about the Australian beer industry is that no matter how much you know, there is always far more to learn. With a history that stretches back millennia and into all walks of life, beer is endlessly fascinating if you decide to head down that particular rabbit hole. And in today's climate, with historic styles and techniques coming to the fore once more and contemporary craft brewers inventing new beers, techniques and flavours seemingly with every passing week, there is always a new niche to explore.

In spending most of my year writing hundreds of thousands of words and, at least until 2015, taking Good Beer Week from the seed of an idea into a festival of global repute, free time to get lost in books and research is few and far between. So it is often through practical experience and conversations with the many wonderful people that make up the beer community in Australia that the knowledge and insight you'll find in these pages is sourced. The key figures who helped me most as I first ventured into the world of beer were credited in *150 Great Australian Beers* so I won't repeat myself here.

I would like doff my cap to a few by name, however, including the Good Beer Week team led by Kate Paterson and including Miro Bellini, Matt Houghton, Siobhan Kerin, Tiffany Waldron, Dereck Hales and Glen Crawford. There's an expanding band of people helping The Crafty Pint grow, thus allowing me the time to write this book, including Nick Oscilowski, Dan Thornbury, Kerry McBride, Matt King, Chris Brady, Fiona Johnston, Claire Ali, Ruth Dawkins, Pia Poynton, Guy Southern, Ross Lewis, Bert Spinks, Will Ziebell, Glen Humphries, Darren Magin, Adrian Boyle and James Graham, several of whom also helped proof this book. Others to offer input to the book were Shawn Sherlock of FogHorn Brewhouse, Costa Nikias of La Sirène and Luke Robertson of Ale Of A Time, while Rihana Ries at Hardie Grant was a very patient wielder of the cattle prod and the likes of Tom, Kate, Shano, Rob, Adrian and Jeff have all played their part in keeping me relatively sane.

About the Author

James Smith was born in the famous brewing town of Burton upon Trent, home of the pale ale, so a career in beer was, perhaps, inevitable. It took a move to Melbourne, Australia, more than three decades later for the immersion in beer to truly begin. A journalist by trade, he landed in Australia as the slow-burning craft beer scene was starting to fire and, unable to find up-to-date information on the industry, set about covering it himself. Now often referred to as 'Crafty' after the beer website he launched in 2010, The Crafty Pint, he writes about beer for a number of national publications, is a founding member and former festival director of Good Beer Week and sponsors the Beer Media Award at the Australian International Beer Awards in the hope of encouraging more people to write and report on the local beer scene.

Published in 2016 by Hardie Grant Books

Hardie Grant Books (Australia)
Ground Floor, Building 1
658 Church Street
Richmond, Victoria 3121
www.hardiegrant.com.au

Hardie Grant Books (UK)
5th & 6th Floors
52–54 Southwark Street
London SE1 1UN
www.hardiegrant.co.uk

A Cataloguing-in-Publication entry is available from the catalogue
of the National Library of Australia at www.nla.gov.au

The Great Australian Beer Guide
ISBN 978 1 74379 139 4

Publishing Director: Jane Willson
Project Editors: Rihana Ries and Loran McDougall
Editor: Lucy Heaver, Tusk Studio
Design Manager: Mark Campbell
Designer: Matthias Lanz/Loupe Studio
Photographer: Chris Middleton
Production Manager: Todd Rechner

Colour reproduction by Splitting Image Colour Studio
Printed and bound in China by 1010 Printing International Limited